Women and the Gothic

Edinburgh Companions to the Gothic

Series Editors
Andrew Smith, University of Sheffield
William Hughes, Bath Spa University

This series provides a comprehensive overview of the Gothic from the eighteenth century to the present day. Each volume takes either a period, place, or theme and explores their diverse attributes, contexts and texts via completely original essays. The volumes provide an authoritative critical tool for both scholars and students of the Gothic.

Volumes in the series are edited by leading scholars in their field and make a cutting-edge contribution to the field of Gothic studies.

Each volume:
• Presents an innovative and critically challenging exploration of the historical, thematic and theoretical understandings of the Gothic from the eighteenth century to the present day
• Provides a critical forum in which ideas about Gothic history and established Gothic themes are challenged
• Supports the teaching of the Gothic at an advanced undergraduate level and at masters level
• Helps readers to rethink ideas concerning periodisation and to question the critical approaches which have been taken to the Gothic

Published Titles
The Victorian Gothic: An Edinburgh Companion,
    Andrew Smith and William Hughes
Romantic Gothic: An Edinburgh Companion,
    Angela Wright and Dale Townshend
American Gothic Culture: An Edinburgh Companion,
    Joel Faflak and Jason Haslam
Women and the Gothic: An Edinburgh Companion,
    Avril Horner and Sue Zlosnik

Forthcoming Titles
Scottish Gothic: An Edinburgh Companion,
    Carol Margaret Davison and Monica Germanà

Visit the Edinburgh Companions to the Gothic website at: www.euppublishing.com/series/edcg

Women and the Gothic

An Edinburgh Companion

Edited by
Avril Horner and Sue Zlosnik

EDINBURGH
University Press

Edinburgh University Press is one of the leading university presses in
the UK. We publish academic books and journals in our selected subject
areas across the humanities and social sciences, combining cutting-
edge scholarship with high editorial and production values to produce
academic works of lasting importance. For more information visit our
website: www.edinburghuniversitypress.com

© editorial matter and organisation Avril Horner and Sue Zlosnik, 2016, 2017
© the chapters their several authors, 2016, 2017

Edinburgh University Press Ltd
The Tun – Holyrood Road,
12(2f) Jackson's Entry,
Edinburgh EH8 8PJ

First printed in hardback by Edinburgh University Press 2016

Typeset in 10.5/13 Sabon by
Servis Filmsetting Ltd, Stockport, Cheshire
printed and bound in Great Britain by
CPI Group (UK) Ltd, Croydon CR0 4YY

A CIP record for this book is available from the British Library

ISBN 978 0 7486 9912 4 (hardback)
ISBN 978 1 4744 2556 8 (paperback)
ISBN 978 0 7486 9913 1 (webready PDF)
ISBN 978 1 4744 0951 3 (epub)

The right of Avril Horner and Sue Zlosnik to be
identified as Editors of this work has been asserted
in accordance with the Copyright, Designs and Patents
Act 1988, and the Copyright and Related Rights
Regulations 2003 (SI No. 2498).

Contents

Acknowledgements   vii

Introduction   1
Avril Horner and Sue Zlosnik

Part I: Family Matters

1. Heroines in Flight: Narrating Invisibility and Maturity in
    Women's Gothic Writing of the Romantic Period   15
    Angela Wright

2. Madwomen and Attics   31
    Laurence Talairach-Vielmas

3. Mothers and Others   46
    Ginette Carpenter

4. The Gothic Girl Child   60
    Lucie Armitt

5. 'A Woman's Place'   74
    Diana Wallace

Part II: Trangressions

6. Wicked Women   91
    Anne Williams

7. The Female Gothic Body   106
    Marie Mulvey-Roberts

8. Spectral Femininity   120
    Rebecca Munford

9. Female Gothic and the Law   135
    Sue Chaplin

10. Female Vampirism   150
    Gina Wisker

Part III: New Directions

11. Queering the Female Gothic   169
    Ardel Haefele-Thomas

12. No Country for Old Women: Gender, Age and the Gothic   184
    Avril Horner and Sue Zlosnik

13. Virtual Gothic Women   199
    Catherine Spooner

14. Formations of Player Agency and Gender in Gothic Games   214
    Tanya Krzywinska

Notes on Contributors   228
Index   232

Acknowledgements

This book is intended to celebrate the work of women writers in the field of Gothic, both creative and critical. We should like to thank all colleagues, past and present, who have offered support and intellectual stimulation over the years. Thanks are also due to generations of conference presenters who have brought new and challenging material to our attention.

This project would not have been possible without the patience and support of Jackie Jones and Adela Rauchova at Edinburgh University Press and the series editors, William Hughes and Andrew Smith. We are most grateful.

Introduction

Since the early debates about 'Female Gothic' in the 1970s and 1980s, inspired by Second-Wave Feminism, the theorisation of gender has become increasingly sophisticated and has resulted in a long interrogation of the category 'woman'. There was, however, a political price to pay for this, in so far as feminism gave way to the problematics of post-feminism, now itself being interrogated by a younger generation of women. The contributors in this volume tackle such conundrums in lively chapters that explore Gothic works – from established classics to recent films and novels – from feminist and/or post-feminist perspectives. The result is a book that combines rigorous close readings with elegant use of theory in order to question some ingrained assumptions about women, the Gothic and identity.

Ranging from late-eighteenth-century Gothic fiction to twenty-first-century science fiction films and Gothic video game-playing, as well as recent novels dealing with virtual reality, this volume offers coverage both of established classics within the Gothic canon (for example, novels by Radcliffe, Braddon, Stoker and du Maurier) and less well-known, more recent texts (work by Yvonne Heidt, Cate Culpepper and Scarlett Thomas, for example). Several rather disturbing key features emerge from the analyses of such wide-ranging material. Despite the considerable economic, social and legal progress (at least in the Western world) made by women, Gothic texts still frequently convey anxiety and anger about the lot of women. Many of the works analysed in this volume reflect women's lack of agency; the continued polarisation of women through patterns of antithesis such as good/ bad, saint/sinner and virgin/ whore; a continued use of stereotypes; and the pathologisation of women who fail to conform to traditional expectations. While these vary in expression and representation across the centuries and across cultures, they are depressingly constant and suggest that women have been and still feel disadvantaged and disempowered. On the other hand, the use of

Gothic effects to celebrate transgressive female energy and iconoclasm is perhaps greater and more subtle now than it was when Charlotte Dacre wrote *Zofloya, or The Moor* in the early nineteenth century.

While works by male Gothic authors are discussed in several of the chapters, the main focus of *Women and the Gothic* is unashamedly on women: women characters within texts; women as Gothic authors; women as readers; women as critics; women as theorists. This is not because we want to return to the ghettoisation of work by women prevalent in the 1970s and 1980s; rather it is because we think that post-feminism has been a mixed blessing that needs challenging. On the one hand, it has allowed a more sophisticated and nuanced approach to gender; on the other hand, it has worked to retrograde effect in eliding misogynist impulses within the text, the academy and the world. For this reason, there have very recently been calls to revive feminism in what seems to be a shift of mood. Examples include the UK Feminista movement, the Everyday Sexism Project (everydaysexism.com), the publication of *Fifty Shades of Feminism*, edited by Lisa Appignanesi, Susie Orbach and Rachel Holmes, in 2013, and the reprinting of Shulamith Firestone's *The Dialectic of Sex: The Case for Feminist Revolution* (1970) by Verso in March 2015. What has become known, since 2013, as 'fourth-wave feminism' sees women engaging with technology to build strong movements online in order to challenge outdated attitudes and to demand social justice for women. This is no doubt because, despite changes to legislation and social practices, women still struggle for equal status with men economically, politically and socially, and misogyny remains deeply ingrained in almost all cultures. This book should be seen as part of that feminist revival; indeed, Gina Wisker in her chapter sees recent Gothic writing by women as indicating a 'new feminist energy'. Collectively, the chapters highlight how Gothic texts either mimic the polarisation of women in Western society or seek to challenge damaging stereotypes and constricting practices – sometimes both in the same text. In examining this cultural phenomenon, the authors of these chapters draw on a number of critical approaches and are not afraid to question orthodoxies. Overall, the volume embraces post-feminism but is not afraid to critique it; draws on feminism while interrogating its shortcomings; and resurrects the body of the Gothic woman in various and multifarious ways.

In bringing together outstanding women critics from different generations we are able to represent and celebrate the place of women in the Gothic as our understanding of it has evolved with the growth of Gothic studies. The first section of the book, 'Family Matters', comprises five chapters that focus on the confinement of women; they illustrate how patriarchal ideology can result in psychological containment at one extreme and actual physical incarceration at the other. Women can by bounded by the home and by an expectation that they will slot easily into traditional roles; refusal to accept this can result in shaming or demonisation. Angela Wright, author of the first chapter in this section, examines the phenomenon of heroines in flight in Gothic texts by women, arguing that although it is a truth well known that mothers are invariably dead or dying when such flights occur, the reasons underscoring that recognised truth require further scrutiny. Wright notes that Jane Austen's narrator in *Northanger Abbey* brilliantly parodies this well-known trope as early as 1797, drawing upon the fictional models of Ann Radcliffe, Maria Regina Roche, Eliza Parsons and Eleanor Sleath. And yet, she suggests, closer study of all these novels reveals that the mothers therein portrayed are less dead than one might imagine; they may be imprisoned, disguised or wronged, perhaps, but they are nonetheless disturbingly present. In this chapter Wright sets out to recover the undead mother and, in doing so, interrogates why so many heroines of women's Gothic take flight during the Romantic period.

The second chapter in this section, 'Madwomen and Attics' by Laurence Talairach-Vielmas, focuses on how mad/bad women during the nineteenth century were generally safely put away in order to maintain the status quo, their imprisonment ending their deviance. Women locked up and/or buried alive in Radcliffean Gothic and Victorian revisions of the genre, such as Charlotte Brontë's *Jane Eyre* (1847), are generally read by feminist critics as representations of woman's social and legal condition, epitomising woman's powerlessness and voicelessness in a patriarchal society. However, in the second half of the nineteenth century, such images of madwomen locked up in attics were revisited, as madness and 'badness' became the object of medical investigation and as research into mental physiology attempted to probe the mysteries of brain mechanisms. Not only did sensation novelists rewrite the clichés of the genre, finding their sources of inspiration in real-life cases and denouncing the wrongful incarceration of women in lunatic asylums (as in Wilkie Collins's *The Woman in White* and Mary Elizabeth Braddon's *Lady Audley's Secret*), but they also incorporated madwomen buried alive due to medical errors into their fictions. Talairach-Vielmas focuses in particular on representations of emotions and on the ways in which definitions of madness changed in the nineteenth century. Moreover, she reveals how madwomen's places of confinement changed during that period, coffins and deadhouses (structures used for the temporary storage of human corpses before burial) replacing the attics of mid-Victorian narratives, allowing authors to both capitalise on current fears of premature interment and offer a more horrifying vision of containment.

In 'Mothers and Others', Ginette Carpenter examines two recent films, exploring the figure of the gothic m/other as a continuing site of textual absence and/or excessive abjection. Ridley Scott's *Prometheus* (2012), prequel to the *Alien* quadrilogy, repeatedly absents the mother in its postulation of a male creationist myth, and the uncanny textual space opened up by its anterior-yet-posterior relationship to its predecessors is overwritten by the predictable effects of penetrative body-horror: the mother as monstrous Other is driven beyond the edges of the text. In contrast to this absenting of the mother, Lynne Ramsay's *We Need to Talk About Kevin* (2011) is saturated with motherly presence, so that the character of Eva Khatchadourian occupies every scene. The tropes of Gothic horror are used to convey a sense of mothering as violent self-erasure and the mother as potential progenitor of an uncontainable monstrous Other. However, the film uses repeated mirrorings of Eva and Kevin that imply a haunting, pre-Symbolic bond that persists in troubling a monolithic reading of the developing mother/son dyad. Drawing on Kristevan and Irigarayan theory, Carpenter argues that both *Prometheus* and *We Need to Talk About Kevin* are examples of a post-feminist Gothic that articulates contemporary anxieties about the increasingly engineered medicalisation and judgemental cultural monitoring of mothering/mothers.

In the fourth chapter in this section, 'The Gothic Girl Child', Lucie Armitt suggests that when Gothic narratives pair up children as sister/brother siblings, the girl child is frequently read as mere shadow (ghost) to her more interesting brother. However, when read in isolation, a far more intriguing narrative emerges. Anxiety about intimacy between girls or between girls and women is evident, Armitt argues, in works such as Elizabeth Gaskell's 'The Old Nurse's Story', Margaret Oliphant's 'The Library Window' and Henry James's *The Turn of the Screw*. A young girl's desire for a female Other is the unspeakable subtext of these and similar stories. Examining Daphne du Maurier's short story 'The Pool', Angela Carter's *The Magic Toyshop*, Stephen King's *Carrie* and Sarah Waters's *The Little Stranger*, Armitt explores both the rivalry between sisters and the self-abjection that can result from the onset of menstruation. A common narrative trope in stories of this kind, she notes, is the double or mirror. The relationship between women and mirrors is often exploited within literature of all kinds, but in Gothic narratives reflections frequently produce skewed images or strange doppelgängers that perhaps represent the fear of a new identity following menstruation or the loss of childhood innocence. Finding that bonds between girls in

Gothic texts are constantly fraught with danger, betrayal and loss and that the Gothic girl child must undergo trauma on her journey towards womanhood, Armitt concludes that it is hard to find positive messages for younger women in Gothic works, a textual feature that perhaps reflects the contradictory attitudes held towards girls by society at large.

In the last chapter in the 'Family Matters' section, 'A Woman's Place', Diana Wallace argues that the Gothic has been the mode of writing that has perhaps most brilliantly articulated and symbolised the terrors of the domestic space. Possession, confinement and loss of identity are all shadows which haunt the home for women, particularly those who inhabit – or fear inhabiting – the roles of housewife and mother. In 'The Uncanny' (1919), Freud explored the ambivalent relationship between the *heimlich* and the *unheimlich*, the way in which the 'homely' doubles the 'unhomely'. In Gothic texts, the homely is often associated with the hellish and with the sense of a split female self. In this chapter, Wallace examines a range of works by Norah Lofts, Christina Stead, Sylvia Plath, Shirley Jackson, Penelope Mortimer, Barbara Comyns and Emma Donoghue in order to explore how they use Gothic tropes and devices to convey women's ambivalence towards the realm of the domestic and their role within it.

The second section of this volume, 'Transgressions', opens with Anne Williams's chapter 'Wicked Women'. She suggests that the villainesses of early male Gothics, such as Lewis's Matilda in *The Monk*, are characters of romance, wherein we expect to find types and stereotypes rather than realistic psychological portraits. They can be unambiguously wicked because they are women in a metaphysical system that blames Eve as the root of all evil. Williams argues, however, that since the 1790s the Gothic tradition has been engaged in challenging and deconstructing the notion of 'wicked women'. Indeed, the Gothic gallery of wicked women offers a guide to evolving cultural notions of female psychology. Having traced such women back to the portrayal of Eloise as irrational woman in Pope's 'Eloise to Abelard', Williams then draws on psychoanalytic theory to examine representations of the sexually desiring woman as 'hysterical', focusing in particular on the figure of the rebellious nun. And although Horace Walpole gives us no wicked women in *The Castle of Otranto*, Williams intriguingly suggests that 'the female' – constructed by patriarchy as instability, materiality, sexuality, irrationality, darkness, evil – is nevertheless housed within Otranto's vaults and hidden chambers. From there she moves to focus on the mother as witch figure, suggesting that many Gothic texts are fraught with anxiety pertaining to mothers and noting that expression of sexual desire by female characters, in texts as diverse as *Zofloya the Moor, Jane Eyre* and *Rebecca,* is associated with an adopted masculinity and with wickedness. Williams concludes by looking at works by Shirley Jackson and Henry James and examining how they exploit the ambiguities inherent in the familiar Gothic conventions of feminine evil.

In 'The Female Gothic Body' Marie Mulvey-Roberts argues that the property and inheritance rights of the early 'transgressive' Gothic heroine could be seized by controlling her body through marriage, domestic violence or imprisonment. Women writers, including Ann Radcliffe and Elizabeth Gaskell, rewrote Perrault's version of the Bluebeard legend to embrace female empowerment and somatic ownership. Rosina Bulwer Lytton's wrongful confinement within an asylum by her Bluebeard husband, the Gothic novelist Edward Bulwer Lytton, appears to have influenced the work of Wilkie Collins and Elizabeth Braddon. Mulvey-Roberts goes on to suggest that throughout history women's bodies have frequently been regarded as sites of monstrosity and she notes that this cultural abjection is represented within the Gothic in various ways, from the gorgon to the vampire. Furthermore, the danger posed by the reproductive female body and anxieties about miscegenation are denoted in the fragmentation of the female monster in Mary Shelley's *Frankenstein.* However, adaptations by feminist novelists, including Shelley Jackson and Elizabeth Hand, celebrate the autonomous patchwork self and scarred female body as representations of a painfully achieved female subjectivity. Literary representations of the Medusa's castrating gaze, from C. L. Moore's 'Shambleau' to Susan Hill's *The Woman in Black* and the misogynist myth of the *vagina dentata*, deconstructed in Angela Carter's short stories, demonstrate how fears of the feminine continue to be articulated through the female body and its constituent parts. Mulvey-Roberts concludes that Gothic fictions embody a dialogue between an unquestioning representation of the female body as threatening and an awareness that such images merely work to sustain a misogynistic patriarchal inheritance.

In 'Spectral Femininity', Rebecca Munford examines the troubling spectres of femininity that have haunted the Gothic imagination since the eighteenth century. Etymologically related as much to the field of looking as to the realm of phantoms, the 'spectre' occupies a vital place in the Gothic's vocabulary of haunting, revenance and (in)visibility. From the repressed daughters and buried mothers of the eighteenth-century Gothic, to the infernal images of wraithlike women in the macabre imaginings of Edgar Allan Poe and Charles Baudelaire, femininity is peculiarly susceptible to 'spectralisation'. With reference to the Freudian uncanny, Derrida's notion of spectrality and the work of Terry Castle, Munford analyses Daphne du Maurier's *Rebecca*, Shirley

Jackson's *The Haunting of Hill House* and Ali Smith's *Hotel World*, in all of which images of spectral femininity are used to explore questions of historical dispossession, experiences of social invisibility, and anxieties about sexual identity and generational conflict. As Derrida reminds us, the spectre 'begins by coming back'; never fully exorcised, the spectral is always that which refuses to be laid to rest. Munford concludes that, while images of spectral femininity often function as sites of dread and anxiety, they also work to signify powerful images of irrepressible female desire and agency.

In 'Female Gothic and the Law', Sue Chaplin argues that the Gothic emerges in the eighteenth century as a potent literary critique of modern Western forms of law – and that the law underwent rapid transformation at the same time as the Gothic began to take shape and rapidly diversify in the eighteenth and nineteenth centuries. She suggests that Gothic writing by women in particular interrogates the ontological instability and physical vulnerability of the female subject before the law and that it does so through repeated evocations, in various historical and cultural contexts, of the relationship between law, sacrifice, trauma and shame. While remaining sensitive to questions of historical and cultural difference in Gothic narratives, Chaplin seeks to identify points of continuity between older modes of Female Gothic and its more contemporary manifestations; she therefore moves from analyses of work by Sophia Lee, Ann Radcliffe and Eliza Parsons to female-authored vampire fictions by Stephenie Meyer and Charlaine Harris. Drawing on Juliet MacCannell's work, Chaplin argues that these diverse narratives articulate the trauma and shame of female subjects constructed in and through the law as sacrificial objects of exchange between 'brothers'. Contemporary female Gothic fictions, she concludes, expose the trauma and shame of the law *itself* as its ontological coherence begins to disintegrate under the conditions of late-modernity.

In the last chapter of this section, 'Female Vampirism', Gina Wisker examines how fictional vampires problematise received notions of women's passivity, 'natural' nurturing skills and social conformity, suggesting that female vampires destabilise such comfortable, culturally inflected investments. Indeed, she argues that performativity, abjection and carnival lie at the heart of their construction and representation so that there is a constant tension between punishment and celebration of their transgressive nature. Ranging across a number of nineteenth-century texts, including Le Fanu's 'Carmilla' (1871–2), Stoker's *Dracula* (1897), Braddon's 'The Good Lady Ducayne' (1896) and Florence Marryat's *The Blood of the Vampire* (1897), Wisker suggests that they can be read as indicating gaps and fissures in social certainties and as nightmares emanating from the zones of patriarchy. Moving into the twentieth century to consider Angela Carter's 'The Lady of the House of Love' and 'The Loves of Lady Purple', Wisker finds powerful female vampires who provide templates for later authors, such that vampires come to embody 'energies of revolt' in work by writers such as Sherry Gottlieb and Nancy Kirkpatrick. In these later texts and in various lesbian vampire fictions, vampires become liberating, feminist figures: sexually transgressive, they undermine received certainties of identity, family, and hierarchy based on gender, sexuality and ethnicity. But they can also represent the energy of social activism: Nalo Hopkinson's culturally inflected 'Greedy Choke Puppy' refocuses the female vampire in a more socially engaged role, playing on concerns about women and knowledge, the community, values, ethics and cosmetic beauty. Wisker's chapter concludes with two recent works: *A Girl Walks Home Alone at Night* (2014), a film directed by Ana Lily Amirpour, and Moira Buffini's play *A Vampire Story* and its film version *Byzantium*, directed by Neil Jordan in 2013. In these works we see vampires becoming angels of mercy and women becoming self-sufficient despite poverty and vulnerability; we also see a skateboarding fearless female vampire who helps clean up the alleys and back streets of the small Iranian dead-end town where she lives in an attempt to eradicate poverty and violence.

The third section of *Women and the Gothic*, 'New Directions', comprises chapters that engage either with new ways of looking at Gothic texts or focus on new media that have appropriated the Gothic mode. The first of these, 'Queering the Female Gothic' by Ardel Haefele-Thomas, examines work by women writers from the 1890s onwards who use the Gothic to create covert and/or overt queer situations and characters – often as a means of exploring larger cultural and social concerns, such as restrictive patriarchal and hetero-normative family structures, the medical pathologisation of female and genderqueer bodies, institutions of racism and sexism within colonial and slave narratives, and contemporary issues surrounding the intersections of sexuality, race, class and gender identity. Haefele-Thomas examines the work of a number of American and British women authors who have employed the Gothic as a proverbial safe space in which to explore these concerns; they include Vernon Lee, Florence Marryat, Carson McCullers, Toni Morrison, Maryse Condé, Jane Chambers, Jewelle Gomez, Sarah Waters, Yvonne Heidt and Cate Culpepper. Not only do their fictions encompass queer characters and scenarios in terms of gender identities outside of the male/female binary and the full spectrum of queer sexual orientation, but these authors themselves, taken as a group, embody the full spectrum as far as gender identity and sexual orientation are concerned.

In 'No Country for Old Women', the editors of *Women and the Gothic*, Avril Horner and Sue Zlosnik, explore Gothic modes of representing older women that either reinforce or challenge the negative images of female ageing that are ubiquitous in many cultures. They suggest that post-feminism is retrograde in its attitude to age and argue that it has served the purpose of a dominant culture that marginalises the older woman and which, through fetishising the youthful body, inevitably produces fears of ageing in the young. They suggest that this fear of ageing is reflected in many popular Gothic texts, including the *Twilight* series, and note that such works can be placed in a long tradition of writing that represents the older woman as sinister, manipulative and predatory. Indeed, they observe that many nineteenth-century authors presented older women (such as the Countess Fosco in Wilkie Collins's *The Woman in White*, Madame Beck in Brontë's *Villette*, and the 'she' of Rider Haggard's eponymous novel) in just that vein. While Daphne du Maurier adopted that template for Mrs Danvers in *Rebecca*, in 'Don't Look Now' she more subtly portrays the older woman through the eyes of a male unreliable male narrator, as strange, wise and emotionally prescient, while simultaneously drawing attention to the fragility of masculinity. The figure of the soucouyant in work by authors such as Jean Rhys, Helen Oyeyeme and David Chariandy allows yet another configuration: that of the older woman as insightful, independent and capable of supernatural transformations. Certain authors, including Stella Gibbons, Edith Wharton and Paul Magrs have used yet another tactic – that of comic Gothic – to subvert conventional attitudes to the older woman. Horner and Zlosnik uncover in their chapter a complex dialogue in and between Gothic texts about the ageing woman – one that reflects the fear, anxiety and revulsion evoked by the ageing female body in many cultures but that also offers counter-narratives that redeem ageing as a time of energy and liberation.

In 'Virtual Gothic Women', Catherine Spooner argues that recurring fictions of uncanny disembodiment and an 'electronic elsewhere' accompanied electronic media throughout the nineteenth and twentieth centuries. She suggests that women's position within this alliance has been complex: often the media through which technologies are Gothicised, as in spirit photography, provide a hinge between the embodied human subject and a pure realm of disembodiment. This uneasy positioning of a Gothicised female subject across the Cartesian mind/body dualism is reiterated in contemporary fictions that engage with the possibilities of digital technologies. Virtual Gothic heroines are liberated into a realm of pure mind, but remain haunted by the needs and sensations of the body. Spooner begins by briefly tracing the relationship between Gothic femininity and technology through the eighteenth and nineteenth centuries, demonstrating how an increasingly disembodied and uncanny femininity was mediated through emergent media such as photography, telegraphy and cinema. Having considered Arthur Machen's *The Great God Pan* (1894), Spooner then focuses on three contemporary novels that provide an insight into the historical development of Gothicised digital technologies and so-called 'virtual' environments since the early 1980s: William Gibson's *Neuromancer* (1984), Neal Stephenson's *The Diamond Age* (1995) and Scarlett Thomas's *The End of Mr Y* (2006). Each of these novels complicates and negotiates the role of the Gothic heroine in the digital labyrinth, while asking searching questions about the role of the body in a culture of disembodiment.

In the last chapter in the volume, 'Formations of Player Agency and Gender in Gothic Video Games', Tanya Kryzwinska explores the connections between the design of player agency and formations of gender within Gothic video games. Having outlined how the conditions of player agency drain power from the more radical and subversive gender formations often found within Gothic fiction itself, Kryzwinska turns to games in which a more subtle, ambiguous or subversive approach to player agency is taken; where alternative methods and contextualising representations are deployed by game designers to create models of player agency that do not, through the usual trope of mastery, align with dominant notions of masculinity or a phallic economy. Her focus in this chapter is therefore mainly on the role of players in the thick of the Gothic game text and the gendered, contextual economy of the power (or powerlessness) that they are afforded. Some Gothic game designers are finding innovative ways of playing with and subverting the conventional, gendered plotting of power that is apparent in games such as *Outlast* (2014), *Painkiller* (2004) and *Quake 4* (2005). *Phantasmagoria* (1995), *Primal* (2003), *American McGee's Alice* (2000) and *Bayonetta* (2009), for instance, draw on narratives told from a woman's point of view. They can, therefore, Kryzwinska suggests, be categorised under the cultural rubric of 'Female Gothic', although she uses the term not to suggest that gender or sex is immanent but to show how gender is constructed and performed through the texts that comprise culture. Such games actively invite the interest of women and girl players. Kryzwinska concludes that certain iterations of Gothic can be used very effectively in games to disquieten and demythologise the thoughtless formations of agency and gender that are perpetuated by many games directed at men and boy players.

The reasons for women's current lack of equality with men economically, socially and politically are manifold, but one of them is the negative way in which women are conceptualised in many cultures. Close analysis of this in Gothic fiction, film and other media illustrates how this negativity is constantly conveyed through powerful myths and images which work to devalue women at an unconscious as well as a conscious level. The Gothic, which has always excelled in the portrayal of the Other, rather horrifyingly reveals how women have been, and continue to be, abjected by the very societies that claim to value them. However, as several chapters in this volume demonstrate, many women authors have used the Gothic mode to critique both negative images of women (as wicked, or threatening or sinister) and the systems of power that effect the hierarchy whereby women are devalued. In this sense, Gothic fictions enact a dialogue between the continued unquestioning use of negative images of women and an awareness that such images merely work to sustain a misogynistic patriarchal inheritance. The Gothic, then, can be used to negotiate inherited, changing and often contradictory female identities rooted deep in the cultural imagination. Its contribution to our awareness of what it means to be a woman is that it exposes – often sensationally, sometimes sinisterly, occasionally comically and frequently horrifyingly – the extreme reaches of the cultural celebration and demonisation of women.

Part I

Family Matters

Heroines in Flight: Narrating Invisibility and Maturity in Women's Gothic Writing of the Romantic Period
Angela Wright

Rack well you hero's nerves and heart,
And let your heroine take her part;
Her fine blue eyes were made to weep,
Nor should she ever taste of sleep;
Ply her with terrors day or night,
And keep her always in a fright,
But in a carriage when you get her,
Be sure you fairly overset her;
If she will break her bones – why let her:
Again, if e'er she walks abroad,
Of course you bring some wicked lord,
Who with three ruffians snaps his prey,
And to a castle speeds away;
Those close confin'd in haunted tower,
You leave your captive in his power,
Till dead with horror and dismay,
She scales the walls and flies away.

(Mary Alcock, 'A Receipt for Writing a Novel', in Poems)

Published in 1799, Mary Alcock's parodic recipe for novel-writing repeats much-echoed commonplace assumptions about the comparative youth, fair complexion, victimisation, nervous constitution and tendency to flight that characterised the Gothic heroine of the 1790s. In playful tone, Alcock's recipe endows the heroine with the superhuman abilities of scaling walls and fleeing tyranny, underlining at the same time the unrealistic expectations that author and reader project onto a heroine. Still, despite the humorous vein, there is something disturbing about the way in which her poem conflates the role of Gothic authorship with the fictional role of villain. The imagined addressee of this poem ('you') holds the heroine captive, like the villain, subjects her to a carriage crash, kidnap, imprisonment and perpetual flight. It is an astute conflation on the part of Alcock, suggesting that any female author's exploitation of a heroine involves, in turn, an abrogation of femininity on their part. In other words, exploiting a heroine for commercial gain is a masculine pursuit, unsuitable for proper women writers.

Of course, Alcock did this in the spirit of parody, in order to distance herself critically from the commercial exploitation of the Gothic heroine. Her recipe was one in a long line of parodies that targeted the unimaginative regurgitation of a heroine as virtuous and blue-eyed. 'Terrorist Novel Writing' (Anon. 1798), 'The Terrorist System of Novel Writing' (Anon. 1797) and Alcock's 'Recipe' all reproduced the stable set of ingredients for composing a Gothic novel, implying that if any author or reader was naïve enough to devour these recipes, then they must already be lacking in imagination and enterprise. 'Terrorist Novel Writing', for example, humorously conflated the unthinking fashionable routines of those female readers who populated spa towns such as Bath with their unimaginative reading habits, advising of the ingredients: 'Mix them together, in the form of three volumes to be taken at any of the watering places before going to bed' (Anon. 1798). The implications were clear; it mattered not in which particular order the three volumes came, or the particular spa town in which they were consumed. The result of reading would always be the same.

Writing almost contemporaneously with the satirists of these articles and poems, Jane Austen too recognised and foregrounded the perils of novel-writing in *Northanger Abbey* as early as 1797. There, she drew upon the fictional heroines of Ann Radcliffe, Maria Regina Roche, Eliza Parsons and Eleanor Sleath as she painted her own heroine, Catherine Morland, in stark contrast to the Emilies, Amandas and Laurettes of her contemporaries. On the first page, Austen's narrator takes pains to draw our attention to Catherine's 'thin awkward figure, a sallow skin without colour, dark lank hair, and strong features' and her inability to 'learn or understand anything before she was taught' (Austen 1995: 13). These characteristics appear to stand in stark contrast to those of the well-read, refined, flaxen-haired, blue-eyed, lachrymose heroines that populated the best-selling Gothic romances of Radcliffe, Roche, Parsons and Sleath in the 1790s.

Such stark contrasts drawn between a conventionally fair Gothic heroine in flight and Catherine Morland's humorously sketched anti-heroine with her sallow complexion has led Deirdre Le Faye, for one, to observe that Gothic heroines are:

> of high birth, angelic beauty, extreme virtue and sensibility, and although usually orphaned and invariably growing up in poverty on some lonely

foreign mountainside, nevertheless are so naturally gifted as to possess all the female accomplishments without ever having any formal tuition. (Le Faye 2002: 205)

As with Alcock's recipe, virginity, sensibility, beauty, threat and flight constitute the consistently reproduced, unimaginative qualities of the eighteenth-century Gothic heroine. These, for many, were qualities that are perceived to be stock, imitative and endlessly reproduced without deviation in women's Gothic writing of the Romantic period.

Ann Radcliffe was certainly not the first author to place a heroine at the centre of her novels. Almost since the inception of the novel, the qualities of heroism were endlessly sculpted and refined by authors throughout the eighteenth century, including the notable examples of Samuel Richardson, the Marquis de Sade, the Abbé Prévost, Jean-Jacques Rousseau and Henry MacKenzie. Radcliffe, however, came to be perceived as exceptional due to the unique fusion of qualities and challenges with which she endowed her heroines. Like Mary Alcock's recipe, her heroines were visions of blue-eyed innocence who were con-tinually confronted with terrors thrown in their way by the villain at the heart of the tale. Radcliffe's original genius was, however, widely recog-nised and praised, with Sir Walter Scott christening her 'the first poetess of Romantic fiction' and Nathan Drake calling her 'the Shakespeare of Romance writers' (see Townshend and Wright 2014: 3–32). Those women authors who dared to follow in the footsteps of Radcliffe, however, attracted critical censure on the basis of slavish imitation and commercial exploitation. Through the financially successful examples of Ann Radcliffe's tales of terror, which earned unprecedented sums of £600 for *The Mysteries of Udolpho* (1794) and £800 for *The Italian* (1797), the uncontaminated virtue, beauty and evasive abilities of the heroine had proven, for many aspiring authors, to be too commercially appealing. Or had they?

When one goes beyond the textual examples of Ann Radcliffe and Jane Austen during the Romantic period, I will argue, the qualities of heroism that I have outlined above become less clear-cut in terms of uncompromising virtue, beauty and age. After a brief survey of how more canonical examples of Gothic fiction in the 1790s first address the stock characteristics of the heroine, I will proceed to examine more closely a less well-known example of Gothic fiction from the 1790s, Eleanor Sleath's *The Orphan of the Rhine* (1798). This was one of the Northanger Horrid Novels that Austen's Isabella Thorpe suggests to Catherine Morland from a reading list supplied by the absent 'Miss Andrews', a name which, to a contemporaneous readership, could only conjure up the conduct book example of Samuel Richardson's famously virtuous servant heroine Pamela Andrews from 1740. Why this name is dropped in so casually by Austen is unclear. Its inclusion suggests that only a character as impossibly virtuous as Pamela Andrews could recommend these works, or else that the works themselves are impossibly virtuous. Whichever the case is, the fictional recommendation of Miss Andrews suggests that *The Orphan of the Rhine* was read with more frequency and gusto when it was published than it is now. From Sleath's novel, I will argue for a revaluation of the representations of women, a revaluation that reverses the easy assumptions both of the Romantic parodies of Gothic fiction and of persistent critical tendencies that accept some of the assumptions about heroism that such parodies propagated.

To some degree, the critical tendencies to accept the stock characteristics of heroism have been challenged before, most notably by E. J. Clery in *The Rise of Supernatural Fiction, 1762–1800*. In an insightful chapter upon Gothic heroism, Clery interrogated what she perceived to be the 'rival hermeneutics' of heroism at work in novels such as Ann Radcliffe's *The Mysteries of Udolpho* where even the villain Montoni sneeringly refers to its self-conscious qualities (Clery 1995: 119). Examining the passage where Montoni tells Emily 'You speak like a heroine ... we shall see whether you can suffer like one' (Radcliffe 1980: 381), Clery observes that while heroism 'is initially projected as an illegitimate and irrational "other" of authority' it nonetheless 'finds justification in the outcome of the narrative' (Clery 1995: 119). Focusing upon the qualities of heroism, which, during the course of the narrative, appear to challenge patriarchal authority without any authority of their own before eventual vindication, Clery argues that Emily survives by 'turning the tables and learning to treat *herself* as a commodity' (122). She continues by focusing upon the heroine's 'exchange value' in the marriage market place, arguing that virtue becomes synecdochical of her humanity and actions, and that the way that a heroine prevails is by valuing her body and virtue as a commodity. Heroism thus becomes a process in self-awareness. Clery's argument is vital in its dissection of the qualities of heroism, for she points up the symbiotic nature of its differing qualities, and how they come together to act as a market force in any successful negotiation towards marriage.

That self-awareness is a painful lesson in what Mary Wollstonecraft had already identified in *A Vindication of the Rights of Woman* as the indelicacy of 'bring[ing] to market a marriageable miss, whose person is taken from one public place to another, richly caparisoned' (Wollstonecraft 1994: 255). Authors who were contemporaneous with

Ann Radcliffe had already exposed the painful lessons and negotiations of the marriage marketplace; Frances (Fanny) Burney's first novel *Evelina* (1778), for example, bore the tight-lipped descriptive subtitle: 'The History of a Young Lady's Entrance into the World'. Neither the title nor the novel itself suggested in any way that this entrance into the world would be one of pleasure; instead, as the novel's epistolary form made clear, that entrance into the world is determined by others, and endured by the heroine. Burney's subsequent novels, *Cecilia* (1782), *Camilla* (1796) and *The Wanderer* (1814), experimented stylistically and thematically with the reasons why the negotiation of a marriage market place was so fraught for females either endowed with fortune or else presented as penniless. The title of her final novel, *The Wanderer, or Female Difficulties* exposed these dangers to greatest effect; with its disowned, rootless, penniless heroine confronted with abject poverty, scorn and disdain everywhere she goes. Burney's wanderer foregrounds in terrifying manner precisely why virtue alone is not enough for any heroine; fortune, family and class are also precious adjuncts to the commodity of virtue.

Whose Perspective?

Gothic writing of the 1790s teaches its readership about both the values of maintaining virtue, and the perils of shedding that self-same commodity. As the decade of the 1790s progresses, however, these polar oppositions of morality are increasingly interrogated, compassionated and blurred. Those shades of representation exist even in Matthew Lewis's 1796 novel *The Monk*, where, as many of its contemporaneous critics protested, female characters who transgressed (Matilda and the Bleeding Nun) were either demons or ghosts. Lewis's convenient spectralisation of the transgressors does not necessarily imply condemnation, however; *The Monk* offers surprising moments of compassion to Beatrice de Las Cisternas in particular. She is the Bleeding Nun who haunts Raymond in place of his promised bride Agnes. Her story is recounted to us from two sources, first Agnes and later the Wandering Jew. Agnes, a fellow female who, like the Bleeding Nun, is upon the brink of being forced into conventual life, confesses to Raymond that she is an 'unworthy Historian' of this transgressive nun who fell prey to her passions and murdered for love. Part of the reason for this, reveals Agnes, is that 'in all the Chronicles of past times, this remarkable Personage is never once mentioned' and that 'unluckily till after her death She was never known to have existed' (Lewis 1980:140). It was only upon death,

Agnes emphasises, that the Bleeding Nun deemed it 'necessary to make some noise in the world' (140). The invisibility of the Nun during her life, forced into a convent in place of a premature marriage, is fore-grounded and criticised through Agnes's choice of words; she can only 'make some noise in the world' upon death as 'unluckily' in life she was not recognised. Furthermore, as Agnes's narrative makes clear, it is only in death that her wishes are respected by those who surround her:

> '... as soon as the Clock strikes One the Door of the haunted Chamber opens. (Observe, that this room has been shut up for near a Century.) Then out walks the Ghostly Nun with her Lamp and Dagger: She descends the stair-case of the Eastern Tower; and crosses the great Hall! On that night the Porter always leaves the Gates of the Castle open, out of respect to the Apparition: not that this is thought by any means necessary, since she could easily whip through the Key-hole if She chose it; But merely out of politeness, and to prevent her from making her exit in a way so derogatory to the dignity of her Ghost-ship.'
> 'And whither does she go on quitting the Castle?'
> 'To Heaven, I hope; But if she does, the place certainly is not to her taste, for She always returns after an hour's absence.'
>
> (Lewis 1980: 141)

The ghost of Beatrice de las Cisternas is here accorded a level of dignity that, Agnes emphasises, she did not receive during her lifetime. The porter leaves the gates open to her 'out of respect' and 'politeness' so that her 'Ghost-ship' can sail through unchallenged and unimpeded. Invisible in life, the reader is forced, through Agnes's account, to see the levels of respect and dignity that the ghost Beatrice receives as the recti-fication of an injustice. Majesty, dignity and reverence characterise her reception in the after-life even as she went unnoticed and uncelebrated during her lifetime.

The version of the Bleeding Nun that Agnes gives us is markedly different to the tale offered to Raymond by the Wandering Jew in *The Monk*. By contrast, the latter develops the narratives of the Nun's trans-gressions more censoriously, concentrating upon her 'warm and volup-tuous character' (173) and her growing 'depravity' (174). The story of the Bleeding Nun, is, as Jerrold E. Hogle insightfully describes it, one of several instances that demonstrate that 'sexuality has lost its juridical base' within *The Monk* (Hogle 1997). Within the competing male and female versions of the Bleeding Nun's story in *The Monk*, we further see how Lewis offers insight into the social causes that underline this; how, for many women, their existence goes unremarked whether they are morally virtuous or 'depraved' in life. Lewis, despite seemingly offering the angel/demon dichotomy in *The Monk*, offers surprising and easily overlooked moments of understanding into the all-too-human failings of his female characters. When read closely, these moments of insight from Lewis illustrate the overarching significance of gender in interpreting and recounting the histories of women.

It may seem odd to raise the example of a male author of Gothic horror, Matthew Lewis, in order to discuss the idea of the heroine in Women's Gothic writing of the Romantic period. I do so, however, with good reason, for the example of Lewis's infamous *The Monk* is published amid the examples of women's Gothic writing that I offer. Perhaps for reasons of propriety (given its lurid depictions of rape, incest and murder) and the accusations of blasphemy that were levelled against the novel by anti-Jacobin critics, it is not mentioned by name in parodies of Gothic in the 1790s, but it nonetheless provides an important conduit for the development of the idea of the heroine in the 1790s (see Wright 2013: 135–40). Prior to Lewis's 1796 shocker, Ann Radcliffe had also begun to examine and portray with remarkable consistency females who were imprisoned, silenced and invisible. Her earliest novels, *The Castles of Athlin and Dunbayne* (1789) and *A Sicilian Romance* (1790), both give remarkably consistent examples of women silenced and imprisoned by tyrannical husbands. In the first, the Baroness Louisa and her daughter Laura are passive prisoners of Baron Malcolm, while in the second novel, Louisa di Bernini is discovered to have been imprisoned by her husband for close on twenty years. Although Radcliffe famously never exploited the supernatural in publication form during her lifetime, there is a sense that the servants' nervous imaginings of ghosts when they espy tapering, wavering lights, or hear an unusual noise, are in fact acts of intuition concerning the imprisoned women. Following on from Radcliffe's examples, without doubt Lewis's Bleeding Nun from 1796 took its cue from the silenced, imprisoned female in Radcliffe's earlier works. And what is more, the bifocal manner in which he chooses to portray the Bleeding Nun (offering versions of her by both a male and female narrator) in turn allows for a more complex approach to questions of virtue, age and domestic imprisonment in subsequent novels.

Although the critical story of Women's Gothic Writing has, to an extent, uncovered the point about hidden histories, what I think remains to be explored is the extent to which Romantic Gothic women's writing, influenced by both Ann Radcliffe's and Matthew Lewis's earlier examples, contained within itself the seeds of critical distancing from the parodic heroinism that it also proposed (see, for example, Doody 1977; Ellis 1989; Hoeveler 1998; Smith and Wallace 2009). If we take first Radcliffe's novel that is published after Lewis's *The Monk*, the opening of the 1797 *The Italian* does not give its readership much cause to hope for any deviation from the conventional Gothic heroinism that the Alcock recipe cited at the beginning of this chapter. Through the focalisation of the hero, Vincentio di Vivaldi, two women who catch his eye in church are offered to the gaze of the readership. We learn that one is the heroine through the glimpses of her afforded to the hero on the second page: '[Ellena's] features were of the Grecian outline, and, though they expressed the tranquillity of an elegant mind, her dark blue eyes sparkled with intelligence' (Radcliffe 2000: 10). The other woman, who we learn later is Signora Bianchi, is repeatedly described through the focalisation of Vivaldi as 'old', an adjective that seems somewhat dispensable to our understanding as we learn that she is in fact the aunt and guardian of Ellena. Notwithstanding, we must learn Vivaldi's opinion that:

> The figure of Signora Bianchi was not of an order to inspire admiration, and a spectator might have smiled to see the perturbation of Vivaldi, his faltering step and anxious eye, as he advanced to meet this venerable lady, as he bowed upon her faded hand, and listened to her querulous voice. (Radcliffe 2000: 31)

Signora Bianchi seems to be there merely as necessary evil, an elderly figure to be circumvented in order to gain access to the beautiful, blue-eyed heroine. It is only upon her untimely death, as Vivaldi examines the 'livid face of the corpse' that he feels any affinity with her; he ruminates that:

> this was the same countenance which only one preceding evening was animated like his own; which had looked upon him in tears, while, with anxiety the most tender, Bianchi had committed the happiness of her niece to his care, and had, alas! too justly predicted her approaching dissolution. (Radcliffe 2000: 68)

Vivaldi's emotions towards the elder of the two women, therefore, move from disdain while she lives, to terror as he looks upon her 'livid face' after death, and culminates, finally, in a misplaced, insincere nostalgia towards her anxiety about her niece Ellena. Only Bianchi's fine display of her feelings for Ellena arouse any pity or sorrow in Vivaldi for her death. Vivaldi's terror at the corpse of the older woman can only be held in abeyance by sentimentalising the relationship of Bianchi to Ellena. In many respects, Vivaldi is Radcliffe's finest hero in terms of compassion, duty and solicitude, but Radcliffe takes care, I think, to reveal slowly his flawed, biased approach to women; his tendency to deify the young and beautiful heroine, and to dismiss all other female characters within the novel as mere adjuncts to the young heroine.

By contrast, Olivia, the older nun who, it transpires, is the long-lost mother of Ellena, is focalised only through her daughter; through her we first learn of her sympathy and sensibility; her tale of woe, involving betrayal and rape, is reserved for the revelatory closure of the tale. The significance of this narrative reversal is that Olivia is first admired and loved; and only secondarily compassionated for her misfortunes and victimisation. Her tale, economically told as it is, serves mostly as necessary plot development in the narrative. It awards Ellena a birthright, accounts for the mysterious bond that draws the older and younger women together, but the order in which it is told does, however, raise important questions about storytelling and perspective within the narrative.

Reframing the Tale

In one respect, Eleanor Sleath's *The Orphan of the Rhine*, first published by the Minerva Press in 1798, seems to fall into the category of one of the many 'vapid and servile imitations' of the 'creative genius' and 'descriptive powers of Mrs Radcliffe' (Anon. 1799: 356). For like Radcliffe's *The Italian*, published a year before, there is the pairing of a younger woman and older woman, the eponymous Orphan of the Rhine and her foster mother Julie de Rubine. This pairing is also doubled within the novel in a strikingly similar way to Radcliffe's *The Italian*. At one point, Julie de Rubine, foster mother of the orphan Laurette, listens to the tale of the Conte della Croisse, who in his youth allowed himself to be seduced and led astray from his wife by a young woman accompanied by an older one:

> [W]e beheld two females come on shore [...] They were both veiled; but the graceful figure of the younger, for the other seemed to have passed the summer of her days, chiefly attracted our regard. Fancy had portrayed a face not less beautiful than the form to which it belonged; and I was anxious to be assured whether she had not been too profuse of her colouring, when a ruder breeze from the water wafted aside the lighter texture of her veil, and discovered the original. (Sleath 2014: 111)

Focused through the male gaze, the older woman is quickly dismissed as having 'passed the summer of her days', whereas the younger's form is referred to in terms of artwork; the Conte wishes to discover whether the original lives up to the face that 'Fancy' has suggested belongs to her. Fancy is personified as female by the Conte, who thereby displaces his own act of salacious objectification. Abstract fancy, art and artistry combine to describe the exquisite beauty of the younger woman, whereas the older woman's faded beauty is referred to in more organic terms. This scene is, of course, remarkably similar to the scene which opens Radcliffe's *The Italian*, where the face of the heroine Ellena is revealed to the panting, eager hero Vivaldi only by her veil being momentarily disrupted, and can then only be described as 'Grecian' in outline. The conventionality of the artistic metaphors in both Radcliffe and Sleath can be read as being inevitably parodic, almost bowed under the weight of artistic metaphor invoked to describe beautiful heroinism in the history of the eighteenth-century heroine-focused novel. With *The Orphan of the Rhine*, however, there is one crucial distinction to be forged, and that is that the male narrator's verbal confession of his partiality to the younger woman whom he espies is conveyed with regret to an older, wiser woman, who frames the narrative. Julie de Rubine, the older, wronged woman, is the female character whom we first love and admire in *The Orphan of the Rhine*. Although seemingly (although misleadingly) morally compromised herself, having a child with no husband to explain it, she is nonetheless the moral core of the tale, and provides the narrative pulse of the story. The name of this moral arbiter comes quite self-consciously from the 1777 novel of Henry MacKenzie, *Julia de Roubigné*. Set in France, MacKenzie's epistolary novel mediated sentiment, in the wake of Jean-Jacques Rousseau's far more famous *Julie, ou la Nouvelle Héloïse* (1761) with the central eponymous heroine dying at the hands of a husband she has married from pecuniary necessity rather than love. As a novel, MacKenzie's epistolary tale has not endured as well as its famous Rousseauvian predecessor, but its plot and epistolary didacticism, where the letters seem to be more lessons in how to conduct oneself with propriety than true situations, clearly influenced Eleanor Sleath.

Sleath presents us with a woman who, 'having met with some peculiar misfortunes, originating from the depravity of those with whom she was unhappily connected, had disengaged herself from the world at that period of existence when it usually presents the most alluring prospects' (Sleath 2014: 3): Julie de Rubine has been abandoned and disowned by the Marchese she believes she was married to; we encounter her as a mother who 'takes refuge from the censure of a rash and unfeeling world'; a world that, despite her strong moral compass, benevolence and good judgement, will judge her on the basis of her compromised virtue. It is in this situation that she receives an extraordinary request from the man who wronged her, the Marchese, to rear an orphan, Laurette, as her own child. Being a woman of strong character, she agrees to do so, and to compromise her own independence by taking possession of one of the Marchese's estates, in the interests of advancing her son and adopted daughter. The resemblance between MacKenzie's 1777 Julia and this Julie are striking, as both heroines unite their fates to men that they do not love out of pragmatism. Indeed, in Sleath's older and wiser version, Julie de Rubine never acquires a love interest, and thus does not correspond to several of the key criteria for heroines in flight that the 1790s parodies provided.

While MacKenzie's 1777 novel suffered commercially from being an epistolary exposition of sensibility as that particular form was declining in popularity in Britain, Sleath harnesses the moral possibilities of the declining epistolary form and grafts them onto a more problematic tale of an older, wiser heroine who is already an experienced mother. Her Julie serves as the moral conduit for tales such as the salacious confessions of extramarital affairs from the Conte della Croisse, she raises another person's child unquestioningly without fretting unnecessarily over its parentage, and takes over the role of the enterprising, young heroine where, at one point in the novel, she penetrates the disused section of the castle, and releases from captivity the Conte della Croisse, who has been held prisoner upon the orders of the Marchese. Age and wisdom also bring fresh perspectives upon classic Gothic situations. During the approach to the castle where she is set to raise her family under the protection of the man who wronged her, she surveys the architecture in a manner strikingly reminiscent of Radcliffe's heroine Emily St Aubert from *The Mysteries of Udolpho*.

> It was at a late hour when the party arrived at their destined abode, and the shades of evening had conspired, with the solitude of its situation, to give an air of gloomy magnificence to the scene.
> The castle, which was seated upon an eminence, about a quarter of a league from the bed of the river, seemed to have been separated by nature from the habitable world by deep and impenetrable woods. (Sleath 2014: 28)

The natural environment offers Julie key warnings about the solitude of her future 'dreary abode' (Sleath 2014: 29). These alarms are further supported by the castle's 'massy walls, that spoke of murder and imprisonment, in which the proud possessor, wrapped in selfish security, listened to the cry of anguish and the groan of death with sullen apathy' (Sleath 2014: 32). Julie anticipates and reads the warnings issued by nature and architecture, but is powerless to do anything about them. As a parent seemingly compromised, suggests Sleath, Julie de Rubine now has little choice but to submit to the Marchese's arrangements for the raising of her family. She must even change her name, to the far less distinguished Madame Chamont. While she is left in peace for a relatively extended period of time to raise her son and adopted daughter into young adults, slowly and surely her identity and freedom become eroded. Espied upon by conspiring servants, encouraged to change her name, slowly and surely this older heroine loses her bearings until, having been discovered in helping the Conte to escape from his dungeon, she is kidnapped abruptly and removed from the narrative space of the novel. Her sudden and unexpected departure makes way for the more conventional heroine of the novel to emerge, Laurette, the orphan of the Rhine. Sleath gradually cedes narrative space to the development of the younger heroine. Towards the close of the novel, although Julie de Rubine is eventually rediscovered, we are forced instead to celebrate the restoration of the orphan's aristocratic, familial origins, and her eventual marriage to Enrico, son of Julie. It is notable that, in the final chapter of the novel, Julie, our heroine and focaliser for such a large part of the narrative space, is not even mentioned by Sleath.

Perhaps Sleath's decision to refocus her tale, to consciously rename Laurette, the younger woman, as 'our heroine', was borne in part from an awareness of the invisibility of older women. Bowing to the commercial pressures of heroine-centred narrative, Sleath's gradual occlusion of the older, wiser woman's tale is indicative of the perceived tastes and preferences of the time. After all, successful Gothic precursors, such as Matthew Lewis in *The Monk*, Ann Radcliffe in many of her Gothic novels, Eliza Parsons in *The Castle of Wolfenbach* and Maria Regina Roche in *Clermont* had all chosen to dispose of the older, mother figure too. Sleath's Julie de Rubine/Madame Chamont survives, however, and we learn that she is 'unequalled in generosity as well as every other mental perfection' (Sleath 2014: 373). Even if she is not a heroine in name, Sleath awards her older protagonist many of the parodied attributes of the heroine. She rescues a man from imprisonment, is terrified, kidnapped, and wronged, *and* she remains the character in the novel who possesses 'mental perfection'.

> [T]o recognise the materiality of the text (in several senses) opens up an awareness of its deceptiveness and instability, even as it also takes on an almost uncanny power to fix and 'materialise' the speaking subject. Thus Gothic texts consistently reveal the uneasy compromise made (or imposed) by the Law of the Father on the material conditions of meaning. (Williams 1995: 66)

Ann Radcliffe's *The Italian*, in the wake of Horace Walpole's *The Castle of Otranto* (1764) and her own earlier tale *A Sicilian Romance* (1790), rely upon the trope of a male figure reading the manuscript of a tale translated by a male student or priest. Thus, any reading of the story that we make is conditioned by the material framing of the tale that is imposed by what Williams terms the 'Law of the Father'. This reconditioning of narration and mediation clearly awards narrative priority to the partial gaze of Vincentio di Vivaldi, but Radcliffe always makes us aware of these masculine frames of meaning. The English male traveller who frames the tale in the Prologue, for example, is immediately presented to us as a pompous and intolerant interpreter of Italian mores; so too Vincentio di Vivaldi is foregrounded as being impetuous, and prejudiced in his approach to the older Signora Bianchi. With Eleanor Sleath's *The Orphan of the Rhine*, however, there is a crucial difference. Her tale is no longer framed by manuscript or any male gaze; instead, her governing centre of narrative authority becomes the sympathetic, compromised and older Julie de Rubine. Named after eighteenth-century heroines from the pens of Rousseau and MacKenzie, she is nonetheless more than a tributary of those male exemplars of sensibility. Unconfined by the epistolary form, she becomes the moral core of this Gothic tale, taking the rightful place as the heroine in content, if not in form.

If the example that Sleath gave of the older, wiser woman in *The Orphan of the Rhine* was not embraced at the time of its publication, this was perhaps because the novel itself seems to have been read superficially by its critics in 1798. Dismissed as a 'slavish imitation' by the *Critical Review* (Anon. 1799: 365), *The Orphan of the Rhine* does not seem to correspond easily to the parodies of heroines or older women that circulated at the time of its publication. Even *Northanger Abbey,* which was unusual for at least acknowledging Sleath's novel, humorously identified Catherine Morland's mother as an exception to the norm of dead, older mothers in Gothic fiction in being 'a woman of plain useful sense, with a good temper, and what is more remarkable, with a good constitution' (Austen 1995: 13). *The Orphan of the Rhine* does not subscribe to this parodic vision. Instead, it gives us vital evidence of how the Gothic interrogates those questions of heroinism, at the same time that it appears to endorse them. The stock attributes of heroinism, and counter-values of fallen women, are often conditioned by narratives framed by male pens of translation and interpretation. Sleath's novel is little short of revolutionary in the way that it breaks an eighteenth-century model of sensibility (Julie de Rubine) from the epistolary frames in which she was captured, and awards her both the characteristics of heroinism and the narrative's moral gaze.

Subsequent examples of older women in women's Gothic writing of the Romantic period are relatively sparse. On one hand, Charlotte Dacre's *Zofloya* (1806) contains a morally compromised mother, Laurina, who is chastised fully for not guiding and educating her daughter, Victoria di Loredani; on the other, Mary Shelley's *Frankenstein* (1818) contains a saintly, over-indulgent mother on the margins of the narrative, who dies prematurely from illness. These nebulous, occasionally menacing presences are, however, conditioned by material narrative frames governed by the Law of the Father. With the example of *Zofloya*, the 'Historian' who traces the causes and effects of the depravity of Victoria seems to be implicitly male; with *Frankenstein*, those male frames become explicit in the novel's recourse to epistolarity. However, *Frankenstein* too contains the seeds of dissent; the sibling addressee of Robert Walton's letters which frame the novel is a 'Mrs Saville', presumably a mother as well as a wife. Her silence upon the narrative does not deny her presence; the compass of the older woman is there. Perhaps, Mary Shelley suggests, the true heroine of the narrative is Mrs Saville, or any other female reader who passes judgement upon the alien, violent world that the three male characters create.

To focus, as parodies did, upon the heroines in flight of women's Gothic writing was fun, playful, and at times justified. However, as I hope that I have demonstrated, this very much depended not only upon whose story was being told, but who was telling the story. In Matthew Lewis's *The Monk*, a novel which parodies the idea of a heroine as much as it endorses it, Agnes describes herself as a 'Historian' of the Bleeding Nun, and offers us a far more compelling version of her than that of the Wandering Jew. Likewise, Radcliffe's *The Italian* and Sleath's *The Orphan of the Rhine* play with and challenge the conventions of storytelling. Freed from the confines of a masculine tradition of storytelling, the precise identity, characteristics and age of the heroine in flight become more varied and complex. We cannot determine precisely the ages of Julie de Rubine, Olivia and others, but their stories at least become increasingly visible. For 'fine ladies', wrote Samuel Johnson in *The Rambler* in 1750, 'age begins early, and very often lasts long'. This may well have been the case, but we note the growing visibility and repositioning of these 'fine ladies' within Women's Gothic writing of the Romantic period.

Bibliography

Alcock, Mary (1799), 'A Receipt for Writing a Novel', *Poems*, London: C. Dilly, Poultry.

Anon. (1797), 'The Terrorist System of Novel Writing', *Monthly Magazine*, August: 102.

Anon. (1798), 'Terrorist Novel Writing' in *The Spirit of the Public Journals for 1797*, London: Richardsons, Symonds, Clarke, Harding, pp. 223–5.

Anon. (1799), Review of Eleanor Sleath, *The Orphan of the Rhine, Critical Review*, 27 November: 356.

Austen, Jane [1818] (1995), *Northanger Abbey*, ed. and intro. Marilyn Butler, Harmondsworth: Penguin.

Burney, Frances [1778] (1982), *Evelina; or the History of a Young Lady's Entrance into the World*, ed. and intro. Edward A. Bloom, Oxford: Oxford University Press.

Burney, Frances [1814] (1991), *The Wanderer; or, Female Difficulties*, ed. Margaret Anne Doody, Robert L. Mack and Peter Sabor, Oxford: Oxford University Press.

Clery, E. J. (1995), *The Rise of Supernatural Fiction, 1762–1800*, Cambridge: Cambridge University Press.

Doody, Margaret Anne (1977), 'Deserts, Ruins and Troubled Waters: Female Dreams in Fiction and the Development of the Gothic Novel', *Genre*: 10.

Ellis, Kate Fergusson (1989), *The Contested Castle: Gothic Novels and the Subversion of Domestic Ideology*, Urbana: University of Illinois Press.

Hoeveler, Diane Long (1998), *Gothic Feminism: The Professionalisation of Gender from Charlotte Smith to the Brontës*, Liverpool and Pennsylvania: Liverpool University Press.

Hogle, Jerrold E. (1997), 'The Ghost of the Counterfeit – and the Closet – in *The Monk*', *Romanticism on the Net*, 8 (November). Available at: http://erudit.org/revue/ron/1997/v/n8/005770ar.html?lang=en (accessed 30 August 2015).

Johnson, Samuel (1750), *The Rambler*, 11 (24 April).

Le Faye, Deirdre (2002), *Jane Austen: The World of Her Novels*, London: Frances Lincoln.

Lewis, Matthew [1796] (1980), *The Monk*, ed. and intro. Howard Anderson, Oxford: Oxford University Press.

MacKenzie, Henry (1777), *Julia de Roubigné, a tale*, in a series of letters. Published by the author of *The man of feeling*, and *The man of the world*, 2 vols, London: Strahan and Cadell.

Parsons, Eliza (1793), *The Castle of Wolfenbach*, London: Minerva.

Radcliffe, Ann [1789] (1995), *The Castles of Athlin and Dunbayne*, ed. Alison Milbank, Oxford: Oxford University Press.

Radcliffe, Ann [1790] (1993), *A Sicilian Romance*, ed. Alison Milbank, Oxford: Oxford University Press.

Radcliffe, Ann [1794] (1980), *The Mysteries of Udolpho*, ed. Bonamy Dobrée, Oxford: Oxford University Press.

Radcliffe, Ann [1797] (2000), *The Italian, or the Confessional of the Black Penitents*, ed. Robert Miles, Harmondsworth: Penguin.

Roche, Maria Regina (1798), *Clermont. A Tale*, 4 vols, London: William Lane.

Rousseau, Jean-Jacques (1761), *Julie, ou la Nouvelle Héloïse* , trans. William Kenrick as *Eloisa: or, a series of original letters collected and published by J.J. Rousseau*, 4 vols, London: Griffiths, Becket and De Hondt.

Shelley, Mary [1818] (1993), *Frankenstein, or the Modern Prometheus*, ed. Marilyn Butler, Oxford: Oxford University Press.

Sleath, Eleanor [1798] (2014), *The Orphan of the Rhine: A Romance*, intro. Ellen Moody, Richmond, VA: Valancourt Books.

Smith, Andrew and Diana Wallace (2009), *The Female Gothic: New Directions*, Basingstoke: Palgrave.

Townshend, Dale and Angela Wright (ed.) (2014), *Ann Radcliffe, Romanticism and the Gothic*, Cambridge: Cambridge University Press.

Williams, Anne (1995), *Art of Darkness: A Poetics of Gothic*, Chicago and London: University of Chicago Press.

Wollstonecraft, Mary (1994), *A Vindication of the Rights of Woman* [1792], in Janet Todd (ed.), *Political Writings*, Oxford: Oxford University Press.

Wright, Angela (2013), *Britain, France and the Gothic, 1764–1820: The Import of Terror*, Cambridge: Cambridge University Press.

Chapter 2

Madwomen and Attics
Laurence Talairach-Vielmas

The solitary life, which Emily had led of late, and the melancholy subjects, on which she had suffered her thoughts to
dwell, had rendered her at times sensible to the 'thick-coming
fancies' of a mind greatly enervated. It was lamentable, that
her excellent understanding should have yielded, even for a
moment, to the reveries of superstition, or rather to those starts
of imagination, which deceive the senses into what can be
called nothing less than momentary madness.

(Ann Radcliffe, *The Mysteries of Udolpho*, p. 102)

In Ann Radcliffe's *The Mysteries of Udolpho* (1794), spectres are often
the product of a nervous young maiden's inflamed imagination or
alarmed fancy. Ghosts are nothing but the heroine's own 'spirits', and
her journey consists, therefore, in learning how to control them before
she can be happily married. To do so, the Radcliffean heroine, driven by
an irrepressible curiosity, is led to unveil the stories of other women, and
gradually realises that the passionate female characters who fail to tame
their wild nature end up locked up in turrets, convents or prisons of
sorts. As Eugenia C. DeLamotte contends, 'the discovery of the Hidden
Woman' is 'a staple of women's Gothic', and:

> Gothic romances tell again and again this story of the woman hidden from
> the world as if she were dead, her long suffering unknown to those outside –
> or sometimes even inside – the ruined castle, crumbling abbey, deserted wing,
> madhouse, convent, cave, priory, subterranean prison, or secret apartments.
> (DeLamotte 1990: 153)

For DeLamotte, just like Sandra Gilbert and Susan Gubar (1984) in the
now classic feminist study of nineteenth-century women writers, *The
Madwoman in the Attic*, the discovered woman who has been buried
alive may fall into one of two main categories, the 'Good Other Woman'

or the 'Evil Other Woman', both the angel and the demon suggesting women's confining roles and the social conditions of Victorian patriarchy (DeLamotte 1990: 153).

Among the numerous examples of locked-up women, the trope of the madwoman in the attic is perhaps one of the most potent images of Gothic fiction. As this chapter will show, the madwoman was first and foremost a conventional sentimental icon. But the trope was repeatedly rewritten in Gothic narratives throughout the nineteenth century, the madwoman confined in the attic uncannily hovering between the Good and the Evil woman, the literal and the figurative, and vigorously participating in the construction of fear – and horror. As shall be seen, the enduring Gothic cliché helped women and male writers define the condition of woman even when – or perhaps especially when – the madwoman resisted being locked up in the attic or when she escaped the garret.

'You shall be removed … to the east turret'

> Ye are to know, Signors, that the Lady Laurentini had for some months shewn symptoms of a dejected mind, nay, of a disturbed imagination. Her mood was very unequal: sometimes she was sunk in calm melancholy, and, at others, … she betrayed all the symptoms of frantic madness. It was one night in the month of October, after she had recovered from one of those fits of excess, and had sunk again into her usual melancholy, that she retired alone to her chamber, and forbade all interruption. It was the chamber at the end of the corridor, Signors, where we had the affray, last night. From that hour, she was seen no more. (Radcliffe 1980: 290)

The madwoman that Emily St Aubert discovers in *The Mysteries of Udolpho* is the passionate Signora Laurentini, driven to insanity and murder out of love for the Marquis de Villeroi. As her description suggests, Signora Laurentini's pathology is hard to frame and shifts from one extreme to the next before the female character ultimately disappears – ironically – when calmed – or tamed. Secreted in a convent and forced to take the veil to repent of her deed, she becomes an image of live burial since her father circulates the rumour that she has been murdered by her husband. Yet, neither dead nor alive, the madwoman is taken for a ghost who haunts the forest around the castle and denies the passing of time, or mistaken for a wax figure endlessly postponing the process of bodily decomposition. As a spectre, Laurentini appears as completely disembodied; as a putrefying corpse, she is all body. The images of the spectre and the wax figure suggest the female character's resistance to being locked up in a category, just as in a coffin. She hovers between the living and the dead, the ethereal and the corporeal, becoming a pivotal character in the Gothic narrative: the mystery around her identity and fate conveys suspense till the very end and enables the heroine to probe the nature of the supernatural just as it allows her to witness another example of woman's limited choices outside marriage and lack of freedom in patriarchy.

Indeed, Radcliffe's madwoman in the convent is one of the motifs that helps the woman writer reflect the heroine's likely fate. The madwoman's confinement illustrates how in Radcliffean Gothic female characters experience the violence of a male-dominated world, foreshadowing or mirroring the ways in which the heroine falls prey to a male villain (see Modleski 1990). As a matter of fact, metaphors of entrapment and literal imprisonment frame the heroine's experience through powerlessness, as the latter is taken time and again to 'her prison' (Radcliffe 1980: 227, 426). Fleenor's definition of 'Female Gothic', which encapsulates and redefines Ellen Moers's initial coining of the term (Moers 1978: 90–110),[1] claims that such Gothic is grounded on the patriarchal paradigm that 'the woman is motherless, defective, and defined by a male God' (Fleenor 1983: 11). The self-divided heroine is a 'reflection of patriarchal values', and her quest frequently leads her to investigate 'whether she is anything but reflection' (Fleenor 1983: 12). Such feminist views posit that, even if the threats jeopardising the life of the heroine are often dispelled by the end of the novel, the plots foreground female victimisation in order to dramatise woman's self-abnegating role within patriarchy. Anne Williams also traces the 'Gothic myth' in the patriarchal family, with Lacan's 'Law of the Father' as the leading principle of the cultural order: 'sexual "difference" is indeed the "key" to the secrets of the patriarchal power structure' (Williams 1995: 43). Threatened with being removed to the east turret if she does not resign her settlements to Signor Montoni, Emily learns both 'the danger of offending a man, who has an unlimited power over [her]' (Radcliffe 1980: 305) and the dangers of woman's fancy or mind. Her encounter with female doubles, both mad and locked up, offers the reader a bleak vision of women's fate in a male-dominated world. In so doing, the meetings reflect the heroine's own madness in a glass darkly, which she must learn to tame before entering matrimony. This is strengthened by the idea that women may be responsible for being locked up: Signor Montoni claims that 'if [Emily] is removed to the turret, it will be her own fault' (Radcliffe 1980: 307) and the heroine regularly 'blame[s] herself for suffering her romantic imagination to carry her so far beyond the bounds of probability', 'endeavour[ing] to check its rapid flights, lest they should sometimes extend into madness' (Radcliffe 1980: 342).

Women constantly flirt with madness, it seems, as if madness and womanhood both define an idealised sensitive femininity and its opposite – the evil woman locked away in a convent to expiate her crimes. Radcliffe's Gothic romance draws upon stereotypical sentimental constructions of woman and borrows from the literary convention of the woman driven to madness out of love, the better to undermine them. The ambiguity of the Gothic madwoman in the convent, as much spectral as corporeal, as much angel as demon, blurs conventional representations of femininity through its contradictions, and evokes mystery and fear for the heroine and prompts readers to question such representations. Radcliffe's madwoman foreshadows here Victorian representations of madwomen in attics, sowing the seeds of a feminist discourse later employed by authors such as Charlotte Brontë. Half a century later, the iconic mad Bertha Mason, locked up in the attic of Thornfield Hall in *Jane Eyre* (1847), also illustrated how Gothic doubles could be used to reflect the heroine's own sense of imprisonment. The mad Bertha Mason functions as a double of the wild Jane, who strives to escape her confining condition through flight, starvation or even madness, as Gilbert and Gubar (1984) have shown. Yet, the corpulent lunatic, towering over men and threatening them with her virile force, did not simply upset the conventional literary stereotype: Brontë's madwoman in the attic also revamped the trope of the madwoman in the turret or convent by reflecting current medical thinking about mental pathologies. Suffering from 'moral insanity', as defined by Esquirol's treatise on insanity, *Des Maladies mentales* (1838), and popularised by J. C. Prichard's *A Treatise on Insanity and Other Disorders Affecting the Mind* (1835) in England, Bertha is considered as morally corrupted, her species of insanity being therefore linked with her immoral behaviour (Small 1996: 163; Martin 1987: 124–39).

Brontë's madwoman in the attic, as a confirmed medical patient regularly surveyed by medical professionals, certainly influenced the sensation novelists of the 1860s.[2] Sensation fiction rewrote many Gothic themes, motifs and plot-patterns, both to foreground the victimisation of women through its sensational madwomen and to challenge gender stereotypes. Unlike Bertha Mason, Mary Elizabeth Braddon's villainess in *Lady Audley's Secret* is a fair-haired, blue-eyed and fragile angel who embodies the feminine ideal while being bigamous and suspected of murder. Like Brontë's madwoman, however, she 'has the cunning of madness, with the prudence of intelligence' (Braddon 1987: 379). Her mental derangement is associated with no lesion of the brain, but results rather from her sinful deeds. Eventually taken to a madhouse – which the female character calls her 'living grave' (Braddon 1987: 391) – Lady Audley, renamed Mrs Taylor (just as Radcliffe's Signora Laurentini had been renamed Agnes) is buried alive in order to 'repent' (Braddon 1987: 391). The sanatorium replaces here Radcliffe's convent or Brontë's attic, and Braddon's madwoman sensationally – and ambiguously – rewrites earlier models of locked-up women. This time, the madwoman in the madhouse is ethereal and innocent-looking, and her secret may well be that she is not even mad.

As Helen Small has shown, the sensational madwomen of the 1860s were inspired by late-eighteenth- and early-nineteenth-century sentimental and stereotypical images of female insanity, such as those of women going mad when they lose their lovers, extolled by novelists, dramatists, poets and painters during the cult of sensibility (Small 1996). Radcliffe's use of women's sentimentality and nervous sensitivity at the end of the eighteenth century was, however, much more sensationally exploited by novelists like Braddon, for instance, whose Lucy Audley is a modern rewriting of Ophelia, the villainess's mental disturbance starting after her husband's desertion, even if the patient is allegedly plagued with hereditary insanity. Furthermore, seminal sensation novels were also deeply ingrained in a period which saw major reform initiatives in the history of insanity. Wilkie Collins's *The Woman in White* was serialised in November 1859, just a few months after two major 'lunacy panics' in Britain: the revelation of the wrongful confinement of sane men and women led to the establishment of a Select Committee of Inquiry, represented by the Alleged Lunatics' Friend Society (Small 1996). In addition, the serialisation of *The Woman in White* corresponded with the publication and widespread discussion of the Parliamentary Select Committee Inquiry into the Care and Treatment of Lunatics and Their Property of 1858–1859 (Taylor 1988: 30). Even though Wilkie Collins was a male writer, he was a known supporter of the asylum reform movement and close to the significant figures connected with psychological medicine, such as Bryan Procter (1787–1874), who was a Lunacy Commissioner between 1832 and 1861 and the dedicatee of *The Woman in White*, just like Charles Dickens, whose villainess, Miss Havisham, in *Great Expectations* (1861), may be seen as a double of Collins's woman in white. Charles Reade, another famous writer associated with the sensation genre, was also involved in lunacy reform, his *Hard Cash* (1863) featuring a parody of John Conolly (1794–1866), an alienist (one who treats mental diseases) much involved in new methods for dealing with the insane in mental homes and who denounced wrongful confinements in private madhouses. In 1865 the establishment of the

Medico-Psychological Association (later to become the Royal College of Psychiatrists) was another landmark underlining the links between the sensational madwomen that were captivating the Victorians at the time and the history of insanity. It was also in 1859–1860 that Henry Maudsley – Conolly's son-in-law – published his views on hereditary insanity for the first time.

By drawing upon sentimental literary conventions and rewriting earlier Gothic representations of the madwoman in the attic, the sensation writers of the 1860s highlighted how women's supposedly weak will inevitably constructed women as typical nervous sufferers. In so doing, they condemned the construction of insanity as 'an extension of [the] female condition' (Small 1996: viii). Because this matched contemporary constructions of femininity, defining women as weak and liable to suffer from debility of the nerves, Victorian madwomen embodied a typically feminine condition, whether they suffered from simple nervous exhaustion, hysteria or even mania. However, Braddon's twist to the eighteenth-century sentimental icon of the love-mad woman indicates how Victorian popular fiction could turn hackneyed clichés on their heads. Braddon may have been inspired by the literary convention of the Ophelian madwoman but the villainess, unlike Wilkie Collins's Laura Fairlie in *The Woman in White*, for instance, no longer embodies ideals of sensibility. Braddon's sensational revision of the trope of the madwoman, as one of the many metaphors that define the feminine ideal, shows how the reworking of such sentimental icons by sensation writers in the 1860s, and their recurrent play upon the gendering of madness as a female condition, was a direct response to the medical discourses that confined women within subordinate positions through defining them as weak and passive beings. The weight of medical discourse that permeates sensation novels indicates the genre's denunciation of the authority of medical science and its infiltration into the social sphere.

From 'Moral Insanity' to Hystero-Catalepsy

Indeed, in the second half of the nineteenth century, the figure of the madwoman in the attic became intertwined with discourses on medical science, most particularly in the popular literature of the period. As neuro-physiology gradually placed the mind at the heart of emotions, emotions were redefined by physiologists 'as a product of sensory perception and material processes'. Physiological research paved the way for the shift from cardio-centric to neuro-centric understandings of emotional experiences (Alberti 2010: 29). With the development of neuro-physiology, therefore, emotions were more and more linked to brain mechanisms. The replacement of the heart by the brain as the organ linked with emotions is manifest in several portraits of Victorian Ophelia-like madwomen. The many rewritings of the figure of the madwoman in the attic of the last decades of the nineteenth century suggest that the madwoman had increasingly become the object of medical investigation. As already argued, use of Gothic tropes enabled sensation writers to engage in debates about insanity. But the evolution of the figure of the madwoman also helped writers denounce inconsistent constructions of madness which underlined woman's lack of willpower while simultaneously incriminating wilfulness in cases of hysteria (see Owen 1989: 147).

This is particularly illuminated by Dickens's woman in white in *Great Expectations*. Dickens's Victorian Ophelia, driven to madness on her aborted wedding day and self-confined in Satis House, typifies the gradual rationalisation and scientific framing of the Gothic heroine's and/or villainess's emotions. As a woman with a 'broken' heart, as she explains to Pip on their first encounter, Miss Havisham appears first and foremost as a mechanical body, the play on the broken heart suggesting parallels between the state of her house, with clocks stopped at twenty minutes to nine, and her physiology, which seems to have gone wrong and driven her to insanity. Moreover, she is compared to 'the ghastly waxwork at the fair' by the young Pip the first time he sees her. The metaphor recalls Radcliffe's parallels between Signora Laurentini and the wax figure of the decomposing body behind the veil, which makes her body hover between life and death. In the nineteenth century, many wax figures were in fact anatomical Venuses, made up of multiple pieces likely to be disassembled,[3] and displayed both in medical museums and at fairs. These models, such as those of the Specola museum, which opened in Florence in 1775, made directly from cadavers and designed as substitutes for corpses, were used in medical education in order to teach the mechanisms of the human body. The wax substitutes enabled medical professionals to teach human anatomy without resorting to corpses at a time when the supply of cadavers was scarce.[4] But Miss Havisham's body is that of a morbid Venus who asks to be laid upon the table after her death, oscillating between the female corpse and the artwork. Indeed, hardly any trace of bodily decomposition ever appeared on the Florentine waxes, the waxworks looking like female sleepers and often even ornamented with rich accessories. Yet, Miss Havisham's 'corpse-like' appearance (Dickens 1994: 59), and the author's comparisons of her to a mummy likely to turn to dust if taken into the natural light (Dickens 1994: 59), compose a death-in-life figure, which constantly signals instability, her body both arrested, therefore, and likely to fall into dust and disappear. Thus, Dickens's madwoman, even when dressed in bridal apparel, remains for ever haunted by her own corporeality, just like Signora Laurentini before her or Brontë's oversized madwoman.

It is the contradictions in Miss Havisham's appearance – both disembodied when Pip first hears her and with a frightening corporeality, both bride and old maid, angel and demon – that terrify Pip on their first encounter. The madwoman participates, indeed, in the construction of an uncanny world which the hero must decode by taming his illusions – or expectations. Dickens's madwoman has the same function as the veiled wax statue in *The Mysteries of Udolpho*, which Emily takes for the murdered body of Signora Laurentini, resisting decomposition. Unlike Radcliffe's passionate Laurentini, mainly characterised by her 'fits of wildness' (577), Dickens's hysterical Miss Havisham, or Braddon's insane villainess, are framed by a medical discourse or defined by objects reminiscent of the medical culture of the times which intimate the conflicting links between woman and the body and the impossibility of locking up the madwoman in a category – or a coffin. This idea would be even more strengthened in late-Victorian popular fiction, which drew upon research into cerebral localisation and studies in craniology and phrenology, most notably through manifold references to the famous physiologists of the second part of the nineteenth century, from John Hughlings Jackson (1835–1911) to David Ferrier (1843–1928).

The Gothic fiction of the last decades of the nineteenth century increasingly showed that:

> [m]uch of the scientific interest in the nervous system was focused on the boundaries of waking, sleeping, and dreaming, and on how far the medical intervention might reveal the mechanism by which body and mind communicated across the mysterious borderland of consciousness. (Wood 2001: 104)

As a result, the madwomen of the end of the nineteenth century pushed the Gothic heroine's hypersensitivity and impressionability to extremes. Instead of producing fainting and loss of consciousness, fear entailed catalepsy – a disease characterised by a sudden fall into a state of apparent unconsciousness, and which was discussed by medical professionals alongside – and sometimes even confused with – hysteria, epilepsy, mesmerism and trance. As early as 1853, Charlotte Brontë used catalepsy as a trope to figure her heroine's repressed feelings in *Villette*:

> Oh, my childhood! I had feelings: passive as I lived, little as I spoke, cold as I looked, when I thought of past days, I *could* feel. About the present, it was

better to be stoical: about the future – such a future as mine – to be dead.
And in catalepsy and a dead trance, I studiously held the quick of my nature.
(Brontë 1985: 175)

As Lucy Snowe reaches a new understanding of herself through a cataleptic trance, Brontë capitalises on a metaphor directly borrowed from
medical discourse: locked up in her own mind, Lucy metaphorically
buries herself alive, and the novel recurrently plays upon such images
of live burial to map out the heroine's repressed nature. As Brontë's use
of catalepsy suggests, the disease became one of the central figurative
tropes of Gothic fiction, essential to scholarly interrogations of Gothic's
psychoanalytic character, as Eve Kosofsky Sedgwick argues (Sedgwick
1986: 23). But catalepsy above all inspired many narratives of premature burial. In 1821, John Galt's 'The Buried Alive' paved the way for
Edgar Allan Poe's cataleptic Madeline Usher in 'The Fall of the House of
Usher' (1839) and other tales such as 'Berenice' (1835), 'The Premature
Burial' (1844), 'The Cask of Amontillado' (1846) and even 'The Black
Cat' (1843), which all drew upon catalepsy and/or the live burial trope.
By the last decades of the nineteenth century, however, the cataleptic
madwomen locked up in their own minds and risking live burial had
become the ideal victims of medical experimentation.

Wilkie Collins's *Heart and Science* (1883) is a case in point. The plot
echoes the old Radcliffean Gothic romance of female victimisation, as
the helpless and friendless Carmina becomes increasingly nervous and
hysterical. Isolated and the prisoner of her aunt, whose cruelty she must
silently and patiently endure, Carmina matches the stereotype of the
feminine ideal. Signs of rebellion appear nevertheless in the submissive
girl, although they are largely restricted to her written confessions to her
old chaperon. Carmina resents her powerless position, both as a ward
subjected to her aunt's authority and as a woman denied a voice of her
own. Though decorum demands that she should never bang doors, she
chokes and suffocates as she is denied any form of personal privacy,
and her anger towards her aunt once drives her to the verge of hysteria.
The nature of woman's will forms a major theme of the narrative. The
heroine is placed in the company of a series of strong-willed women who
exhibit similar signs of hysteria, highlighting once again clashing definitions of insanity and of woman's relationship to willpower (Talairach-
Vielmas 2009). As suggested, instead of fainting or losing consciousness
as in Radcliffean Gothic, Carmina becomes cataleptic and falls into the
hands of the mad scientist of the novel, Dr Benjulia:

The shock that had struck Carmina had produced complicated hysterical
disturbance, which was now beginning to simulate paralysis. Benjulia's

profound and practised observation detected a trifling inequality in the size of the pupils of the eyes, and a slightly unequal action on either side of the face – delicately presented in the eyelids, the nostrils, and the lips. Here was no common affection of the brain, which even Mr. Null could understand! Here, at last, was Benjulia's reward for sacrificing the precious hours which might otherwise have been employed in the laboratory! From that day, Carmina was destined to receive unknown honour: she was to take her place, along with the other animals, in his note-book of experiments. (Collins 1994: 290)

Catalepsy was particularly seen as resulting from 'moral shocks' (Maudsley 1880: 74). The deathlike spells it produced were regarded as characteristic of certain hysterical disorders – for example, the 'lucid hysterical lethargy' distinguished by the French neurologist Gilles de la Tourette (1857–1904), who worked with Charcot at the Salpêtrière from 1884. In such cases, the patient's pulse rate fell, the heartbeat became inaudible, and the patient grew pale, still and cold, often remaining in that state for several days and facing the risk of live burial (Bondeson 2002: 251). Catalepsy was seen as a form of 'hysterical ecstasy' (Maudsley 1880: 56) which typified double consciousness since it illustrated a complete the loss of control over the mind and could lead to madness.

Collins's play with catalepsy to create tension and fear in the narrative seems to have been directly inspired by the medical and popular literature of the time. The association of the cataleptic patient's sharp awareness of the events around him (Ellis 1835: 129) and his powerlessness and lack of volition, made him an ideal victim who could be handled at will, an idea that flourished in Victorian fiction as well as in medical articles, in which medical professionals drew upon a set of tropes to depict their patients often using generic stereotypes of the Gothic. Collins's choice of catalepsy to revamp the Gothic madwoman reflects the medical reality of the period, as medical professionals investigated the signs of death and attempted to distinguish real from apparent death.[5] Collins had already touched upon the subject in *Jezebel's Daughter* (1880), when one of the female characters believed dead is taken to a deadhouse (a structure used for the temporary storage of human corpses before burial) and comes to life again. But the cataleptic female patient enabled him to reactivate the Gothic cliché of the madwoman. It drew upon Gothic conventions while simultaneously pointing out the increasing gendering of hysteria, its mysteries, contradictory definitions, and above all its capacity to reveal the violence of medical science, as women became ideal subjects for medical experimentation – or worse, were doomed to be buried alive.

This Gothic trope is even more striking in Bram Stoker's *Dracula* (1897), where the vampirised Lucy Westenra is subjected to several experimental treatments and eventually 'buried alive' (Stoker 1997: 180). The novel is punctuated by stories of individuals who were buried alive, the narratives appearing as soon as Dracula enters England, as if to foreshadow Lucy's premature interment. Whitby Abbey is associated with the nun Constance de Beverley in Walter Scott's 'Marmion' (1808), who ends up walled up alive in the dungeon. Later on, Van Helsing attempts to explain vampirism through stories of entranced people buried alive and resurrected, such as that of the Indian fakir (172), and a character is bricked up by Dracula in the churchyard of St Peter at the end of the novel. Lucy has been vampirised during a sleepwalking trance as she escaped the house in her nightdress. Her predisposition to somnambulism intimates the character's weak will; it anticipates as well the parallels between the mysteries of vampirism and brain mechanisms the novel draws upon. Furthermore, Mina's fears for Lucy's reputation when she finds her, just as her concern that the news may unsettle her mother who suffers from a heart disease, are telling. Lucy's nightly adventure/encounter with the vampire is likely to induce a moral shock. Consequently, Lucy is increasingly aligned with stereotypical representations of hysterical women, a comparison that climaxes when the vampire finally dies, writhing like one of Charcot's hysterics.

Indeed, the novel as a whole explores research into the understanding and mapping of the brain and directly cites figures like John Scott Burdon-Sanderson (1828–1905) and David Ferrier. Near the beginning of the novel, Mina Harker, worried about her husband's health, consults Dr Van Helsing, because her *fiancé*, Jonathan Harker, had 'a sort of shock' in the Carpathians, when he 'thought he saw some one who recalled something terrible', an experience which induced a brain fever (Stoker 1997: 165). Although the doctor believes that Harker's constitution makes him a patient not likely 'to be injured in permanence by a shock' and contends that his 'brain and heart are all right' (Stoker 1997: 167), his medical verdict foregrounds the novel's concern with late-nineteenth-century investigations of the brain. Throughout the narrative, the medical professionals investigate the origins of brain disease, aligning the heart and the brain in their explanations of their patients' illnesses. Suffering from vampirism, the characters – Jonathan Harker and Lucy Westenra – become hypersensitive and exhibit symptoms very close to Dr Seward's patient, Renfield. Heartbreaks are defined as 'wounds' which refuse to 'becom[e] cicatrised' (Stoker 1997: 170) and reopen, drawing comparisons with the vampire's bites – small punctured wounds on the victims' throats – while emotions are represented as blood being 'drain[ed] to the head' (Stoker 1997: 120), as when the poor emaciated Lucy turns crimson at the remembrance of Dr Seward's marriage proposal. As I have suggested, the debate between the heart and the brain which *Dracula* points to is a long one, but the *fin-de-siècle* novel, figuring medical practitioners holding post-mortem knives to remove young women's hearts and medical experts dreaming about carrying out vivisection on human beings to advance the knowledge of the brain, is a blatant illustration of the medicalisation of emotions and the secularisation of psychology on which the novel capitalises in its revision of the vampire myth. Stoker's madwoman in the coffin intimates, in fact, that by the end of the nineteenth century, the literary convention of the Ophelian madwoman was no longer an empty senti-mental trope: it not only followed contemporary medical research into emotions and debates around the roles of the heart and brain, but was also more and more used to foreground the contradictory construction of woman as both ethereal and corporeal, anaemic and bloody, virginal and sexual – the angel and demon tracked and unveiled by feminist critics such as Nina Auerbach (1982) and Gilbert and Gubar (1979), a being defined and confined by medical science, and a potent and threatening image of fear, especially when the woman resisted being imprisoned in the attic, madhouse or coffin, and came back to haunt or bleed her tormentors.

Madmen in Attics

However, the example of *Dracula* shows that at the turn of the century men were just as likely to suffer from shock and hysteria as women. The attic was, indeed, likely to be inhabited by women and men alike. The sensation novelists who had used insanity to epitomise the female condition rewrote their madwomen to remain in line with contempo-rary constructions of mental diseases. This is, for instance, the case in several of Mary Elizabeth Braddon's novels of the turn of the nineteenth century and beginning of the twentieth century, such as *The Golden Calf* (1883), in which Braddon describes the male protagonist's degeneration and his gradual descent into *delirium tremens*, developing a theme she had already raised in *Eleanor's Victory* (1863) and *Thou Art the Man* (1894), in which the male protagonist suffers from hereditary epilepsy and eventually becomes mad, or *Dead Love Has Chains* (1907), in which the hero is found mad after a nervous breakdown and has to go into a nursing home. Braddon's choice of a mad male character whose pathol-ogy matched current constructions of mental disturbances marks the popular writer's move away from the sensational characters and plots that had made her fame half a century before. For, as argued, if women were defined as nervously debilitated, men were, on the contrary, supposed to incarnate the bourgeois ideal of manliness that implied mental and physical strength – an ideal that was to be reinforced in late-Victorian imperialist fiction, such as Henry Rider Haggard's imperial Gothic.

In *Dead Love Has Chains*, in particular, Braddon chooses a male character to play the part of the Ophelian madwoman, deliberately undermining dominant Victorian gender representations. The novel is focused on Conrad Harling's 'love-madness' (Braddon 2014: 46) or 'melancholy madness' (47). Conrad Harling is 'a romantic young man, full of high-flown sentiments and wild Quixotism' (31), an 'impassioned' 'Preux Chevalier' (34), whose sensitivity may be reminiscent of Radcliffe's valiant knights. But his 'highly emotional temperament' (51) makes him vulnerable to mental disease. The hero thus collapses when he finds himself deserted by his *fiancée*, and the narrative relates his struggle with madness. Braddon's choice of a madman illuminated changing visions of insanity at the turn of the twentieth century, especially related to the description of an emotional shock provoking physical lesions in the brain. However, the portrait of an insane and hypersensitive man in a masculinist culture enabled Braddon to offer a more sympathetic approach to nervously susceptible men. This move away from conventional representations of the madwoman in the attic typifies the role that Victorian writers played in negotiating tensions and challenging the very stereotypes that informed their works and that were so quintessential to the Gothic.

Notes

1. Moers's definition only takes into consideration Gothic narratives written by women. Her point is that Female Gothic triggers physiological dread, meant to express fears related to childbirth. Fleenor enlarges her definition by focusing on the patriarchal paradigm inherent in all Gothic narratives by women.
2. Many of Mary Elizabeth Braddon's works refer to *Jane Eyre*, for instance. 'The Mystery at Fernwood' relates the story of twin brothers, one of whom is insane and locked up on the top floor of Fernwood. His insanity results from a fall, which caused a fatal injury to the brain. In 'The Flight from Wealdon Hall', Braddon has the governess help the mad wife to escape. Braddon even wrote an essay on Charlotte Brontë (Braddon 1906).
3. Miss Havisham also recalls one of the most famous mechanical automata displayed in the nineteenth century: Madame Tussaud's Sleeping Beauty – Madame du Barry's wax model. Du Barry's 'breathing' wax model had a mechanical beating heart, and her chest could be seen rising as she lay asleep on a sofa, disturbingly disrupting the boundaries between the real and the artificial as between the animate and the inanimate.

4. From 1832 changes in the legislation, with the Anatomy Act regulating dissection, facilitated the supply of cadavers in England.
5. Research into the clinical reality of death was prevalent in the nineteenth century, but as early as the seventeenth century, the works of Jacob B. Winslow (1669–1760) (*Morte incertae signa* (1740)) and Jean-Jacques Bruhier (1685–1756) (*Dissertation sur l'incertitude des signes de la mort* (1746–49)), who translated and rewrote Winslow's work, focused on cases of live burial and illuminated fears of live burial. In France in 1787, the physician François Thierry, like Bruhier a century before, made proposals to develop morgues for the recently deceased throughout the country, while in Austria in 1788 Johann Peter Frank (1745–1821) supported the building of communal deadhouses in every town. In the 1790s, Christoph Wilhelm Hufeland (1762–1836) was the first to draw plans for a Weimar deadhouse (*Leichenhaus*). Waiting mortuaries were then established in many cities throughout the German states. See Bondeson 2002: 53, 55, 60, 88–92.

Bibliography

Alberti, Fay Bound (2010), *Matters of the Heart: History, Medicine and Emotion*, Oxford: Oxford University Press.

Auerbach, Nina (1982), *Woman and the Demon: The Life of a Victorian Myth*, Cambridge, MA: Harvard University Press.

Bondeson, Jan [2001] (2002), *Buried Alive: The Terrifying History of Our Most Primal Fear*, New York: Norton.

Braddon, Mary Elizabeth (1906), 'At the Shrine of "Jane Eyre"', *Pall Mall Magazine*, 37: 174–6.

Braddon, Mary Elizabeth [1907] (2014), *Dead Love Has Chains*, ed. Laurence Talairach-Vielmas, Kansas City: Valancourt Books.

Braddon, Mary Elizabeth [1862] (1987), *Lady Audley's Secret*, Oxford: Oxford University Press.

Brontë, Charlotte [1853] (1985), *Villette*, London: Penguin.

Collins, Wilkie [1883] (1994), *Heart and Science*, Stroud, Glos: Alan Sutton.

DeLamotte, Eugenia, C. (1990), *Perils of the Night: A Feminist Study of Nineteenth-Century Gothic*, Oxford: Oxford University Press.

Dickens, Charles [1861] (1994), *Great Expectations*, Oxford: Oxford University Press.

Ellis, Andrew Esq. (1835), 'Clinical Lecture on a Case of Catalepsy, occurring in the Jervis-Street Hospital, Dublin', *The Lancet*, 2 May: 129–34.

Esquirol, Jean-Etienne Dominique (1838), *Des Maladies mentales, considérées sous les rapports médical, hygiénique et médico-légal*, Paris: J.-B. Baillères.

Esquirol, Jean-Etienne Dominique (1845) *Mental Maladies: A Treatise on Insanity*, trans. with addition by E. K. Hunt, Philadelphia: Lea and Blanchard.

Fleenor, Juliann E. (ed.) (1983), *The Female Gothic*, London: Eden Press.

Gilbert, Sandra M. and Susan Gubar [1979] (1984), *The Madwoman in the Attic: The Woman Writer and the Nineteenth-Century Literary Imagination*, New Haven, CT: Yale University Press.

Martin, Philip (1987), *Mad Women in Romantic Writing*, New York: St Martin's Press.

Modleski, Tania [1982] (1990), *Loving with a Vengeance: Mass-Produced Fantasies for Women*, London: Routledge.

Maudsley, Henry [1857] (1880), *The Pathology of Mind*, New York: D. Appleton & Company.

Moers, Ellen [1976] (1978), *Literary Women*, London: The Women's Press Limited, pp. 90–110.

Owen, Alex (1989), *The Darkened Room: Women, Power, and Spiritualism in Late Victorian England*, Chicago: University of Chicago Press.

Prichard, J. C. (1835), *A Treatise on Insanity and Other Disorders Affecting the Mind*, London: Sherwood, Gilbert and Piper.

Radcliffe, Ann [1794] (1980), *The Mysteries of Udolpho*, Oxford: Oxford University Press.

Sedgwick, Eve Kosofsky [1980] (1986), *The Coherence of Gothic Conventions*, London: Methuen.

Showalter, Elaine (1987), *The Female Malady: Women Madness and English Culture, 1830–1980*, New York: Pantheon Books.

Small, Helen (1996), *Love's Madness: Medicine, The Novel, and Female Insanity, 1800–1865*, Oxford: Clarendon Press.

Stoker, Bram [1897] (1997), *Dracula*, ed. Nina Auerbach and David S. Skal, New York, London: Norton & Company.

Talairach-Vielmas, Laurence (2009), *Wilkie Collins, Medicine and the Gothic*, Cardiff: University of Wales Press.

Taylor, Jenny Bourne (1988), *In the Secret Theatre of Home: Wilkie Collins, Sensation Narrative and Nineteenth Century Psychology*, London: Routledge.

Williams, Anne (1995), *Art of Darkness: A Poetics of Gothic*, Chicago: University of Chicago Press.

Wood, Jane (2001), *Passion and Pathology in Victorian Fiction*, Oxford: Oxford University Press.

Chapter 3

Mothers and Others

Ginette Carpenter

The discursive panopticon that monitors and proscribes performances of femininity is particularly vigilant in relation to mothering. The pressures attendant on contemporary motherhood have been documented extensively in texts such as Naomi Wolf's *Misconceptions* (2002), Susan J. Douglas and Meredith W. Michaels's *The Mommy Myth* (2004) and more recently in Kat Banyard's *The Equality Illusion* (2010: 179-202) and Rebecca Asher's *Shattered* (2012). These accounts all suggest that advance of feminism is precarious and that women continue to be defined and constrained by tenacious models of the maternal that merge with a loudly trumpeted post-femininity to overwrite patriarchal confinement with illusions of choice (McRobbie 2008: 1–5; Power 2009: 29–37). This chapter reads two contemporary films through the prism of women's Gothic to demonstrate the maintenance of a hegemonic version of the maternal that offers only compliance or abjection. Since Ellen Moers's famous claim that Mary Shelley utilised the fantastic potential of the Gothic to covertly represent the hidden horror of pregnancy and mothering (Moers 1978: 91–9) the figure of the monstrous m/Other has been identified as a site of rupture that serves a dual function: voicing the obfuscated experiences of maternity while simultaneously reinscribing the fictions that maintain the occlusion. Gothic texts (and their monsters) have always performed this contradiction, both policing and transgressing the borders between ideological inscription and resistance (Botting 2014: 8–12) and the films under discussion here operate in this way, both reasserting and troubling constructions of the m/Other and thereby articulating a range of anxieties that attend their maintenance.

Ridley Scott's *Prometheus* (2012) and Lynne Ramsay's *We Need to Talk About Kevin* (*WNTTAK*) (2011) seem at first to have little shared territory depicting, respectively, a dystopically imagined future and a realist nightmare. *Prometheus* is set in the late-twenty-first century on a high-tech spaceship and a desolate, inhospitable planet; *WNTTAK* is almost entirely enacted within the mundane, and primarily domestic, spaces of contemporary America. However, the films' representations of the maternal and the monstrous – of mothers and Others – can be seen to reflect corresponding cultural anxieties about the production, maintenance and interrogation of twenty-first-century gender roles and the continued surveillance of maternity. In both films these are evocations channelled through the conventions of Gothic: their generic instabilities, use of excess, overlapping of past and present and depictions of uncanny and abject monstrosity combine with the visual tropes of the horror film to create unsettling depictions of feminine embodiment, pregnancy, birth and mothering.

The readings that follow are theoretically underpinned by a model of maternal abjection, mobilising the paradigms offered by Julia Kristeva, Barbara Creed and Luce Irigaray in order to demonstrate the extent to which contemporary Gothic texts are still invested in a process of Othering the mother. In *Powers of Horror* Kristeva outlines her conception of the 'archaic mother' as a source of 'generative power' which 'patrilineal filiation has the burden of subduing' (Kristeva 1982: 73). The abject thus erupts as that which potentially transgresses 'the boundary between semiotic authority and symbolic law' (73). In her seminal account of Kristeva's thesis, Barbara Creed argues that 'Kristeva stresses her [the archaic mother's] double signifying function as both source of life and the abyss. In both aspects she is constructed as abject in order to ensure the constitution of subjectivity and the law' (Creed 1993: 25–6). Creed's concept of the monstrous-feminine, 'of what it is about woman that is shocking, terrifying, horrific, abject' (1) maps Kristeva's ideas directly onto horror films of the 1970s and 1980s to argue that '[v]irtually all horror texts represent the monstrous-feminine in relation to Kristeva's notion of maternal authority and the mapping of the self's clean and proper body' thus 'signify[ing] a split between the two orders: the maternal authority and the law of the father' (13). The work of Kristeva and Creed highlights the ways in which the maternal is contained and confined by patriarchal law, but these psychoanalytic readings uphold the necessity of the separation between semiotic and symbolic as a process of becoming a functioning subject, thereby maintaining the Othering of the mother. Irigaray offers a more materialist critique by arguing that the 'the whole of our western culture is based upon the murder of the mother' (Whitford 1991: 47) and that '[t]he mother has become a devouring monster as an inverted effect of the blind consumption of the mother' (40). For Irigaray the power of the maternal is culturally abjected and made monstrous – 'And the things they threaten us with! We are going to swallow them up, devour them, castrate them' (50) – via the consuming mechanisms of discourse and language so only a defused, unthreatening and proscribed space remains for woman to inhabit: 'her confinement behind the door of a house. Where almost nothing happens except the (re)production of a child' (64). Like Kristeva and Creed, Irigaray observes the fully embodied experience of the maternal as excluded and culturally abjected, as 'shameful flow' (64), but positions the culturally permitted performance of maternity as being repeatedly being 'torn to pieces' (38) while 'remain[ing] forbidden, excluded' (39). The maternal must be both abjected and assimilated by patriarchal law: the mother is simultaneously, and paradoxically, rejected and incorporated. The value of Irigaray's thesis is in its move beyond the confines of psychoanalytic analyses to interrogate the underlying discursive structures that maintain maternal abjection for, as Judith Halberstam contends, 'the unconscious itself and all of its mechanisms are precisely the effects of historical and cultural production' (Halberstam 1995: 8). For Irigaray, psychoanalytic discourse can only ever be complicit in the maintenance of a historically enacted and continuing matricide. *Prometheus* and *WNTTAK*'s mapping of these contradictory evocations of maternal abjection and incorporation reveal the tenacity of the archetype of the all-consuming m/Other.

Compared with *WNTTAK*, *Prometheus* is critically s/mothered. It is also haunted by its filmic antecedents returning repeatedly to the *mise-en-scène*, imagery and narrative structures of its predecessors. In this regard the film itself has an uncanny effect as it simultaneously replicates and deviates from these antecedents; it is both familiar and resoundingly *Other*. The story concerns two anthropologists – Elizabeth Shaw and Charlie Holloway– who claim to have found the origin of humanity, via a series of globally distributed cave paintings that show humans worshipping giant beings ('Engineers'). Peter Weyland, head of the multinational Weyland Corporation, funds an expedition to fulfil his dying wish to meet his maker/s. The events then follow a very familiar arc from the first two *Alien* films: a crew travel in hyper-sleep, on the craft *Prometheus*, to their destination, where they are awoken – this time by an android-caretaker, Weyland's 'son' David – and set out to explore an abandoned spaceship, thereby awakening an alien species that is housed and breeding there. The monster then proceeds to annihilate several of the crew in conventional horror mode, as they gradually discern that this is not the Engineers' planet, but one which they used as a storage facility for alien DNA as bio-weaponry. Weyland is killed by a reanimated Engineer, who also dismembers David, and others die in a heroic act of self-sacrifice as they crash the *Prometheus* into the escaping Engineer spaceship, bound to destroy Earth. The intertextual symbolism of the film is heavily laboured, with all involved in the overreaching mission punished for this transgression. The parallels between the Engineers and Victor Frankenstein are clear – humankind as a monstrous creation that its architects seek to destroy – but this interestingly mirrored depiction of Othering is stifled by the excessive effects of the gratuitously gory body-count and the meandering narrative and its overblown concerns. The film ends with the only human survivor, Shaw, and the decapitated head of David embarking upon a further journey to discover why humanity's creators were so determined to annihilate their offspring, a clear indication of a sequel.

Shaw is the little girl lost at the centre of the narrative, an orphan questing for meaning and faith in a disordered and ultimately faithless universe. She is in many ways a Ripley-clone and, like Ripley in *Alien* (dir. Ridley Scott, 1978), she is positioned as what Anne Williams describes as a 'plucky Gothic heroine' (1995: 250), but her carefully detailed back-story encourages a degree of sentimental identification that is importantly absent from the quadrilogy. While Shaw is in hyper-sleep, David watches her dreams to reveal that following the premature death of her mother she was raised by her father, until his demise, and that she still wears his cross. This marker of faith is tellingly removed by David as he attempts to turn Shaw into a scientific experiment, employing her as an incubation unit for an alien foetus. Shaw's abortion of the foetus is, arguably, the central and most horrific scene of the film with regard to its depiction of the female body and its return to *Alien*'s paradigms of abjection that have been overwritten by more complex models of femininity and mothering in the later films (see Constable 1999; Stacey 2003; Melzer 2006; Botting 2008). The operation deliberately invokes and replays key scenes from its predecessors: the original film's infamous (and misnamed) 'chest-bursting' scene, where Cain gives 'birth' to the monster; *Alien3*'s (dir. David Fincher, 1992) climactic matricide, as Ripley clutches her own erupting alien baby to her chest while deliberately plunging to her death; and the Ripley-clone's reluctant killing of her child-alien at the end of *Alien Resurrection* (dir. Jean-Pierre Jeunet, 1997). Yet Fincher's and, in particular, Jeunet's films offer more nuanced and shifting possibilities for maternal identification as Patricia Melzer argues convincingly in *Alien Constructions*: '[t]he conflation of the monstrous and the maternal in the *Alien* series results in an appropriation of the position of the Other by Ripley in the fourth movie' (Melzer 2006: 136). However, Shaw's abhorrence for the alien foetus she is housing returns *Prometheus* to the dated binaries of *Alien* and *Aliens*, whereby the borders between subject and abject, mother and monster, are rigorously patrolled. The character's location as orphan means that the film reinforces what Melzer has identified as the 'patriarchal ideology of the mother as a nurturing member of the nuclear family' (132) and jettisons the transgressive embracing of a monstrous m/Other suggested by the latter two films of the quadrilogy. Yet the explicit enactment and attendant horror of the act of aborting the alien fœtus also resonates uncomfortably with vehement contemporary pro-life discourses (Banyard 2010: 196–202), positioning abortion as an act of unremitting violence. Birth *and* its refusal are evoked as similarly monstrous.

Prometheus's refutation of feminine monstrosity – the outright rejection of Kristeva's 'archaic mother' (Kristeva 1982: 77) – is underlined by the specifics of Shaw's abortion. The procedure is executed by a medipod stored on-board to nurse the geriatric Weyland and 'calibrated for male patients only'. Shaw can therefore only instigate the intervention via a male model: 'Surgery. Abdominal. Penetrating injuries. Foreign body'. The messiness of female embodiment, and its accompanying 'horrors', is thus literally reinscribed as male, and pregnancy (re)located as abject and forcibly ejected from the symbolic realm; there are no words. The camera, however, speaks fluently to a range of embodied anxieties as it hovers voyeuristically over Shaw's honed form while she disrobes, readies herself and is operated upon. Historical – and hysterical – fears about the shape-shifting pregnant body are therefore conflated with a highly contemporary body fascism, as Banyard observes: '[w]omen's and girls' bodies are objectified and stigmatised on a scale as never before … it is a spectrum on which having your flesh cut, sucked and sliced for non-medical purposes is a logical act' (Banyard 2010: 43). The abortion itself can be read as a grotesque parody of cosmetic surgery, whereby the female body is sculpted and literally, in Shaw's case, stapled together again. The fact that her form is tightly bikini-bandaged throughout this sequence connotes her as simultaneously vulnerable and desirable and the deployment of old-school body horror further provokes and reaffirms the male gaze. The intense focus on Shaw's pulsating midriff as it is prepared, sliced and the skin and muscle neatly rolled back encourages a very particular type of Gothic voyeurism – what Halberstam might label a 'skin show' (1995) – where that which is hidden is exposed. The scene therefore problematises conceptions of inside and outside, of self and Other. Yet the potential of monstrosity to 'represent[s] the disruption of categories, the destruction of boundaries, and the presence of impurities' (Halberstam 1995: 27) is stapled shut in the same way that Shaw's stomach is returned to its pre-gestational tautness. The uncanniness attendant on both pregnancy and inner anatomy – the most intimately familiar as unfamiliar – is rejected in favour of the recirculation of a damagingly pernicious version of twenty-first-century embodied femininity.

Meredith Vickers – the other key female character in the film and Weyland's biological daughter – presents an even more impossibly perfected version of the female body, her tight muscles and sharp edges used to underpin the cold, unbending efficiency with which she manages the *Prometheus*. Vickers is visually aligned with the metallic lines of the spaceship, her body chiselled and worked to athletic perfection and her decisions made without compassion or empathy. She performs a particular version of ruthless, solipsistic masculinity and her eschewing of stereotypical feminine traits is demonstrated by her brutal torching of Holloway, her sexual predation of Janek and her single-minded attempt at escape, all of which are punished, in classic horror mode, by her premature demise. As a female character she is contrapuntally cast against the far more emotional and humane Shaw and this contrast is emphasised physically in the juxtaposition of the tall blonde with the petite brunette. Vickers' appearance is also used to visually align her with her 'brother' David – a 'child' far more esteemed by their father – and many of her actions can be read as mirroring or mimicking David in her quest for an ever-absent parental praise.

These restrictive and confining representations of femininity would seem to locate *Prometheus* as an example of what Williams, in relation to the first three films, labels Male Gothic (Williams 1995: 249–52). Williams argues that, despite their science-fiction pedigrees, the films replicate the patriarchal family structure and Ripley is the '"good woman"' (251) who purges the ships (*Alien*, *Aliens*) and colony (*Alien*³) of the monstrous feminine, thus adhering to the pattern apparent in the Male Gothic tradition as a whole: that the horrible, the abject, is identical with the 'the female,' the alien energy that poses a dreadful danger to man, society and the Law of the Father (252).

This reading is clearly compatible with the ways in which *Prometheus* is damagingly haunted by its antecedents, but Shaw's journey also has clear resonances with the model of Female Gothic, as the motherless child explores the corridors of spaceships avoiding predation. Moreover, monsters come in many guises and an alternative reading, a reading through the gaps, suggests that, despite the prevalence of textbook alien monsters – devouring, unstoppable and endlessly invasive – it is David who is the most unnerving monstrous Other. 'Born' by human design, David is the perfect child who cannot exist: biddable, obedient, non-confrontational and conventionally attractive. The mutated monstrosity of Fifield and Holloway, in all their embodied grossness, is less unnerving than David's perfection. In many ways he is, for the majority of the film, uncanniness personified, a living doll that apes embodiment while unfettered by the messy demands of the human body. His objective rationalism and profit-driven instrumentalism serve as a cipher for both the rampant expansionist policies of the Weyland Corporation and of dominant, unbending patriarchal power. Yet David exists in a far more liminal space than his actions suggest, his appearance engendering a familiarity that belies his 'otherness', and his inability to die, his fractured *return* (like that of his predecessors Ash, Bishop and Cal in the earlier films), makes him an ultimate figure of Gothic monstrosity. He has more in common with the vampire or the zombie than with his human inventors. David's narrative arc is a movement from uncanny to abject, from robotic perfection – beautiful, unmarked, intellectually masterful – to a torn, dismembered head. He begins the film in a position of authority and control, watching and tending to the sleeping crew, while filmed in probing close-up perfecting his Lawrence of Arabia hairstyle and his mastery of languages: the anti-abject. He ends the film literally ripped apart, in pieces. David's trajectory reverses that of Frankenstein's monster as he journeys from a humanised consumer of texts and expert communicator to a collection of improvised body parts, speech bubbling falteringly through disconnected wiring, as abject monstrosity overwrites the performance of symbolic assimilation. David's head becomes a visual signifier of Weyland's 'workshop of filthy creation' (Shelley 1992: 53), of man's overreaching search to mimic birth. Yet David's dismemberment also invokes Irigaray's figure of the 'the woman who was torn to pieces between son and father' (Whitford 1991: 38) and can be read as an enactment and inversion of the process of maternal abjection, as the android 'birthed' by man is made monstrous by man's creator/father (an Engineer). Moreover, Shaw's cradling of David's head, as she apologises for having to shut him in a rucksack, inverts *her* abjection of the alien foetus as David becomes her monster to carry, the weight on her back rather than in her belly. If David is the monstrous spectre that stalks the corridors of this film, then Elizabeth Shaw's final act (and the name she shares with Victor Frankenstein's wife can be no coincidence) gestures towards a recognition of alterity. Both Shaw and David are broken by this point of the film – the former held together by staples and tape – and thus Shaw invokes not only Victor's wife but also his monster's desired female companion, a fellow wanderer of the wild, desolate wastes of outer space.

The confined, crowded, domestic *mise-en-scène* of WNTTAK is far removed from the sweeping, widescreen landscapes of *Prometheus*: Ramsay's film is Shelley's 'trauma of afterbirth' (Moers 1978: 93) imagined within a realist frame. The film narrates the story of Eva

Khatchadourian, whose son, Kevin, on his sixteenth birthday, methodically executes seven of his classmates and wounds several others by locking them in the school gym and targeting them with a crossbow. Prior to this he has also murdered his younger sister, Celia, and father, Franklin. As in Lionel Shriver's novel, published in 2005, the patricide and sororicide are disclosed at the dénouement, requiring the viewer to confront their own complicity in any simplistic models of judgement and blame. Ramsay has ruthlessly pruned Shriver's book and the film lacks some of the novel's ambiguity, sacrificing unreliable narration for a more precise evocation of a monstrous relationship between parent and child. However, the claustrophobia of the epistolary form has been maintained by the fact that Eva appears in every scene: this is very deliberately the mother's tale. The film works back and forth between Eva's life post-massacre, as she determinedly remains in the same small-town community, visiting Kevin in jail weekly, and the history to the central acts of violence via vignettes of her courtship, marriage and Kevin's upbringing. These timeframes are rapidly overlapped – the use of analepsis is at times dizzying – with only the length of Eva's hair as clue to whether the events portrayed are past or present, and this palimpsestic conflation emphasises the trauma of the events. Eva's past is ever-present, but she is also entirely defined by events that cannot be altered, only endlessly replayed, as Peter Bradshaw observes in his review of the film: 'Swinton portrays Eva as a ghost, haunting her past and haunted by it' (Bradshaw 2011). What haunts Eva the most is her failure as a mother, and the flashbacks are all to events where she, and/or her husband have ignored or repressed signs of Kevin's monstrosity. For Kevin is a truly monstrous child: resistant, unresponsive and deliberately destructive. He appears to pursue the course of action that will cause the most distress, particularly to his mother, from endless crying to a refusal to talk and a rejection of any attempts at potty-training. Yet Franklin, absent from the daily grind of mindless parenting, can see only 'a sweet little boy' who does 'what boys do' and this determined refutation of his son's proclivities for violence and pain is tragically played out when Kevin callously assassinates him by the very means – archery – that his father has encouraged as a suitably boyish pursuit. *WNTTAK* thus engages directly with the discursive construction of motherhood, from the overriding pressure to be a mother to the isolation and sense of failure that often attend the role: Irigaray's 'confinement behind the door of the house' (Whitford 1991: 64). However, the unspoken, yet omnipresent, question that underpins the novel – what happens if you give birth to a monster? – is more forcefully foregrounded in the film by virtue of its recourse to the cinematic conventions of Gothic horror.

Ramsay creates an overpoweringly threatening sense of domestic Gothic by defamiliarising the mundane and the everyday: the sound of sprinklers becomes an ominous refrain that merges with the whirring blades of circling police helicopters; strawberry jam spills excessively over pristine kitchen surfaces; the expensive, suburban, family home – labelled 'our very own castle' by Franklin – is clinically cold and cavernous. The arrival of Kevin instantly shatters Eva's life as she transforms from globe-trotting, travel-company director to stay-at-home Mum. The sense of imprisonment she feels is conveyed by the contrast with her initial depiction at Spain's La Tomatina – the excessive tomato-throwing festival – where she is held aloft by other revellers in a Christ-like pose, a visual symbol of how her life will be sacrificed to her future child. The focus on a mass of writhing bodies drenched and wallowing in a sea of red tomato flesh clearly foreshadows Kevin's murderous acts; although this opening scene is the most gory of a film in which horror is intimated rather than overtly displayed, as it is, by contrast, in *Prometheus*. Red is deployed menacingly and increasingly throughout *WNTTAK* from splashes of violent colour against more muted backgrounds – a red ball, a red shirt – to the use of filters until, by the concluding scenes, as she lies on her too-small sofa recalling the day of the massacre, Eva is filmed in a red wash, her immersion in the colour a structural counterpoint to her earlier, ecstatic baptism at the Tomatina. In Eva's first scene in the present, the interior of her home is similarly bathed in a red glow, as it is revealed that her house and car have been drenched in gallons of red paint, a crude signifier of her son's act and her perceived collusion in the monstrosity by virtue of being his mother. The narrative returns regularly to scenes of Eva scrubbing the paint from windows, porch and doors, a seemingly endless task and one that symbolically transfers the paint to her face and hair. The allusion to Lady Macbeth's obsessive hand-washing is clear and this cleverly associates her with a heinous crime, marking her as complicit. The tropes of the horror film are astutely parodied and mobilised by Ramsay – the fleshly excess is tomatoes, the oozing gore is strawberry jam, the blood that cannot be washed out is paint – to intensify the uncanniness of the performance of suburban domesticity. In a characteristically wry shot, Ramsay returns to tomatoes to film Eva in close-up in the supermarket against a Warholesque wall of identical tomato soup cans, used, as Hannah McGill observes, to signify Eva's transformed life, post-massacre: '[h]er adventures have all been contained; her life reduced and confined' (McGill 2011). However, arguably, this confinement begins with Kevin's birth. The sense of entrapment, failure and self-blame is nothing new. If, as Bradshaw argues, 'Eva's only identity is now that of someone who

gave birth to horror' (Bradshaw 2011), then this is the outward manifestation of the inward sense of alienation and despair that have defined
her since Kevin's conception.

Eva's pregnancy is marked by discomfort with the way in which
her body is being shaped from the inside out by forces that elude her
characteristic control. This is evoked by a scene in her gym (another
ironic foreshadowing) changing rooms where Eva sits, centre-frame,
fully clothed, surrounded by other expectant women who are all standing and conversing, their naked baby bumps crowding Eva's head. As
is typical of Ramsay's oeuvre, meaning resides in the image, not the
dialogue and Eva is Othered by her framing. The sense of dislocation
that Eva feels while pregnant is not the abject horror experienced by
Elizabeth Shaw, it is not a desire to rid herself violently of the Other
she carries, but rather an evocation of the unendingly uncanny state of
gestation as the body is occupied by that which is both of itself and not
of itself, what Wolf labels a 'benign possession' (Wolf 2002: 25). There
is nothing benign, however, about Kevin, and the chaos he wreaks on
Eva's psyche can be read as a realist manifestation of the rampaging
aliens of *Prometheus*. For Eva, Kevin is the ultimate 'Other', yet, until
the massacre, he is insistently present, troubling, and often provoca-
tively transgressing, the mother/child boundaries that are delineated
with entry into the symbolic order. His rejection of toilet-training – he
is still wearing nappies post-kindergarten – is a clear manifestation of
this and the film's focus on bodily excess and very specifically on excre-
ment, can be read through and against Kristeva's model of abjection and
the imposition of matrilineal authority (Kristeva 1982: 71–2). Kristeva
argues that 'maternal authority is experienced first and above all ... as
sphincteral' (71) and that the mother's authority teaches 'the differentia-
tion of proper-clean and improper-dirty, possible and impossible' (72).
Kevin's refusal to recognise 'the self's clean and proper body' (72) is a
refusal of the imposition of maternal law and, thus, also of the law of the
father, for the first must precede the second. There is an inversion here
of Creed's reading of Kristeva – '[b]y refusing to relinquish her hold on
the child, she [the mother] prevents it from taking up its proper place in
relation to the symbolic' (1993: 12) – for it is not the mother who refuses
the break, but the child. Kevin's eventual compliance is in response to an
act of extreme violence by Eva, as she throws him across the room and
breaks his arm, an act engendered by his deliberately provocative soiling
of a newly changed nappy. The scene is filmed to alternately assert
Kevin's control and his vulnerability as leeringly defiant close-ups are
juxtaposed with high-angle shots. Similarly, the sympathy that is evoked
for Eva, as she is confronted by the monstrously rude and resistant child,

is undercut by horror at a mother's outburst so extreme that it leaves her child crumpled in a corner, nursing a twisted limb. When in prison, Kevin will inform Eva that this most anti-maternal of deeds was the 'most honest thing you've ever done' as the child willingly embraces the irruption of the culturally abjected monstrous m/Other.

Eva's violence sees her manipulated into an unspoken pact with her son as he tells his father that he 'fell off the changing table'. Yet this understanding between Eva and her son, symbolically secured in this mutual adherence to the lie, has always existed in parallel to Eva's ongoing despair at Kevin's Otherness. The film emphasises the links between them, using shot-reverse-shot techniques to mirror their inter-actions and devoting far more screen time to Eva and Kevin than to their relationships with either Celia or Franklin, both of whom are really only peripheral players. The 'transgressive sexual relations' that George E. Heggarty identifies as 'an undeniable common denominator of Gothic' (Heggarty 2004: 1) are apparent in the developing intimate dyad between Eva and Kevin: as a child he interrupts Eva performing fellatio on her husband to announce he has 'poopy pants'; when a scowling teenager he leaves the bathroom door open while masturbating, mockingly taunting Eva as she pauses horrified while he fails to miss a beat (pun intended). These moments of rupture, of the destabilisation of legitimate familial relations, are reinforced by the knowingness that exists between Eva and Kevin as he performs a fake version of himself for his father; his sideways glances and collusive sneers are a seeming confirmation of the accuracy of Eva's assessment of his actions. The audience is positioned as witness to these asides and, as such, is implicated in a horror narrative that Franklin not only fails to observe but completely rejects, clinging to his version of middle-class domesticity and telling Eva that she needs to 'talk to someone'. Of course, Franklin is punished for his inability to recognise his son's monstrosity by his murder on the immaculate lawn of the very domestic idyll that he himself has built and Kevin's warped romancing of his mother is underscored by this brutal act of patricide. Franklin's corpse is a grisly signifier of his inert parental role and his death yet again excuses him from the sheer amount of labour that has attended and will continue to attend Kevin's upbringing. Eva's role as mother now burgeons horrifically to encompass atonement for her child's sins, including the loss of her own spouse and daughter. And the millstone gains yet more weight as Eva becomes a willing repository for the community's anger and blame, assuming her son's role as monstrous Other – pilloried, attacked and shunned she becomes another contempo-rary version of Frankenstein's monster, driven to the edges of madness by the knowledge of her own monstrosity.

Eva's willingness to accept the positon of abjected Other is symbolised by her Gothicised body and home, whereby the attempt to monitor the borders between inside and outside, between chaos and control, is represented as an ongoing battle. The neatness of Eva's life pre-massacre, her designer clothing and the minimalist (albeit uncanny) lines of her huge home are replaced by oversized T-shirts and tracksuit bottoms and a crowded, dishevelled house that wears the marks of domestic breakdown. The camera returns to linger time and again over the detritus of Eva's meals for one, over half-finished glasses of wine, cold omelettes and a pile of pill bottles as she sleeps fitfully on the sofa, occupying the no-man's-land between asleep and awake, present and past, life and death. Kevin's crime zombifies Eva and she becomes uncanniness personified: she is simultaneously herself and not herself, here and not here, whole and shattered. The focus on parts of her body – she is rarely filmed in longshot in the 'present' timeframe – reinforces her fragmentation, her dislocation from herself, and the repeated emphasis on her naked feet signifies her loss of balance. Like Shaw, she is patched together, with only the most strained of metaphorical staples preventing her injuries from bursting open. However, unlike Shaw, she has not only lived with, but also actively nurtured, her monster for many years and is thus unable to separate herself from his crimes; she is dismembered by her son's act. Eva's fracturing is evoked by the poignant image of an omelette she makes with eggs that have been maliciously smashed by the mother of one of Kevin's victims. Kevin's act has scrambled her life beyond recognition. The final scenes of the film see her attempting to regain some control by (re)assuming the trappings of domesticity as she decorates a bedroom for Kevin, irons and folds his clothes, makes his bed. Yet these are mere sticking plasters applied to gaping wounds; the horror of Kevin's acts has caused an irrevocable breach and the only way in which the community can heal is to abject Eva. Despite her excessive uncanniness, her role as mother means that she is publicly cast as monstrous feminine, as Creed's 'witch': 'an implacable enemy of the symbolic order ... dangerous and wily, capable of drawing on her evil powers to wreck a community' (1993: 76). Unlike David, there is no one to cradle Eva and she is left to wander the liminal wastes of her desert alone.

Prometheus and *WNTTAK* mobilise Gothic conventions in various ways, not least in their inculcation of fear and anxiety. The former achieves this more viscerally through repeated representations of awe-ful monsters and penetrative body horror, whereas *WNTTAK* produces its effect through the disturbing scenario of the horror residing at home. This chapter has demonstrated that these texts can be read as foregrounding cultural concerns that inform the discursive construction of mothers and Others. Despite its science-fiction pedigree, futuristic setting and twenty-first-century production values, *Prometheus*, in many ways, returns us to an enactment of early Second-Wave femininity, whereby women are superficially represented as equal but are actually scripted and confined by stubbornly embedded patriarchal structures: bodies are perfected, birth abjected. By contrast, *WNTTAK* offers more problematic versions of both femininity and mothering, as bodies fail to conform and both mother and child struggle to perform or adhere to their allotted roles, implying that the pre-symbolic bond continues to trouble the coherence of the father's law. *Prometheus* seems to evoke a proscribed and bound version of the m/Other in comparison to *WNTTAK*'s insistent problematisation of the maternal and the monstrous. Yet the stereotypical alterities of *Prometheus* are, at least in part, overwritten by the android David's dismemberment, which foregrounds the monstrous operations of patriarchal power and also offers Shaw an opportunity to embrace, literally, and care for a monstrous Other, akin to filling the 'hole' in the 'bellies ... and in the site of ... identity' that women endure within the symbolic order (Whitford 1991: 41), engendered by the cultural abjection of the maternal. Conversely, the potential of *WNTTAK* to interrogate the discourses that allow 'the [male] subject [to] use, explore, fragment, speculate the other' (Whitford 1991: 61) is undercut by Eva's acceptance of the mantle of her child's monstrosity. Their final acceptance of their delineated roles in the symbolic – signified by their embrace at the close of the film – can only result in Eva's abjection, her being cast out and away, as evoked by the final fade to white.

Filmography

Alien, directed by Ridley Scott, USA: Twentieth Century Fox, 1979.
Alien3, directed by David Fincher, USA: Twentieth Century Fox, 1992.
Alien Resurrection, directed by Jean-Pierre Jeunet, USA: Twentieth Century Fox, 1997.
Prometheus, directed by Ridley Scott, USA: Twentieth Century Fox, 2012.
We Need to Talk About Kevin, directed by Lynne Ramsay, UK: Artificial Eye, 2011.

Bibliography

Asher, Rebecca (2012), *Shattered: Modern Motherhood and the Illusion of Equality*, London: Vintage.

Banyard, Kat (2010), *The Equality Illusion: The Truth About Women and Men Today*, London: Faber & Faber.

Botting, Fred (2008), *Gothic Romanced: Consumption, Gender and Technology in Contemporary Fictions*, London: Routledge, pp. 152–80.

Botting, Fred (2014), *Gothic*, Abingdon, Oxon: Routledge.

Bradshaw, Peter (2011), 'We Need to Talk About Kevin: review', *Guardian*, 20 October. Available at: http://www.theguardian.com/film/2011/oct/20/we-need-to-talk-about-kevin-review (accessed 20 October 2014).

Constable, Catherine (1999), 'Becoming the Monster's Mother: Morphologies of Identity in the *Alien* Series', in Annette Kuhn (ed.), *Alien Zone II: The Spaces of Science Fiction Cinema*, London: Verso, pp. 173–202.

Creed, Barbara (1993), *The Monstrous Feminine: Film, Feminism, Psychoanalysis*, London: Routledge.

Douglas, Susan J. and Meredith W. Michaels (2004), *The Mommy Myth: The Idealisation of otherhood and how it has Undermined all Women*, New York: Free Press.

Halberstam, Judith (1995), *Skin Shows: Gothic Horror and the Technology of Monsters*, Durham, NC: Duke University Press.

Heggarty, George E. (2004), 'Mothers and Other Lovers: Gothic Fiction and the Erotics of Loss', *Eighteenth Century Fiction*, 16(2): 1–16.

Kristeva, Julia (1982), *Powers of Horror: An Essay on Abjection*, New York: Columbia University Press.

McGill, Hannah (2011), 'We Need to Talk About Kevin', *Sight and Sound*, 21(11): 16–19.

McRobbie, Angela (2008), *The Aftermath of Feminism: Gender, Culture and Social Change*, London: Sage.

Melzer, Patricia (2006), *Alien Constructions: Science Fiction and Feminist Thought*, Austin: University of Texas Press.

Moers, Ellen (1978), *Literary Women*. London: The Women's Press.

Power, Nina (2009), *One Dimensional Woman*, Ropley, Hants: Zero Books.

Shelley, Mary [1818] (1992), *Frankenstein*, London: Penguin.

Shriver, Lionel (2005), *We Need to Talk About Kevin*, London: Serpent's Tail.

Stacey, Jackie (2003), 'She is not herself: the deviant relations of *Alien Resurrection*', *Screen*, 43(3): 251–76.

Whitford, Margaret (1991), *The Irigaray Reader*, Oxford: Blackwell.

Williams, Anne (1995), *Art of Darkness: a Poetics of Gothic*, Chicago: The University of Chicago Press.

Wolf, Naomi (2002), *Misconceptions*, London: Vintage.

Chapter 4

The Gothic Girl Child
Lucie Armitt

Critical interest in the Gothic child has been vibrant since the new millennium. In 2004, Steven Bruhm and Natasha Hurley edited *Curiouser: On the Queerness of Children*, in which three of the fourteen essays associate queer children, in whole or part, with the Gothic. In one, Kathryn Bond Stockton identifies an innate 'queerness' in all children, simultaneously recognising that 'We are in a world not ready to receive this historical formulation' (Stockton 2004: 281). The collection as a whole understands 'queer' as 'sexual alterity' and also 'deviation from the "normal"' (Bruhm and Hurley 2004: x) and Stockton extends that terrain to include 'the lurking child, the shadowy child, the indirect child ... the obedient-child-as-fearful child, the not-stopping-what-other-boys-begin child' (Stockton 2004: 284).

In my book, *Twentieth-Century Gothic*, I argue that questions of haunted childhood especially differentiate contemporary Gothic narratives from their antecedents. We create our Gothic monsters to give shape to what are otherwise vague but preoccupying social anxieties. Thus, in the face of the ever-increasing tabloid media fascination with child disappearances, child deaths and child abuse, children and death populate many recent Gothic literary and cinematic texts. Thus do we trace out 'an obsession in society which cannot make up its mind whether it is appalled or enthralled by children and the dangers by which, in their name, we are haunted' (Armitt 2011: 46–7). It is in this paradoxical manner that the Gothic girl child is best understood: as an enigma; a cipher for the appealing nature of things not always fully understood; one who is alluring, but potentially dangerous. In essence, one might argue that she, above all characters, best embodies the very attractiveness of Gothic literature itself.

In this chapter I examine ten fictional treatments of the Gothic girl child, published between 1845 and 2009. In researching the chapter I was surprised to discover that, though the narrative form develops in line with societal shift during that period, and though the sociocultural expectations of women have shifted dramatically since the mid-nineteenth century, the girl child of 1845 shares much common ground with her twenty-first-century sister, for Gothic literary depictions of girls remained surprisingly unchanged.

So what *is* a Gothic girl child? According to James R. Kincaid, all children are slippery to define: '[A]nyone between the ages of one day and 25 years or even beyond might, in different contexts, play that role' (Kincaid 1992: 5). Similarly Margarita Georgieva argues that the term 'child', in literary texts, can extend to include: 'persons of unstable perception ... [those] lacking affective maturity ... [the] vulnerable and helpless' (Georgieva 2013: 2). Especially in relation to girls, beyond literature, definitions of adulthood are driven (perhaps overly) by questions of sexual consent, but even then, slipperiness persists. At the time of writing, the age of sexual consent in the UK is sixteen. Since 1969, and the passing of the Family Reform Law, a girl 'comes of age' at eighteen; before then she did so at twenty-one. In 1800, however, girls could legally marry at twelve, which means that our assumption that a literary bride must have acceded to womanhood cannot be assumed when reading nineteenth-century texts. Leaving legal definitions aside, our expectations about children and playtime are utterly inconsistent. When Sigmund Freud expresses surprise, in 'The "Uncanny"' (1919), when 'a woman patient declare[s] that *even at the age of eight* she had still been convinced that her dolls would be certain to come to life if she were to look at them in a particular, extremely concentrated, way' (Freud 1990: 355; my emphasis), my surprise is not at her declaration, but at his response.

Despite Freud's bewilderment, however, in Gothic narratives it is much more common for girl children to become ensnared in patriarchy's refusal to let them mature. Edgar Allan Poe's story, 'The Oval Portrait' (1845), becomes a kind of allegory for this refusal. Our narrator is a lone male traveller, who stops off at an isolated chateau in the Italian Apennines. His chamber is hung with paintings, differentially revealed to him by the flickering light of his hand-held candelabrum. Eventually he spots one 'of a young girl just ripening into womanhood'. The use of the present continuous ('just ripening') is significant, for this subject is fixed at a point of 'becoming'. To our narrator she is both a bride and 'a young girl', infantilised and arguably dehumanised as he appraises her as being 'frolicksome as [a] young fawn' (Poe 1986: 251, 252).

In the accompanying catalogue, the traveller learns the painter was the bride's husband and so absorbed was he by his art that he failed to notice her 'pin[ing] visibly' before him. Liquid imagery permeates the tale, 'light dripp[ing] upon the pale canvas only from overhead', the paint daubing colour as her life ebbs away (Poe 1986: 252). Elisabeth Bronfen's reading of Poe's story imbues a rivalry between nature and art: the bride's beauty rivals the artist's creation and thus she must die (Bronfen 1992: 112). What Bronfen does not discuss, however, is (for us) the extreme youth of the bride, which adds another hue to the painter's self-absorption. Because the bride has not yet fully matured, the extent of beauty is not yet determined. Hence the painter's urgency: he must work fast to 'perfect' her before she outstrips the 'likeness'.

Irrespective of age, the Gothic infantilises many of its female protagonists. Even Ellen Moers, the feminist literary critic often credited with coining the term 'Female Gothic', defines her heroines as 'maidens' who are 'forced to do what they could never do alone', who 'scurry' across landscapes unchaperoned and 'scuttle' along the corridors of gloomy chateaux (Moers 1986: 126). Such verb choices seem hardly appropriate for adult heroines; nevertheless, they resonate across many a Gothic text. Take, for example, our first encounter with the otherwise adventurous Catherine Earnshaw/Heathcliff/Linton (as she variously inscribes herself in her 'unformed childish hand' upon the window ledge of her chamber (Brontë 1978: 16)), in Emily Brontë's *Wuthering Heights* (1847). Our representative and narrator here is another lone traveller, Mr Lockwood, Heathcliff's new tenant at Thrushcross Grange, forced to shelter from the storm at Wuthering Heights. As he drifts to sleep, the letters of Cathy's name swarm before him, 'as vivid as spectres'; woken later by the persistent tapping of a branch against the window, Lockwood forces his fist through it, only for his fingers to close on Cathy's 'little, ice-cold hand' and his eyes to see 'a child's face looking through the window'. Reporting his terrifying experience to Heathcliff, Lockwood's initial intrigue in Cathy's 'spirited' behaviour turns quickly to horror. Now, he tells him, she is a 'little fiend', and a 'changeling – a wicked little soul' (Brontë 1978: 15, 20, 22). The same slippage we identified in Poe's story pertains here: Catherine dies a married woman, but returns in Lockwood's dreams as a ghost-child. A further slippage intrudes, however, one in which an enchanting child is quickly reconceived as a dreadful monster, and such transformations are surprisingly common in literary depictions of the Gothic girl child. She is typically out of place or time and, here, Cathy is both. Lost on the moors and returning home dead, her pleading at the window figuratively encapsulates her borderline status as a child-woman.

There are a number of similarities between *Wuthering Heights* and Elizabeth Gaskell's 'The Old Nurse's Story' (1852). Like Cathy, Gaskell's child ghost is lost out in the wilds and 'beat[s] against the window-panes, as if she want[s] to be let in' (Gaskell 2000: 24). Equally Hester, the 'old nurse' of the title, is to some extent a version of Ellen Dean, Lockwood's housekeeper at the Grange, who tells him Cathy and Heathcliff's story. Gaskell's Hester was nursemaid to the orphaned Rosamond, a job she took on at the tender age of eighteen, though she tells her tale to Rosamond's children much later. On the death of Rosamond's parents, she and Hester came under the protection of an extended family circle of older relatives. Prominent among them is Miss Furnivall, a great beauty in her own youth, when she was known as Miss Grace. Locked into a bitter rivalry with her now dead sister, Miss Maud, the two women had split over their shared love for one man. Gaskell's treatment of the nature of the bonds between girls is intriguing. In the case of the young Misses Grace and Maud, sisterly love and sisterly hatred are shown as two sides of one coin: a kind of magnetic attraction connects both. Nor does this depiction shift across generations. Rosamond is also magnetically drawn to another girl, whom she describes as being 'not so old' as she is and 'so pretty and so sweet' (Gaskell 2000: 22). As in *Wuthering Heights*, however, what may appear an enticing sweetheart soon proves a Gothic monster. This ghost-girl longs to lure Rosamond to her death and, such is the power of the magnetism, when Hester interposes her body between them the ghost becomes violent, breaking down the door 'with a thundering crash'. Hester's only option is to cling to Rosamond 'tighter and tighter, till I feared I should do her a hurt; but rather that than let her go' (Gaskell 2000: 30, 31). Gaskell's message, then, is disappointingly reactionary: girls cannot trust the allure of their own kind.

Despite its Victorian origins, Hester's reaction to this threat is identical to what remains a very modern fear: (mis)adventure will befall children once let out of our sight and adults must keep them close. Hence, as Michael Morpurgo observes, the distance we permit children to roam today is one-ninth of what it was in the Middle Ages (Cunningham and Morpurgo 2006). Stories such as Gaskell's draw on the Victorian belief that pre-pubescent girls were particularly close to the spirit world and possessed clairvoyant powers. In *The Darkened Room*, a cultural history of nineteenth-century spiritualism, Alex Owen also discusses the role played by so-called 'child spirits', again emphasising this seductive allure. At the same time, she notes that spiritualism, despite the apparent powers it attributes to girls and women, does little to offset the imbalance of power between the sexes: 'the most powerful medium was the most powerless of women, the final coinage of exchange being the apparent abdication of self for possession by another' (Owen 1989: 231–3).

Similar questions of power versus powerlessness can be found in

Margaret Oliphant's *fin-de-siècle* story 'The Library Window' (1896). This young female protagonist sits with her maiden aunt, staring through the window into the house opposite. Therein she spies an attractive young man. On confiding in her aunt, the latter turns storyteller. Long ago, she tells her, a scholar was so compulsively driven by his studies that he ignored the attentions of a young female suitor. On finding her heartbroken, her brothers attacked and killed the scholar. By implication the man across the street is the scholar's ghost and the spinster aunt his lovelorn suitor. As in Gaskell's tale, then, the uncanny attaches itself to close bonds between female characters, but in Oliphant's story an uncanny quality also surrounds the aunt, who reads her niece's ability to see the man as proof of their shared clairvoyance and identifies her as being a 'wom[a]n of our blood' (Oliphant 1988: 328). The darkly murderous tale meets its match in the ever-dimming light in the room, and the atmosphere, coupled with the intensity of the bond between the young woman and her aunt, results in the protagonist becoming over-wrought and, just like Hester in Gaskell's story, her mother intervenes and takes her home. Thus is the niece propelled unambiguously back into childhood ('how can a girl say I will not, when her mother has come for her') and more rivalry, this time between mother and aunt, is implied. That she arrives 'quite unexpectedly, and said she had no time to stay' (Oliphant 1988: 329–30) adds a sense of the urgent need to instil social propriety back into her daughter's life. Again, female intimacy, in a Gothic context, is suggested to be dangerous and, as here, may result in the need for respectability to be restored.

Seeing and shame are twin preoccupations, also, in Henry James's 1898 novella *The Turn of the Screw*. Here the Gothic girl child is Flora who, along with her older brother Miles, is looked after by a new governess, our narrator for most of the narrative. Though much critical opinion has tended to focus upon Miles, Flora's role is far more important than that of a simple accomplice. According to Georgieva, a Gothic child's name 'functions as a capsule, containing the essence of the child and its purpose in the plot' (Georgieva 2013: 37). Certainly, on first meeting, Flora seems to embody all the floral loveliness of her name, her governess delighting in 'the radiant image' of this 'rosy sprite' (James 1986: 153, 155). However, she also epitomises all the afore-mentioned slipperiness of the Gothic child, even her innocence being called into question. The main threat to the children in *The Turn of the Screw* derives from two adult apparitions, the Master's former valet, Peter Quint, and Miss Jessel, the former Governess. Jessel, in particular, seeks out Flora and that the attraction is mutual is more than implied. Fearful on Flora's account, the new governess tries but fails to keep

Flora close and, as she disappears from view again, her protector uncannily observes, 'at such times she's not a child: she's an old, old woman' (James 1986: 235). This age-related comment derives from the uncomfortable manner in which Flora's playfulness often appears to be a form of 'knowingness'. Outside, Flora crafts two blocks of wood into a basic toy boat. Looking on, her governess spies Jessel approach, but being too nervous to look at Jessel direct, instead she watches Flora, looking for evidence of her awareness of Jessel's presence. Though none presents itself, Flora's continued but silent play chills her governess still more. The fear is that Flora is 'playing dumb', an anxiety multiplied at the possibility that Flora may have used her craft(iness) to attract Jessel to her.

In all these nineteenth-century Gothic texts, the difficulty facing their authors is how to convey taboo or unspeakable material in narrative form. As the twentieth century progresses, increasing degrees of freedom are afforded writers wanting to explore the physical nature of the Gothic girl child's identity. By the time Daphne du Maurier wrote her 1959 story 'The Pool', there was enough freedom for her to tackle menstruation, which is clearly the most important rubicon for all adolescent girls, but even here she could only do so by writing 'between the lines'. Deborah, her protagonist, is on holiday at her grandparents' house, because Deborah's mother died giving birth to her younger brother Roger and their father works away in London. Borders and thresholds are the structural underpinning of the narrative, most of which takes place in the garden. At its centre lies a pool, to which Deborah is repeatedly drawn. When she looks into the water, its undulating surface provides her with a skewed mirror: '[I]t was not the face she knew, not even the looking-glass face which anyway was false, but a disturbed image, dark-skinned and ghostly' (du Maurier 1994: 61). This skewing effect takes hold in later twentieth-century women's fiction. As Mary Russo reveals in *The Female Grotesque*, any girl might find herself grotesque at any moment, especially if she fails to remember to 'contain' herself, resulting in 'a kind of inadvertency and loss of boundaries' (Russo 1994: 53). In Deborah's case the lack of containment initially seems self-willed, though as the narrative progresses we find her increasingly unable to determine its consequences.

Deborah's attraction to the pool is as magnetic as the attractions faced by her nineteenth-century forebears, but it is also far more sensually conveyed, amounting to a recurrent flirtation with death. Deborah's motherless state proves crucial to our understanding here, for as Barbara Creed warns, in Gothic texts mother 'is also aligned with death. She gives life, the infant enters the world from her womb, and in her role as Mother Earth she takes life back' (Creed 2005: 16). In texts where the mother is dead, the girl's development may be achieved only by separating off from her grief. The first time she plunges into the pool, Deborah encounters a woman at a wicket-gate who permits her entry and a small blind child 'trying to find her way.' Recognising the child as 'herself at two years old ... when her mother died' we realise, also, that the gate-keeper is her mother (du Maurier 1994: 69).

The skewed mirror of the pool's surface has enabled Deborah to recognise herself in the lost child and, conversely, to realise that she is no longer that (or any) child. In bed later, Deborah reflects on a 'dragging, terrible darkness, and the beginning of pain all over again', a pain every female reader will identify as that of menstruation. On the second night a storm brews and the torrential flow of the pool seems almost to boil over, as 'bubbles sucked at the surface, steaming and multiplying' (du Maurier 1994: 70, 79). This time, though, Deborah re-enters the pool, the wicket-gate remains closed and the woman and child leave her behind. Deborah's banishment here confirms her access to anatomical womanhood. Immersion was both an arrival and a departure, a letting-go of the child in herself in order to embrace the woman she will become, the cost of which involves letting her mother go. The story ends with her grandparents' decision to fence off the pool, closing off any future possibility of Deborah returning. Though Deborah's near-drowning might seem an extreme version of how a girl experiences her first menstrual period, her final thoughts strike an everyday chord: 'What had happened to her was personal. They had prepared her for it at school, but nevertheless it was a shock' (du Maurier 1994: 80).

This deathly relationship between mother and girl is also the catalyst for the Gothic in Angela Carter's *The Magic Toyshop* (1967). Melanie is fifteen and, like Deborah, pubescent. For Melanie, however, adolescence is a delight:

> For hours she stared at herself, naked ... And then she would writhe about, clasping herself, laughing, sometimes doing cartwheels and handstands out of sheer exhilaration at the supple surprise of herself now she was no longer a little girl'. As the 'cartwheels and handstands' make clear, however, Melanie remains torn between the world of womanhood and the world of play: 'Edward Bear ... beadily regarding her from the pillow and Lorna Doone splayed out face down in the dust under the bed. (Carter 1967: 12)

Melanie begins the novel as a teenager inhabiting a comfortable middle-class family existence and it is perhaps the 'normality' of that world that tempts her into an act of fatal transgression. Her mother has accompanied her father abroad on a business trip and Melanie exploits her mother's absence to don her wedding dress. Drawn outside, like Deborah, similarly seductive dangers pertain: 'The dewy grass licked her feet like the wet tongues of small, friendly beasts' (Carter 1967: 15, 17). Also like Deborah, she finds herself locked out, this time literally. Still wearing the wedding dress, she scales an apple tree and clambers back through her bedroom window, landing in a heap on the floor. In the morning, 'stiff with horror', she realises 'She had bled far more than she realised' and the dress is despoiled. At this spillage of sexually charged blood the house suddenly seems haunted 'and the back of her neck twitched when she heard chance thumpings and creakings' (Carter 1967: 22, 23–4). As with Deborah, the price Melanie pays for accessing womanhood is the loss of her mother, for in the morning she learns both parents have been killed in an air-crash. At this point the novel takes a sustained Gothic turn as she and her younger siblings, Jonathan and Victoria, are sent to live with Uncle Philip in his London toyshop.

Toys, for all their 'Edward Bear' homeliness, frequently take on a sinister aspect in Gothic narratives and, according to Freud, 'the impression made by waxwork figures, ingeniously constructed dolls and automata' is one of the most common sources of the uncanny (Freud 1990: 347). Writing about *The Magic Toyshop*, Helen Carr makes the intriguing observation that 'Carter ... loves [toys'] garish inventiveness, but can't forget that the home of toymaking is Nuremberg' (Carr 1986–7: 41).[6] In Carter's novel, however, it is less the toys themselves that are sinister and more their manipulation in the hands of Uncle Philip. Innately lascivious, Philip insists on Melanie auditioning to play Leda to his swan puppet:

'You're well built for fifteen ... Do you have your periods?'
'Yes,' she said, too shocked to do more than whisper.
He grunted, displeased.
'I wanted my Leda to be a little girl. Your tits are too big.'
(Carter 1967: 143)

According to Lorna Sage, *The Magic Toyshop* is 'about growing up' (Sage 1983: 207), but as this exchange with Philip demonstrates, the situation is not quite so clear-cut. What begins at home with Melanie's innocent delight in her impending womanhood becomes tarnished at the toyshop, such that Paulina Palmer argues Melanie mourns her childhood. Palmer's reading derives from a scene of holiday licence when, with Philip away on business, Melanie and her Aunt Margaret dress up for a party. Melanie gives Margaret her mother's pearls to keep, 'hop[ing] her aunt would grow so attached to the pearls during the day that she would think they had always been her own' (Carter 1967: 189). Palmer draws attention to the inherent ambiguity in Carter's choice of the pronoun 'they'. Superficially referring to the pearls, Palmer suggests it also refers to Melanie and her siblings: Melanie wishes for Margaret to accept her as her child (Palmer 1987: 192).

Again such desires are complicated by sisterly rivalry. Aunt Margaret already adores five-year-old Victoria and persistently babies her, treating her like a toddler, complete with 'nice towelling bib with a green frog on it' (Carter 1967: 71). Much like James's Flora, however, Victoria is only superficially cute: to Melanie she has always been 'a dreadful secret in the back bedroom ... pushing her indecent baby face against the banisters' (Carter 1967: 7–8). When inside the toyshop, Melanie repeatedly imagines Victoria behind bars: in the 'rat-trap' of her cot or 'napp[ing] in her cage' (Carter 1967: 135, 146). As Victoria sits up in bed, partly dressed, with her genitalia exposed, Carter describes her outer labia as a 'pink female fold [which] smiled longwise between her squatting, satiny thighs'. The image resonates uncannily with an earlier memory of Melanie's: a Jack-in-the-box that Philip sent her, which, when opened, presented her with 'a grotesque caricature of her own face [that] leered from the head that leapt out at her' (Carter 1967: 182, 12). Victoria, in these terms, already embodies Russo's female grotesque, with its 'open, protruding, irregular, secreting, multiple, and changing' form (Russo 1994: 8).

Even before they arrive at the toyshop, Melanie's resentment of Victoria is such that the younger child takes on a kind of profanity in Melanie's eyes. In church, while Melanie prays 'Please God, let me get married. Or, let me have sex', Victoria, Melanie contemplates, has 'nothing to pray for' and thus entertains herself by '[tearing] the fringes off the hassocks and [eating] them' (Carter 1967: 8, 9).

In *The Magic Toyshop* such references to profanity are fleeting and, in this instance comedic, but at the horror end of the Gothic spectrum, more specifically in Stephen King's 1974 novel *Carrie*, profanity and its connection with the Gothic girl child becomes a sustained study. Carrie is a year older than Carter's Melanie, but far less self-assured. Melanie lacks female companions of her own age, but King's novel suggests their absence might prove beneficial, for Carrie's victimisation is inflicted on her by other girls: 'They stared. They always *stared*' (King 1974: 4; emphasis in original). It is striking how, despite all the social advances of feminism, Gothic narratives continue to resist any positive reading of sisterhood. Here, the girls inflict upon each other their shared fear of self-abjection, which Julia Kristeva describes as 'A massive and sudden emergence of uncanniness, which ... harries me as radically separate, loathsome' (Kristeva 1982: 2) Certainly it is with such a 'massive and sudden emergence' that

King opens his novel, setting it in the girls' locker room during 'Period One'.

Driven from the showers by the PE teacher, Carrie finds blood pouring down her legs. Then the girls set up a carnival chant:

> '"*Per*-iod!"
>
> ...
>
> "*PER*-iod!"
> ... Someone in the background ... was yelling '*Plug it up!*' with hoarse, uninhibited abandon.
> "*PER*-iod, *PER*-iod, *PER*-iod!"'

(King 1974: 6)

Carrie operates through the inverted logic of what Allon White identifies as the 'postromantic carnival of the night', whereby 'power is eroticised by the "abjectifying" of an object' and is often played out most savagely against 'women or ethnic minorities' (White 1981: 61, 67). At sixteen, Carrie is the last of the girls 'to start' and, having done so, any possibility that she might prove to be 'like' them must be denied her. It is a scenario ripe with what David Punter considers to be a recurrent pattern in King's writing: 'a sense of danger which, unconsciously, requires the elaboration of fantasies of further damage' (Punter 1996: 138). Much of the Gothic horror of the novel emerges from Carrie being endowed with telekinetic powers. As part of King's narrative approach he amalgamates a variety of fictional newspaper, medical and autobiographical accounts to try to integrate a form of fictional authenticity into the horror content. The medical account he constructs pursues a hypothesis that the gene which, in boys, produces haemophilia can, in girls, produce telekinesis, particularly if combined with a traumatic initiation into menstruation. Moreover, the account returns us to the irony often employed in naming Gothic literary characters: 'If the offspring is female, the result will be a daughter who is a [C]arrie[-]r' (King 1974: 100).

It is at the school Spring Ball that Carrie's final destruction is planned. King successfully maintains a lack of clarity about how many of Carrie's classmates are 'in' on the joke, but Christine, Carrie's nemesis, and her male accomplice, Billy, set in train a complicated chain of cause and effect designed to maximise Carrie's ultimate humiliation. Apparently out of a sense of contrition (though equally possibly as part of Christine's 'game'), one classmate, Sue, persuades her own boyfriend, Tommy, to partner Carrie to the dance. In a surprise gesture of acceptance, Carrie and Tommy are voted Prom King and Queen, an accolade involving them being crowned centre-stage. Meanwhile, Christine and Billy have rigged up an ingenious double pulley system suspending two buckets of sows' blood directly above them. At the moment of crowning, Christine pulls the string and drenches Carrie from head to foot in blood. Ironically, in doing so she sets into reverse that original locker-room chant: 'Plug it *up*' (King 1974: 8; emphasis in original). In line with the medical hypothesis, Carrie's telekinetic powers are fully and finally unleashed by this trauma. Utilising occult means, she seals the exits, engulfs the hall in flames, and embarks on a murderous trail of destruction across town.

Blood-letting has always been a key aspect of Gothic horror, but in Carter's short-story collection, *The Bloody Chamber* (1979), it also becomes associated with bestial transformation. Wolf-Alice, the titular character of Carter's final story, is a 'ragged girl' and 'young enough to make the noise that pups do, bubbling, delicious'. Neither 'fully animal nor human', she lives by day in the castle of an old, lycanthropic Duke, whose nocturnal existence ensures they never meet. When menstruation starts, however, she goes searching for rags, only to encounter her own reflection in a mirror. Never having seen it before, she thinks she beholds a companion and 'nuzzle[s]' it, then 'nos[es] it' before 'ask[ing] this creature to try to play' (Carter 1979: 119, 123). Ignorance exists as a sort of freedom for Wolf-Alice, for as Jenijoy La Belle observes, 'For some women their consciousness that they exist at all is dependent on seeing themselves in the glass' (La Belle 1988: 24). Much like the rippling surface of du Maurier's 'The Pool', Carter's mirroring moment operates as both an opening into knowledge and a foreclosure from innocence. Suddenly aware of her isolation, Wolf-Alice puts on a wedding dress discarded by one of the Duke's victims and joins him in his profane churchyard activities. Shot at by local villagers, the Duke is seriously wounded but Wolf-Alice's new relationship with blood enables her to apply her mouth to his wounds. Thus the final image of Carter's collection is a type of profane resuscitation: 'Little by little, there appeared within [the mirror], like the image on photographic paper ... the face of the Duke' (Carter 1979: 126). If development is the process with which Carter leaves us, however, it raises more questions than it answers for the future of the Gothic girl child, for if she is peering into a mirror and seeing only the Duke's face, does he attain life only at the price of her own?

Carter's project, in *The Bloody Chamber,* is driven by an active interest in women's sexual appetites. Although controversial, the Gothic allowed her and many twentieth-century writers the opportunity to extend the limits of social acceptability through extending the physiological and psychical limitations of the human form. Now, in these early decades of the twenty-first century, Gothic writers are returning to a consideration of ghosts, especially when writing about children and child death. That is not to say, however, that the political interests explored by writers such as Carter have gone into abeyance. For the lesbian feminist writer Sarah Waters, the Gothic affords her an especially valuable opportunity to explore the multiple meanings of the word 'queer' already identified above. *The Little Stranger* (2009) is, however, the first of her novels to involve children. Set in the 1940s, immediately following the First World War, the novel focuses upon the upper-class Ayres family and its social, financial and personal demise. Three girl children appear in the book: fourteen-year-old Betty, the maid; Gillian Baker-Hyde, who is 'eight or nine' and the daughter of the Ayres's *nouveau riche* neighbours; and Susan, the first-born daughter of Mrs Ayres, who died from diphtheria at the age of seven. Though all of them contribute to the Gothic plot of the narrative, it is Susan, the ghost-child, who propels the uncanny to the surface of the text. Like Cathy in *Wuthering Heights*, Susan is a scribbling child. When her ghost begins to scribble the letter 'S' repeatedly across the walls, the family is forced into a type of game of hide-and-seek to try to seek out the source of the mystery.

Caroline, Mrs Ayres's living daughter, is 'twenty-six or twenty-seven' and a 'natural spinster' (Waters 2009: 9). Her dislike of children is reiterated and best encapsulated in her irritable resentment, during post-war rationing, at 'the little wretches getting their hands on all the oranges' (Waters 2009: 92). In part, Caroline's irritation is a response to an obsessively heterosexist post-war Britain, with its emphasis on 'family housing policies ... marriage and motherhood' (Armitt 2009: 36). In addition, however, it may simply be motivated by sibling jealousy. In being dead, Susan is the ideal 'little girl', one who will never develop into the awkwardness of adolescence or become 'noticeably plain' like Caroline (Waters 2009: 9). Dead before Caroline was born, there are no grounds on which Caroline can compete with Susan for her mother's attention: death is Susan's final victory. This paradox may also explain the otherwise utterly uncharacteristically childish outburst of Caroline's at Susan's ghostly antics. Instructed by her mother to 'Cover it up' as their search gradually reveals Susan's inscriptions, Caroline exclaims at the walls: 'It's no good your teasing us! We simply shan't play!' (Waters 2009: 304). Caroline has learnt to accept she is not her mother's favourite, but she refuses to brook any kind of rivalry that might require her to contest her supremacy in relation to the 'queer'.

Taking all these various Gothic girl children into account, a remarkable but perhaps disappointing consistency attends their depiction, from 1850 to the present day. Though all the narratives discussed here are richly conceived, compulsively engaging and undoubtedly influential upon the Gothic literary tradition, it is hard to find in them positive messages for younger women. Though magnetic attraction sometimes defines the bonds between girls in these narratives, such bonds are consistently fraught with danger, betrayal or loss. Repeatedly, the Gothic girl child must undergo trauma on her journey towards womanhood, and blood, that fluid especially associated with the female adolescent, plays a particularly horrific role in narratives such as *Carrie*. If Moers is right and the Gothic especially offers its heroines adventures they cannot find elsewhere, the price it seems they must pay for having them is learning to go it alone.

Note

1. Nuremberg was the German city in which the Nazi Party held its annual rallies during Adolf Hitler's rise to power in the 1920s and 1930s. It has also been 'a toy city of world renown' since the medieval period (http://museums.nuremberg.de/toy-museum; accessed 10 January 2015).

Bibliography

Armitt, Lucie (2011), *Twentieth-Century Gothic*, Cardiff: University of Wales Press.

Armitt, Lucie (2009), 'Garden Paths and Blind Spots, *New Welsh Review*, 85: 28–36.

Armitt, Lucie (2013), 'Women Writers in the Haunted House of Fiction', in Claire Whitehead (ed.), *Critical Insights: The Fantastic*, Ipswich, MA: Salem Press, pp. 99–116.

Bronfen, Elisabeth (1992), *Over Her Dead Body: Death, Femininity and the Aesthetic*, Manchester: Manchester University Press.

Brontë, Emily [1847] (1978), *Wuthering Heights*, London: Dent.

Bruhm, Stephen and Natasha Hurley (eds) (2004), *Curiouser: On the Queerness of Children*, Minneapolis: University of Minnesota Press.

Carr, Helen (1986–7), 'Wayward Magic', *Women's Review*, 14/15: 41.

Carter, Angela (1967), *The Magic Toyshop*, London: Virago.

Carter, Angela (1979), *The Bloody Chamber*, Harmondsworth: Penguin.

Creed, Barbara (2005), *Phallic Power: Film, Horror and the Primal Uncanny*, Carlton, VIC: Melbourne University Press.

Cunningham, Hugh (2006), *The Invention of Childhood*, London: BBC Books.

Cunningham, Hugh and Michael Morpurgo (2006), *The Invention of Childhood*, BBC Radio 4, episode 2.

du Maurier, Daphne (1994), 'The Pool' [1959], in Richard Dalby (ed.), *The Virago Book of Ghost Stories, Vol. Two*, London: Virago, pp. 57–80.

Freud, Sigmund (1990), 'The "Uncanny"', *The Penguin Freud Library, Vol. Fourteen*, pp. 335–76.

Gaskell, Elizabeth (2000), 'The Old Nurse's Story' [1852], in Laura Kranzler (ed.), *Elizabeth Gaskell: Gothic Tales*, Harmondsworth: Penguin.

Georgieva, Margarita (2013), *The Gothic Child*, Basingstoke: Palgrave.

James, Henry [1898] (1986), *The Turn of the Screw* in *The Aspern Papers and The Turn of the Screw*, Harmondsworth: Penguin, pp. 143–262.

Kincaid, James R. (1992), *Child-Loving: The Erotic Child and Victorian Culture*, New York: Routledge.

King, Stephen (1974), *Carrie*, New York: Doubleday.

Kristeva Julia (1982), *Powers of Horror: An Essay in Abjection,* trans. Leon Roudiez, New York: Columbia University Press.

La Belle, Jenijoy (1988), *Herself Beheld: The Literature of the Looking Glass,* Ithaca, NY: Cornell University Press.

Moers, Ellen (1986), *Literary Women*, London: The Women's Press.

Oliphant, Margaret [1896] (1988), 'The Library Window: The Seen and the Unseen', in Merryn Williams (ed.), *A Beleaguered City and Other Stories*, Oxford: Oxford University Press, pp. 287–331.

Owen, Alex (1989), *The Darkened Room: Women, Power and Spiritualism in Late Victorian England*, London: Virago.

Palmer, Paulina (1987), 'From "Coded Mannequin" to Bird Woman: Angela Carter's Magic Flight', in Sue Roe (ed.), *Women Reading Women's Writing*, Brighton: Harvester, pp. 179–205.

Poe, Edgar Allan [1845] (1986), 'The Oval Portrait', in David Galloway (ed.), *The Fall of the House of Usher and Other Writings*, Harmondsworth: Penguin, pp. 250–3.

Punter, David (1996), 'Problems of Recollection and Construction: Stephen King', in Victor Sage and Allan Lloyd Smith (eds), *Modern Gothic*, Manchester: Manchester University Press, pp. 121–4.

Russo, Mary (1994), *The Female Grotesque: Risk, Excess and Modernity*, New York: Routledge.

Sage, Lorna (1983), 'Angela Carter', in Joy L. Halio (ed.), *The Dictionary of Literary Biography, Vol. Fourteen*, Detroit: Bruccoli Clark, pp. 205–12.

Stockton, Kathryn Bond (2004), 'Growing Sideways or Versions of the Queer Child', in Stephen Bruhm and Natasha Hurley (eds), *Curiouser: The Queerness of Children*, pp. 277–315.

Waters, Sarah (2009), *The Little Stranger*, London: Virago.

White, Allon (1981), 'Pigs and Pierrots: The Politics of Transgression in Modern Fiction', *Raritan*, 2: 51–70.

Chapter 5

'A Woman's Place'
Diana Wallace

In Norah Lofts's story 'A Curious Experience' (first published in *Woman's Journal* in 1971) a young writer goes to live in a rented house in suburban Suffolk while her husband is away in New York. She is not, as she tells her husband when he proposes, 'the domestic type' but the newly married couple have been 'happy as larks' (Lofts 1974: 110). The house is rented fully furnished at a rent so 'astonishingly low' as to arouse the narrator's 'darkest suspicions' (111) because the arthritic owner is confined to a 'Home'. The 'rot set[s] in' (113), however, when the narrator, anxious to finish her second novel, is overtaken by a curious compulsion to clean the house. The 'good spirit' had 'gone from me' (113), she writes, that 'Deadly' loss, 'The thing we [writers] all fear' (113). Over the next weeks she does so much cleaning – shining windows, tackling the 'offensive' (115) cupboard under the sink, and taking loads of linen to the launderette – that she damages her wrist. Finally, she makes a surprising diagnosis:

> I never studied psychology, but I had read enough to know what was wrong with me. Fundamentally, I thought, I did not like, or was not satisfied with the story on which I should be working. [...] And I was taking refuge from my predicament by pretending to be busy with other things. (Lofts 1974: 116)

Her novel, she recognises, should be written in the first person and not third. But just as she starts to type again, the owner's niece, Mrs Willis, arrives to announce that she must move out because the owner has finally found a housekeeper, which will enable her to return 'home'. Struck by a thought, the narrator asks, 'Would you call your aunt a dominant personality? [...] And was, I mean *is* she house-proud?' (118). Answered in the affirmative she realises, 'I knew what had got into me, I'd been for a month *possessed*' (118; my emphasis). On one level a comic allegory about writerly procrastination, this story also deftly exploits the language of the Gothic – 'darkest suspicions', 'rot', 'spirit', 'haunting', 'deadly', 'fear' – to explore how women can become 'possessed' by the domestic. As Anne Sexton puts it in 'Housewife' (1962), 'Some women marry houses' (Sexton 1991: 64) and Lofts's narrator struggles to resist precisely this kind of entrapment.

If a woman's place is allegedly in the home, the Gothic has been the mode of writing which has perhaps most brilliantly articulated and symbolised the terrors of that domestic space. Possession, confinement, penetration, loss of identity are all shadows which haunt the home for women, particularly those who inhabit – or fear inhabiting – the roles of housewife and mother. If, as Freud suggests in 'The Uncanny' (1919), the *'heimlich'* and the *'unheimlich'*, the homely and the unhomely, double each other through a process of repression and compulsive recurrence, then the Gothic, with its haunted houses and ghostly alter egos, is the ideal vehicle with which to figure the way in which women have traditionally been required to 'bury' their creative energies in order to 'marry houses'. Moreover, their daughters have risked repeating such confined lives: 'A woman *is* her mother', as Sexton puts it, 'That's the main thing' (Sexton 1991: 64). For such women and girls, then, the home is an uncanny space haunted by lost possibilities and shadowed by patriarchal power.

These issues were particularly intense for the post-war generation of mainly white and middle-class women in Britain, America and Australia who were expected to find their ultimate fulfilment, as Betty Friedan (1963) showed, through the 'feminine mystique'. But the 'feminine mystique', as Friedan wrote, was simply a new version of an old image: 'Occupation: Housewife' (Friedan 1982: 38). It made 'certain concrete, finite domestic aspects of feminine existence' – cooking, cleaning, washing, bearing children – into 'a religion, a pattern by which all women must now live or deny their femininity' (38). As one woman interviewed by Friedan put it: 'In the past 60 years we have come full circle and the American housewife is once again trapped in a squirrel cage' (25). Hannah Gavron's *The Captive Wife* (1966) found similar patterns of repression, frustration and fear of repeating their mother's lives among housebound young mothers in London. The modern or drugstore Gothic, with its iconic cover showing a young woman in period costume fleeing a brooding castle, was one popular response to this predicament. But another, rather less discussed, was to use the language, tropes and motifs of the Gothic within ostensibly realist contemporary texts to expose and name women's frustration and anger.

This latter mode is what Joan Lidoff in her pioneering essay on Christina Stead's *The Man Who Loved Children* (1940), a brilliantly black dissection of terminally dysfunctional family life, named the 'Domestic Gothic' (Lidoff 1983: 109–22). In another important essay, Gina Wisker analyses Sylvia Plath as a 'mid-century exponent' of the Gothic, 'a missing historical link' (Wisker 2004: 105), whose work uses Gothic imagery and tropes – hauntings, the witch, the vampire, the devil, split selves – to expose women's entrapment within the domestic. Yet, as I will argue here, Stead and Plath are only two of several mid-twentieth-century women writers (often critically neglected) who developed and reconfigured the domestic Gothic to explore the predicament of the housebound wife and mother and her daughter.

Written by women who can be characterised as the last pre-second-wave-feminist generation, the domestic Gothic texts I want to discuss here anatomise the terrors of a daytime world in which women are isolated in their houses, with or without children, while men are at work, and where the primary outlet for female creative energies is the perfecting of their 'feminine mystique'. The domestic Gothic, as Lidoff characterises it, draws on the imagery of women's daily lives within the home. It 'mines the fantasies of the confined inner world, overcomes the ban on aggression and thus releases energies for creative use: it is a style humorous as well as aggressive, and profusely creative' (Lidoff 1983: 122). Thus it can encompass the comic Gothic of Lofts's women's magazine stories, the domestic poetics of Sylvia Plath or Anne Sexton, and the maternal Gothic of Penelope Mortimer's *The Pumpkin Eater* (1962), as well as the satiric Gothic of Shirley Jackson's *The Sundial* (1958) and *We Have Always Lived in the Castle* (1962) or the magic realism of Barbara Comyns's *The Vet's Daughter* (1959) and *The Skin Chairs* (1962).

The earliest of these texts, Stead's *The Man Who Loved Children*, is perhaps unsurpassed in what Angela Carter called the 'single-minded intensity of its evocation of domestic terror' (Carter 1982). In teenage Louie, her manipulative father Sam Pollitt and his second wife, long-suffering Henny, Stead updates the classic female Gothic plot of orphaned heroine with a cruel stepmother and controlling, potentially incestuous patriarch, and locates it in suburban Washington, DC. Marriage here is far from a happy ending. Repeated childbearing and domestic drudgery have transformed Henrietta from a 'beautiful, dark, thin young lady' (Stead 1970: 70) into the 'grubby, angry Henny', a querulous and embittered figure with a 'deathlike face, drawn and yellow under its full black hair' (70). Monstrously self-regarding, Sam Pollitt, the 'Nobodaddy' of the novel, uses a sickly improvised language all his own, a mix of baby-talk, cant words and pet names ('Womey [Evie, a younger daughter] won't come en scratch m'yed', he whines, 'Womey is mean to her pore old dad' (63), to manipulate his children and victimise his wife.

In a letter home from Singapore, Sam tells Louie about a series of appalling wall paintings he has seen depicting 'A Buddhist Bluebeard Tale': 'There were two women who wouldn't do what their husbands told them. They were tied down on a bench and two demons (men-demons, of course) were hacking their heads off' (259). What is meant as a morality tale for Louie exposes Sam as an American suburban Bluebeard with semi-Fascist ideas about gender roles. Tellingly, in the context of 1940, he remarks, '[I]f I were a Stalin or Hitler, I would abolish school altogether for children [...] and would form them into communities with a leader, something like I am myself, a natural leader' (36). Stead, Lidoff argues, uses domestic Gothic techniques to 'create a narrative voice which, though self-denigrating, is aggressive in its expression of anger' (Lidoff 1983: 121). This is a mode, she suggests, shared with Plath and Sexton. In an early pre-1956 poem, Plath also identifies the dangers of the 'Bluebeard' father who would 'make love to [her]', 'x-ray' her heart and 'dissect' her body, and rejects his seductive power: 'I am sending back the key that let me into bluebeard's study' (Plath 1981: 305). In her late 'Daddy' she develops this Gothic imagery to identify this over-powerful patriarch explicitly with Fascism: 'A man in black with a Meinkampf look/ And a love of the rack and the screw', he is a 'devil' and a 'vampire' who haunts and confines his daughter (Plath 1981: 224).

In very different genres, Lofts's story, Stead's novel and Plath's poetry exemplify the three main domestic Gothic themes on which I want to focus: *unheimlich* houses; the domestic arts; and the murderous nature of family life.

Unheimlich Houses

If the Female Gothic, as Norman Holland and Leona Sherman, among others, have argued, is defined by its central image of 'woman-plus-habitation' (Holland and Sherman 1977: 279) then the mid-century domestic Gothic is distinguished by its focus on ordinary families in sub-urban houses rather than on exotic castles. For Lofts, 'the essence of a good ghost-story, like the essence of the horror-story, should lie in what lurks behind the ordinary, often pleasant façade' (Lofts 1974: 12). Thus her collection *Is There Anybody There?* (1974), in which 'A Curious Experience' was republished, circles round her 'obsession with houses' (11) to explore women's uncanny, often indefinable, discomfort with the domestic space. These stories uncover the ways in which women are not 'at home' in houses, suggesting either a fear of penetration by the male or fear of nothingness. 'The Watchers', for instance, explores Meg's fear of living alone while her husband is away. She feels 'under a close and hostile inspection' (142) and resorts to painstaking strategies – locking doors, drawing curtains, sleeping tablets – to get through the night alone. It is left ambiguous as to whether she is just neurotically over-imaginative or whether there really is something sinister at work in the house. Her stammer suggests the unspeakable nature of these obscure fears. Conversely, in Lofts's 'A Visit to Claudia', Claudia invokes the protection of a friendly ghost against 'Whatever it is that women living alone dread. Feeling lonely or burglars' (128). Lofts's stories frequently expose the gendered nature of this fear. In 'Mr Edward', for instance, a house is haunted by the lustful ghost of a man who used to prey on housemaids; and in 'A Visit to Claudia' the narrator meets ghostly opposition from a former friar, 'one who found his vow of chastity hard to keep' and so hated all women (136). In various ways, then, these houses are rendered *unheimlich* by their associations with male power, both economic and sexual.

The symbolic identification of women with houses noted by Holland and Sherman is developed by Stead in particularly complex ways. Living in a comfortable Washington mansion, Henny is one of those women who 'marry houses': Henny 'belonged to this house and it to her. Though she was a prisoner in it, she possessed it. She and it were her marriage. She was indwelling in every board and stone of it' (Stead 1970: 45). The house is both possession and prison. While Sam's rooms are open and visible, Henny's is a mystery with 'locked cabinets with medicines and poisons, locked drawers with letters and ancient coins [...] a jewel case, and so on' (69) in which the children are only allowed to 'fossick at intervals' (69). Freud's comment that jewel cases often represent the female genitals seems particularly apposite here. Yet the Washington house was paid for by Henny's father and after his death the Pollitts are forced to move to Eastport. The new house, an 'ugly old castle comedown' (331), is more obviously Gothic – 'a dark cavern of horrors' (376) – and explicitly *un*homely: 'How odd', Henny reflects, 'that this tumbledown windy mansion in which she had to live with a despised man was home!' (456). As Stead's play with the word suggests, women's lack of financial power renders them vulnerable to being 'possessed' by the houses they 'marry'.

The Gothic house as a figure for the gendered links between property and power as well as the enforcement of domestic ideology is also central to Shirley Jackson's novels, particularly *The Sundial* and *We*

Have Always Lived in the Castle. The traditional Gothic question of inheritance is raised in the opening sentence of *The Sundial*: 'After the funeral they came back to the house, now indisputably Mrs Halloran's' (Jackson 2014: 1). Shockingly, Mrs Halloran has gained the house by pushing her son Lionel, the rightful heir, down the stairs. Built by the first Mr Halloran as a monument to his own wealth, the mansion is created as a world of its own, standing in extensive lands surrounded by a stone wall. An explicitly Strawberry Hill-esque folly, it has a grotto, ornamental lake and maze, as well as extensively decorated rooms and a library of 10,000 volumes (although Mr Halloran does not care for books).

As her given name Orianna (a sobriquet given to Elizabeth I) indicates, Mrs Halloran is now a matriarchal monarch ruling a household made up mainly of women, with the exception of her invalid husband and her ineffectual lover, Essex. Yet her granddaughter, Fancy, is already planning to inherit: 'When my grandmother dies all this is going to belong to me' (18), she asserts. It is Orianna's spinster sister-in-law, Aunt Fanny (sister of her dead husband), who is the mechanism by which these plans for female ownership are frustrated. In an uncanny encounter in the mist-enshrouded garden, she meets an apparition of her father who warns of impending apocalypse: 'Tell them in the house that they will be saved. Do not let them leave the house' (26). Thus patriarchal power is re-imposed and the women literally confine themselves to the house as they wait for the end of the world.

A rich and underrated novel, *The Sundial* is, as Bernice Murphy notes, a 'knowing homage to eighteenth-century Gothic, a satire of millenarian religious beliefs and a reflection of Cold War anxieties' (Murphy 2005: 10). It looks forward to the rather different handling of a post-homicidal matriarchy in *We Have Always Lived in the Castle*, where, after the deaths of the rest of their family, Constance and Merricat Blackwood live with their invalid Uncle Julian in the big house their father has surrounded by a wire fence and locked gate. Again, the Blackwood house is a symbol of class privilege: 'The people in the village have always hated us', asserts Merricat (Jackson 2009: 4). Unlike the Hallorans' Gothic folly, the Blackwood house is built on 'a solid foundation of stable possessions' brought by the Blackwood women:

> as soon as a new Blackwood wife moved in, a place was found for her belongings, and so our house was built up with layers of Blackwood property weighting it, and keeping it steady against the world. (Jackson 2009: 1)

For Constance and Merricat this matriarchal space is founded on a celebration of the feminine domestic arts. It is the advent of their cousin Charles, who penetrates the house seeking to establish himself as patriarch – occupying their father's room, wearing his watch and courting Constance – which threatens their fragile possession of the home.

Jackson's most widely discussed Gothic text, *The Haunting of Hill House* (1959), has been seen by Claire Kahane as a paradigmatic Female Gothic text in which the heroine confronts the spectral body of the dead/undead mother. The haunted house in which the protagonist Eleanor is entrapped is thus a symbol of the maternal body. Ultimately, Kahane argues, the Female Gothic an 'essentially conservative genre' (Kahane1985: 342), in which the heroine must either resume a quiescent role or be destroyed. This reading of the Gothic, however, focuses on the daughter confronting the maternal at the expense of the mother's own story.

In contrast, the underrated work of Penelope Mortimer is especially interesting for its focalisation through the mother and its use of houses to emblematise her fractured sense of maternal self. In her short story 'The Skylight' (1960), an unnamed woman and her five-year-old son find themselves locked out of the house in France where they are holidaying. The story is suffused by an ominous sense of gloom, the child over-tired and fractious, the mother strained and afraid, feeling herself 'disintegrate from the heat' (Mortimer 1966: 7). The house is grey and mean-looking, surrounded by dead grass and rat-haunted. Stranded with no key, the woman lowers her son in through a tiny skylight, but he doesn't appear to open the downstairs window as instructed. Hours later, having enlisted neighbours to break in, she discovers he has fallen asleep on the floor, and, frantic with pent-up worry, slaps him. As she stumbles away, both of them crying, 'The dead house was full of sound' (27). It was only years later, Mortimer recorded, that she realised that the story was 'about' a miscarriage she had just experienced (Mortimer 1993: 74). Here, then, the Gothic house is reconfigured to express the terrible co-existence in a single body of maternal love, grief *and* ambivalence.

The Domestic Arts

The 'superficial subjects' of Stead's domestic Gothic, Lidoff argues, are 'domestic commonplaces constructed from the details of everyday life – housework, eating, playing, shopping' (Lidoff 1983: 111), but these are rendered Gothic by the emotional and metaphorical excesses which express the violent forces beneath ordinary family life. If the 'feminine mystique', as Friedan suggested, made the domestic activities of cooking, cleaning, washing and bearing children into 'a religion, a pattern' (Friedan 1982: 38), then writers of domestic Gothic expose the horrors underlying these activities, the mess and dirt which have to be repressed. They also associate such activities with the black arts and witchcraft. Within the home, as Wisker has written of Plath's poetry, 'the removal or undercutting of the dependable domestic is the stuff of horror' (Wisker 2004: 107) and is often closely connected to the split female self.

Much of women's work involves the repetitive cleaning of people, houses and things. *The Man Who Loved Children* exposes the 'dirt' of family life, and of the female body, which is at such odds with the dreams of romance. As Henny rages: 'Life's nothing but rags and tags and filthy rags at that. Why was I ever born?' (Stead 1970: 205). Discovering Louie listening to their gossip, Henny and her mother decide that Louie is now old enough to listen to their conversation: 'let her hear the dirt' (206). To her children, Henny is a 'charming, slatternly witch, their household witch' (376). But to her they represent the dirt that she has endlessly to combat: '"The baby's eating dirt [...]"', her children tell her, '"The baby's eating his own crap"' (459–60). Similarly, Plath's poetry lays bare the dirt of domesticity and its intimate relation to the underside of familial relations. 'Lesbos' delineates 'Viciousness in the kitchen!' while 'The potatoes hiss' (Plath 1981: 227). The battle between husband and wife, like that between Sam and Henny, is played out against 'the stink of fat and baby crap' while 'The smog of cooking' becomes 'the smog of hell' (228). Husbands can escape the domestic, of course. In 'Lesbos' the 'impotent husband slumps out for a coffee' (228) while Stead's Sam pontificates that '"a little scientific method would eliminate all work from the household"' (Stead 1970: 380) before he slips off to lie in the sun. But women's female bodies tie them to the house.

Lidoff cites Mary Douglas's work to show how these images of dirt, both domestic and bodily, relate to gendered power structures:

> Dirt is symbolically equivalent to disorder. Women who are assigned by a culture to the daily tasks of chasing dirt are perpetually immersed in chaos. [...] Moreover, the traditional association of feminine reproductive biology with dirtiness reflects a cultural denigration of femininity. (Lidoff 1983: 116)

Henny's body is Gothicised through association with domestic dirt: 'A dirty cracked plate: that's just what I am!' she laments (Stead 1970: 50–1). As Lidoff comments: 'During their reproductive years, the shape of these women's lives is determined by immersion in dirt' (116). So, also, is the shape of their bodies: 'My back's bent in two with the fruit of my womb' (Stead 1970: 284), Henny claims. As Louie gets older, she is also seen by Henny as grotesque: 'the great big overgrown wretch with her great lolloping breasts looks as if she'd rolled in a pigsty or a slaughterhouse' (442). Yet this recognition of their shared monstrosity as female bodies is also what draws Henny and her (step)daughter into an uneasy alliance. It suggests their function as Gothic doubles, projections of the split female self.

The alleged horrors of the over-fertile female body are also at the heart of Mortimer's novel *The Pumpkin Eater* (1962). The nursery rhyme-inspired title invokes the entrapment of women within the domestic sphere: Peter 'Pumpkin eater' (the sobriquet suggesting the husband's devouring of both food and the female body) can't 'keep' (in both senses of the word) his wife until he puts her in a pumpkin shell. Mortimer's protagonist, known only as 'Mrs Armitage', is in the midst of a breakdown and unable, despite sessions with a psychoanalyst, to pinpoint the source of her fear: 'Thirty-one years old, healthy and whole, married to a fourth husband (why four?) who loved me, with a bodyguard of children (why so many?) – what was I frightened of?' (Mortimer 1964: 32). She believes that it is her husband, Jake, by whom she has been 'absorbed' (122), of whom she is afraid: 'He increased monstrously, became the sky, the earth, the enemy, the unknown' (33). In contrast, both Jake and the doctor attribute her sudden collapse in Harrods to her not having enough housework to do and to her allegedly insane '"obsession"' (38) with having another child. Manipulated into an abortion and sterilisation, however, she discovers that Jake has impregnated another woman.

After leaving Jake she goes to a tower, 'a cell of brick and glass' (151), that they have built in the country, where she waits for him, 'as you wait on a hill, in a tower, in the mist, for an enemy' (155). But it is the children, sent ahead by Jake, who come up out of the mist, 'swarming round the tower' (157) and breaking in, so that when Jake arrives she 'accept[s] him at last, because he was inevitable' (157). This painfully ambivalent ending with its Gothic overtones and over-determined Freudian phallic tower was, to Mortimer's distress, radically altered in the 1964 Columbia film, written by Harold Pinter. The emotional and physical 'mess' of family was cleaned up, with the 'fantasy hordes of children' (Mortimer 1993: 102) reduced to three. Instead of being 'tracked down and captured by her innumerable children', the protagonist, played by the beautiful Anne Bancroft in couturier clothes, simply succumbs to the sight of Jake, played by the 'thoroughly decent' Peter Finch (103). In the film version even Mortimer 'couldn't see what [the protagonist] had to complain about' (102). This sanitising of Mortimer's painful account of a woman's descent into the domestic abyss suggests the conservatism of the mid-1960s and the repressed discontent which led to the outbreak of Second-Wave feminism.

Conversely, the domestic arts of cleaning, cooking and shopping represent the imposition of female order on a patriarchal world in *We Have Always Lived in the Castle*. With the patriarch already dispatched by arsenic poisoning, Jackson's novel opens with what is, from the point of view of the narrator Merricat, a semi-idyllic female world. She and her sister Constance order their world through ritualised domestic routines – cleaning and 'neatening' (Jackson 2009: 41) the house, growing and cooking food – which are likened both to the creative arts and the black arts of magic and witchcraft. The cellar is full of preserves made by previous generations: food transformed into 'a poem by the Blackwood women' (42). Food, its preparation and consumption, is fetishised in the novel, a logical extension of the transformation of the domestic arts into a 'religion' noted by Friedan. Indeed, it is no accident that death is often dealt through food in the domestic Gothic – arsenic in the sugar in *We Have Always Lived in the Castle*, tea laced with cyanide in *The Man Who Loved Children* – reversing the nurturing associated with the domestic feminine. Family meals are often where the repressed underside of idealised family life is exposed. It is being sent to bed without supper by her father that precipitates Merricat's murder of her parents, brother and aunt. While Constance is acquitted of the murder, her washing of the sugar bowl after the deaths suggests her complicity in her sister's crime.

The rituals of cleaning are part of Merricat's attempts to protect their domain. Carrying their broom, dustpan and mop, the sisters are 'like a pair of witches walking home' (69). Merricat has developed a system of magical rituals – powerful words and buried objects – by which she attempts to safeguard their space from intruders. When Charles, 'a demon-ghost' (87), penetrates the house and 'dirt[ies] it' (76), Merricat resorts to the purifying power of fire, tipping his pipe into a wastebasket, to make the house 'clean [...] and fair again' (96). While this drives Charles out, it also destroys the upper storey, transforming the house into 'a castle, turreted and open to the sky' (120). Barricaded into this 'tomb' (140), the sisters now neaten and clean this space to create 'a whole new pattern of days' (132). '"We are so happy,"' Merricat repeatedly asserts, in what is an uncannily idyllic ending.

Families Can Be Murder

Familial murder is, of course, a typically Gothic theme. The murder of the mother by the father is a motif familiar from Ann Radcliffe's *A Sicilian Romance* (1790) onward. But these domestic Gothic texts frequently reconfigure the familial murder in unexpected ways. Surprisingly often it is teenage girls, like Merricat Blackwood and Louie Pollitt, who are the parricidal figures. In Lofts's 'Pesticide', for instance, teenage Jenny engineers the death by suffocation of the over-bearing patriarch Mr Jenkins, an Elder of the 'Chosen of Abraham' (Lofts 1974: 45), who bullies his wife and objects to Jenny wearing trousers. Such murders suggest the violent repressions, including incestuous desires, which underlie the façades of suburban domesticity.

A key figure here is Lizzie Borden, who appears in Jackson's *The Sundial* as 'Harriet Stuart', the 'enshrined murderess' who has killed her parents and two younger brothers with a hammer but been acquitted because she was 'only fifteen' and no jury could 'really *believe* she did it' (Jackson 2014: 71). After Harriet's death the house becomes a tourist attraction, listed in local guidebooks as 'a spot of some grisly interest' (74). The unanswered question, however, is motive: 'no one knew why she did it' (71). Jackson revisits this question in *We Have Always Lived in the Castle*, which is a kind of fictionalisation of the aftermath of the Lizzie Borden case. The answers lie in the *unheimlich* tensions buried beneath the domestic, which Stead disinters with perhaps even greater clarity.

As 'one of the great articulators of family life', Carter has argued, Stead's 'loathing of the rank futility of home and hearth is equalled [...] only by that expressed by the Marquis de Sade' (Carter 1982). *The Man Who Loved Children* ends, inevitably, with the death of Henny. This ending brings together two key Gothic themes: the motif of incest within an oedipal plot, and the confrontation with the dead-undead mother (Kahane 1985: 335–6). While it is Louie who laces her parents' tea with cyanide, it could be argued that Sam Pollitt, that suburban Bluebeard, has already killed his second wife. Already apparitional, Henny knowingly drinks the lethal tea, telling Louie and Sam, 'you pair of beasts, my womb is torn to pieces with you' (504). But she also asserts Louie's innocence: 'she's not to blame [...] your daughter is out of her mind' (504).

As Louie enters sexual maturity, the incestuous potential of Sam's struggle for power over her has become clear. He talks to her about sex, reacts with confused rage to the story of a local man accused of incest with his daughter (387), and tells Evie, 'Little-Womey, soon you got to be my wife' (392). Identifying with Beatrice in Shelley's tragic drama of incest and patricide, *The Cenci* (389), Louie writes a play entitled 'The Tragedy of the Snake Man, or Father' in an invented language which trumps Sam's own dialect. Translated, the play tells the story of father–daughter incest and ends:

ANTEIOS: I am only embracing you. My beloved daughter. (But he hisses.)
MEGARA: Mother, father is strangling me. Murderer! (She dies). (409)

For Stead, then, as in the domestic Gothic more generally, family life is a 'patriarchal cage' (Carter 1982) and the only way to break out of that cage is through violence. With Henny, her Gothic mother-double, dead, Louie asserts that '"I'm my own mother"' (521) and leaves the Pollitt house.

A similarly Gothic family romance is enacted in Barbara Comyns's *The Vet's Daughter* (1959) but with a different ending. Set in Edwardian London, the novel is narrated by Alice Rowlands, the daughter of a callous veterinarian and the terrified down-trodden wife he married for her dowry. The *unheimlich* nature of their house is indicated by its macabre furnishings: a rug made from a skinned Great Dane, a monkey's skull on the mantelpiece (Comyns 1981: 2). Comyns similarly exploits the uncanny presence of dismembered bodies in a domestic setting in *The Skin Chairs*. Like Mr Rowlands' animal remains, the eponymous chairs, covered in human skin, represent 'all those victims who are finally crushed by the weight of human aggression, neglect or indifference' (Horner and Zlosnik 2004: 95). Equally crushed, the dying Mrs Rowlands is 'put to sleep' (38) by her husband, who then installs his mistress in the house.

For these Bluebeard fathers, however, the daughter's place is interchangeable with that of the mother, whether as housekeeper or possession. Like Stead's Louie, Alice is exploited by her father. When he discovers Alice can levitate, Mr Rowlands orchestrates a bizarre performance on Clapham Common, where Alice, dressed like a bride, is to 'rise up' (170), preparatory to becoming a music-hall act. Alice does levitate 'simply to escape the horror of my father' (187), but then falls to the ground and is trampled to death. As Horner and Zlosnik conclude, this 'grotesque parody of the wedding service' suggests that 'marriage for many women leads to the death of the self' (2004: 93), as it has for Alice's mother. Alice's levitation can be read as an attempt to rise above the domestic space in which she (and her mother) are trapped: 'Nothing could be worse than home' (90), Alice thinks. Comyns's surreal use of the supernatural tips the domestic Gothic towards magic realism, but it is also a highly effective way of symbolising the *unheimlich* which underlies the ordinary.

Perhaps the most compellingly succinct articulation of this domestic Gothic theme of father–daughter abuse is Plath's 'Daddy', in which the speaker exorcises both the vampire-devil patriarch who has confined and terrified her and his double, the husband-vampire who 'drank [her] blood for a year' (Plath 1981: 224). 'Daddy, I have had to kill you', the speaker tells the Fascist father, concluding triumphantly: 'Daddy, daddy, you bastard, I'm through' (224). 'Daddy', Wisker argues, works through 'Plath's own sense of haunting by the father' who died when she was young (2004: 109). However, read against the wider context of these domestic Gothic texts, especially against Stead's *The Man Who Loved Children*, the poem looks less like a confession of Plath's personal pathology and more like a highly politicised analysis of women's repressed status in mid-twentieth-century culture and society. While the final line of 'Daddy' is ambiguous, it is noticeable that in Plath's late poems, the 'little toy wife' with 'Four babies and a cocker!' of 'Amnesiac' (Plath 1981: 234) increasingly mutates into the vengeful, undead Lady Lazarus who 'eat[s] men like air' (247).

Coda: Emma Donoghue's *Room* (2010) as 'Fourth Wave' Domestic Gothic

While critics such as Holland and Sherman have seen the modern Gothic as 'deeply conservative' (Holland and Sherman 1977: 286), these domestic Gothic texts are politically radical. They prefigure the work of writers such as Angela Carter, Fay Weldon and Toni Morrison, now associated with Second-Wave feminism. However, I want finally to leap forward to a recent text published during what is now being called 'Fourth Wave' feminism. Emma Donoghue's *Room* (2010) takes the themes, motifs and language of the domestic Gothic and reconfigures them in a redemptive celebration of the power of mother-love. The story of five-year-old Jack who lives in a single locked room with his Ma was inspired by 'ancient folk motifs of walled-up virgins who give birth' as well as 'the Fritzl family's escape from their dungeon in Austria' (Donoghue website). Imprisoned in a fortified garden shed and impregnated by 'Old Nick', Ma has created an entire world for her son within the 11-foot-square space. Jack's world is peopled by personified objects ('Rug', 'Wardrobe', 'Meltedy Spoon'), his 'friends' are television cartoon characters, and his day is structured by the routines Ma creates for him.

Here the Gothic is domesticated to transform the hellish into the homely. The locked room of the Gothic novel becomes 'a metaphor for the claustrophobic, tender bond of parenthood' (Donoghue website). The devilish 'Old Nick' is the Gothic villain who visits Ma after dark in a nightmare version of the Psyche and Cupid myth, which Anne Williams (1995) argues underlies the Female Gothic paradigms. In Ma, however, Donoghue reworks the captive Gothic heroine as a capable, inventive and loving mother who refuses to be victimised and who rewrites the Gothic script to protect her child and engineer their escape. Like Plath's 'Lady Lazarus', Ma is both a symbol of recovered female liberty who rises above her victimisation, and 'just a good, plain, very resourceful woman' (Plath 1981: 294).

Bibliography

Carter, Angela (1982), 'Unhappy Families', *London Review of Books*, 4(17) (16 September): 11–13. Available at: http://www.lrb.co.uk/v04/n17/angela-carter/unhappy-families (accessed 7 October 2014).

Comyns, Barbara [1959] (1981), *The Vet's Daughter*, London: Virago.

Comyns, Barbara [1962] (1987), *The Skin Chairs*, London: Virago.

Donoghue, Emma [2010] (2011), *Room*, London: Picador.

Donoghue, Emma, '*Room*', Emma Donoghue website: http://www.emmadonoghue.com/books/novels/room-the-novel.html (accessed 7 October 2014).

Freud, Sigmund [1919] (1990), 'The "Uncanny"' in *Art and Literature*, The Penguin Freud Library, vol. 14 [1985], Harmondsworth: Penguin, pp. 339–76.

Friedan, Betty [1963] (1982), *The Feminine Mystique*, Harmondsworth: Penguin.

Gavron, Hannah [1966] (1968), *The Captive Wife*, Harmondsworth: Pelican.

Holland, Norman N. and Leona F. Sherman (1977), 'Gothic Possibilities', *New Literary History*, 8(2): 279–94.

Horner, Avril and Sue Zlosnik (2004), 'Skin Chairs and other Domestic Horrors: Barbara Comyns and the Female Gothic Tradition', *Gothic Studies*, 6(1): 90–101.

Jackson, Shirley [1959] (1984), *The Haunting of Hill House*, Harmondsworth: Penguin.

Jackson, Shirley [1962] (2009), *We Have Always Lived in the Castle*, Harmondsworth: Penguin.

Jackson, Shirley [1958] (2014), *The Sundial*, Harmondsworth: Penguin.

Kahane, Claire (1985), 'The Gothic Mirror', in Shirley Nelson Garner, Claire Kahane and Madelon Sprengnether (eds), *The (M)other Tongue: Essays in Feminist Psychoanalytic Interpretation*, Ithaca, NY, and London: Cornell University Press, pp. 334–51.

Lidoff, Joan (1983), 'Domestic Gothic: The Imagery of Anger in Christina Stead's *The Man Who Loved Children*', in Juliann Fleenor (ed.), *The Female Gothic*, Montreal and London: Eden, pp. 109–22.

Lofts, Norah (1974), *Is There Anybody There?* London: Corgi.

Murphy, Bernice M. (2005), 'Introduction' in Bernice M. Murphy (ed.), *Shirley Jackson: Essays on the Literary Legacy*, Jefferson, NC, and London: McFarland.

Plath, Sylvia (1981), *Collected Poems*, London: Faber.

Mortimer, Penelope [1962] (1964), *The Pumpkin Eater*, Harmondsworth: Penguin.

Mortimer, Penelope [1960] (1966), 'The Skylight', in *Saturday Lunch with the Brownings*, Harmondsworth: Penguin, pp. 7–27.

Mortimer, Penelope (1993), *About Time Too: 1940–1978*, London: Weidenfeld and Nicolson.

Sexton, Anne [1988] (1991), *The Selected Poems of Anne Sexton*, London: Virago.

Stead, Christina [1940] (1970), *The Man Who Loved Children*, Harmondsworth: Penguin.

Williams, Anne (1995), *Art of Darkness: A Poetics of Gothic*, Chicago and London: University of Chicago Press.

Wisker, Gina (2004), 'Viciousness in the Kitchen: Sylvia Plath's Gothic', *Gothic Studies*, 6(1): 103–17.

Part II

Transgressions

Chapter 6

Wicked Women
Anne Williams

Etymology says it all. 'Wicked' derives from the Old English *wicce*, a witch. Thus any discussion of Wicked Women in the Gothic demands what Mary Daly has called 'the process of freeing words from the cages and prisons of patriarchal patterns' (Daly 1987: 3). Nowadays 'wicked' sounds archaic, evoking 'Snow White', or 'Hansel and Gretel', or the Wicked Witch of the West in *The Wonderful Wizard of Oz* (1900). ('Wizard', though defined as 'a male witch', is derived from the Middle English *wys* or *wis*, meaning 'wise' or 'smart'.) L. Frank Baum's Wizard was a fraud, but his witches have real power over nature, and like those of the Brothers Grimm imply children's anxieties about mothers' possibly supernatural powers. Older witches express men's fears of emasculation. The witch hunter's manual, *Malleus Maleficarum* (1486), reports one who kept a collection of penises in a bird's nest – the largest belonging to the local priest (Kraemer and Sprenger 2013: 108). The witchy women of Gothic fiction usually threaten not literal but more symbolic forms of castration: rebellion against their patriarchal roles as dutiful daughters, faithful wives and self-sacrificing mothers.

The history of wicked Gothic women is a history of rebellion and subversion and a demonstration that representing female subjectivity requires a revolution in literary form. The first epoch of Gothic fiction (1764-c. 1820) coincided with women beginning to publish their writing in great numbers. In portraying their gender, they began to explore and eventually to escape their assigned 'female' role as patriarchy's dark, dangerous 'Other'. Paradoxically, however, the literary foremother of these Gothic wicked women is a female impersonation: Eloisa, in Alexander Pope's *Eloisa to Abelard* (1717). Writing a heroic epistle, an Ovidian genre authorising a male poet to write as a woman abandoned by her lover, Pope paraphrased John Hughes's translation (1713) of the twelfth-century nun Héloïse's letters to her lost, beloved Abelard. Pope's poem exploits the patriarchal stereotypes of women obsessed by romantic love and the interior of the female self as secret and dark, complex and irrational. Thus he places Eloisa, whose convent was Romanesque in style, within a Gothic structure, where literal stone and verbal vows are equally claustrophobic. As a woman imprisoned by the Law of the Father, she is driven virtually mad by unresolvable conflicts. (In *The Rape of the Lock* (1712) Pope had described Umbriel's epic descent into the Cave of Spleen, matrix of hysteria, where binaries dissolve, libidinal energies are liberated, and reason avails nothing.) Not only do readers share Eloisa's confinement, she cries out with the hysteric's 'unnatural' strength. Like the voice of the *castrato* (the eighteenth-century operatic superstar), Pope as 'male soprano' imparts masculine strength to the female vocal register. But Eloisa also adumbrates the Freudian hysteric, seeking relief through a 'writing cure'.

In appropriating the space of patriarchy's 'Other', Pope unleashed disruptive Gothic energies two generations before Walpole's *Castle of Otranto* (1764). Though the poem's sexual politics may now seem obvious, eighteenth-century readers found Pope's portrait of female rebellion powerfully compelling. Horace Walpole designed a section of Strawberry Hill (which would inspire *The Castle of Otranto*) as a tribute to her. In 1753 he wrote to Horace Mann: 'My house is so monastic that I have a little hall decked with long saints in lean arched windows with taper columns, which we call The Paraclete in memory of Eloisa's cloister' (Lewis 1960: 381). And Eloisa's substantial influence is evident a century later when teenaged Percy Bysshe Shelley published *Zastrozzi: A Romance* (1810) and *St. Irvyne: or The Rosicrucian* (1811). These jumbled works constitute his personal play list of 'Gothic's greatest hits' selected from Walpole, Ann Radcliffe, M. G. Lewis, and Charlotte Dacre. His semi-Radcliffean Eloise in *St. Irvyne* has been seduced and abandoned by the villainous Nempère, and bears his bastard child. In a characteristically rebellious gesture, Shelley allows her a happy ending because he sees her, like her prototype, as much victim as violator of the patriarchal rules.

As Juliet Mitchell argues, hysteria is a universal human response to unbearable trauma, a creative attempt to reconfigure an intolerable reality (Mitchell 2000: 41–2). The disruptions that Umbriel observed in the Cave of Spleen signify regression into the pre-Oedipal, the infant's mind prior to entrance into the patriarchal symbolic order where the acquisition of language privileges the logical, the hierarchal and the binary. Fortuitously, Héloïse's history actually included the condition necessary, according to psychoanalysis, for hysterical regression: castration. Abelard's castration, ordered by Héloïse's vengeful uncle, also literalises the medieval fantasy of the witch who steals the embodiment of male authority. Pope seems to have unconsciously intuited what it would be like to experience the world *before* the Law of the Father imposes order. Eloisa defiantly refuses to subordinate body to spirit, passion to reason, female to male, love to Law. Confined by God, Abelard and her own words, Eloisa nevertheless finds imaginative freedom within herself by writing about these irreconcilable opposites. Pope's poem interpolates the reader into this usually repressed dimension of the mind ruled by unregulated desire. 'Eloisa' implicitly suggests models for generations of wicked Gothic women.

In seeking to escape from her socially imposed roles, Eloisa is most outrageous as a rebellious nun, and as such would inspire a favourite early incarnation of the Gothic wicked woman. In her 'Index to Gothic Motifs' Ann B. Tracy lists thirty indeterminate 'villainesses' and another thirty 'loose women', but creates separate entries for the 'bad abbess' (sixteen) and for novices or nuns who are 'debauched' (eight), 'eloped' (two), 'ruined' (five), or just 'wicked' (five) (Tracy 1976: 196–205). In *The Monk* (1796) M. G. Lewis runs through a gamut of possibilities: Agnes, forced to take the veil but becoming pregnant and then mad after her infant dies; the 'Domina', her relentlessly cruel abbess; the Bleeding Nun, ghost of Beatrice, who took a lover, murdered him, and now haunts the hapless Lorenzo; and Matilda, mistress of disguise, who modulates from the novice Rosario to a seductress to a sorceress to a demon sent from hell to destroy Ambrosio, the Monk.

From the Reformation until the final defeat of the Jacobites in 1745, Roman Catholicism posed a real threat to Protestant Britain. The nun was inevitably a focus of anxiety and a figure of mystery. The Church's 'unnatural' demand for celibacy was in fact in essence what patriarchy demanded of all 'good women'; but the female reader could relish the transgressions of a Bride of Christ without realising that she was enjoying a challenge to the system that confined herself. The Church was also organised as a patriarchal family — priests were 'father', abbesses 'mother', and so on. Thus Gothic fictions could explore familial conflicts and cruelties without appearing to do so. Beginning with Father Jerome in *Otranto*, priests and nuns are frequently unmasked as characters' actual relatives, the plot doing the work of psychoanalysis. Furthermore, these female rebels in religious disguise appropriated 'masculine' traits, such as licentiousness and rebelliousness, while also often enforcing the Father's Law with disconcertingly masculine strength; Lewis's Domina pitilessly punishes Agnes for her pregnancy; in haunting Lorenzo, the Bleeding Nun enforces the 'performative' power of the word, even though his vow was spoken to what he believed to be Agnes merely masquerading as her ghostly double. (For a thorough survey of Gothic anti-Catholicism, see Hoeveler's *The Gothic Ideology* (2014).)

Horace Walpole was fascinated by the theatrical 'gloomth' (his own word) he associated with the Roman Church, and acknowledged Eloisa's influence in designing the dream house that inspired his house dream and *The Castle of Otranto*. But there are no overtly transgressive women in this first 'Gothic story'. Matilda and Isabella are innocent damsels in distress, although Manfred 'accidentally' murders his daughter when he mistakes her for Isabella, who has rejected his advances. He despairs at his lack of a male heir, but he never impugns his ageing wife Hippolita's virtue. (Walpole would not directly confront a 'wicked woman' until *The Mysterious Mother* (1768).) *Otranto* dramatises the consequences of the Father's Law for men. Because Manfred's grandfather had murdered Alphonso and usurped his identity as Prince of Otranto, his unfortunate grandson is punished.

But 'the female'– constructed by patriarchy as instability, materiality, sexuality, irrationality, darkness, evil – is housed within Otranto's vaults and hidden chambers. Indeed, Walpole created the Gothic as we know it by inviting his readers to explore the haunted castle, a potent dream symbol for both patriarchal culture and the (masculine) self in the Age of Enlightenment: a defensive structure confining the dangerous 'Other' it has created by simultaneously exploiting and harnessing woman's 'natural magic', the power to give birth. Without sons there would be no more fathers, but if the sons are 'illegitimate', the structure collapses. The words 'castle' and 'castration' are both rooted in the Indo-European *kes*, meaning 'to cut'. (Other Gothic preoccupations also trace their lineage to this syllable: 'chaste', 'caste', 'castigate', and 'incest'.) The castle walls represent patriarchy's ancient power and hide the fatal secrets that prophesy its fall.

In imagining female 'otherness' confined within an ancient, complex structure, Walpole moved the witch from the wild woods 'out there' to the civilised 'in here'. He carried the symbolic bride across the threshold, enforcing a dangerous proximity with her 'Otherness'. Confining the potentially wicked female within the castle creates conditions favourable to producing what Freud – whose essay published in 1919 drew many insights from the Gothic tales of E. T. A. Hoffmann – called 'the uncanny'. *Das Unheimliche* erupts when the familiar becomes terrifying. When his ancestral Otranto is invaded by disjointed pieces of gigantic armour, Manfred learns that his castle is *not* his home. The uncanny, as Nicholas Royle writes:

> Is a crisis of the proper (from the Latin *proprius* 'own') and a disturbance of the very idea of personal or private property, including the properness

of proper names, one's so-called 'name' … [and] of places, institutions and events. (Royle 2003: 1)

The patriarchal position of woman is inherently uncanny; she must submit to confinement within a narrow range of acceptable roles, their very narrowness a symptom of the fear she arouses.

Eloisa's frank expressions of sexual passion were another aspect of her rebelliousness. She refuses to deny the presence of her body, even though as a nun she has renounced sexuality altogether. M. G. Lewis, creator of the Bleeding Nun, founds his Gothic 'horror' on the female body; *The Monk* abounds in terrible mothers, including Agnes, who in her madness, cradles the maggot-infested infant for whose death she is responsible, and Elvira, the unknown mother whom Ambrosio murders when she interrupts his attempted rape of Antonia, his own sister. (Elvira had abandoned him as a baby.) And the very name of the 'Bleeding' Nun implies superstitious dread of the monthly process that signifies female fertility. Wicked women use their bodies to seduce, to horrify and to destroy. In early Gothic these characters most typically have access to supernatural powers, but as Adriana Craciun observes, in novels such as *Zofloya: or, The Moor* (1806), Charlotte Dacre celebrates a female protagonist, Victoria, who explores the implications of a fatal woman devoted to 'corporeal pleasure and destruction' (Craciun 2003: 111). Dacre admired M. G. Lewis, adopting the pseudonym 'Rosa Matilda', and her Victoria inspired several characters in Shelley's youthful novels. But it seems that a merely human female villain was too uncomfortable for readers to contemplate, for during the nineteenth century, destructive corporeality migrated back into the supernatural with the birth of the vampire. This creature not only imperilled the human body and soul, it also threatened patriarchy's founding distinction: that between 'male' and 'female'.

Six years after *Zofloya*, Byron published *The Giaour* (1813) which contains a melodramatic curse on his eponymous 'infidel':

Thy corse shall from its tomb be rent;
And ghastly haunt thy native place,
And suck the blood of all thy race,
There from thy daughter, sister, wife,
At midnight drain the stream of life.

(Byron 1986: 227, ll. 56–60)

Byron felt he needed to include a footnote explaining what this unfamiliar vampire was. In response to his ghost-writing challenge at the Villa Diodati in July, 1816, he himself began and abandoned a novel about a vampire, which his physician John Polidori plagiarised and published as *The Vampyr* in 1819. Hinting that it was Byron's work, he created a European sensation for vampire stories, vampire plays, even vampire operas. Polidori's Lord Ruthven is not much different from any predatory libertine, though he causes his victims material rather than merely social 'ruin'. But Byron's notion that the vampire is cursed to violate the incest taboo by feeding on his own family offers a clue to the origins of this fantasy. In *Totem and Taboo* (1913) Freud argued that the incest taboo enables the infant's separation from its mother (source of both pain and pleasure), and creates the foundation on which culture rests. As it happened, the group at the Villa Diodati were reading Coleridge's just-published 'Christabel' aloud. When Shelley heard the lines, 'A sight to dream of, not to tell!', describing the 'witch' Geraldine's hideously deformed bosom, he shrieked and ran from the room, later telling Polidori that he had suddenly envisioned Mary's nipples replaced with eyes, a not uncommon fantasy of infantile confusion of the mother's face and breast (Hilton 1992: 56).

Byron's guests called Geraldine 'the witch', but today she seems more obviously a vampire. Coleridge's fragment is fraught with anxiety pertaining to mothers. Christabel leaves her father's castle at midnight to pray for her absent lover beneath a 'broad-breasted old oak tree', but there finds Geraldine, and carries her over the castle threshold, oblivious of the signs that she may be 'evil'. In rescuing Geraldine, Christabel has acted as a good mother. But her 'child' fends off the ghost of Christabel's mother, her guardian spirit. While Christabel sleeps in Geraldine's arms, some vampiric exchange of energy occurs. Christabel awakes feeling guilty, while Geraldine is full of energy and proceeds to disrupt the relationship between Christabel and her father Sir Leoline. In imagining Geraldine, Coleridge was quite possibly remembering Robert Burton's tale of Lamia in *The Anatomy of Melancholy* (1621), a nightmare figure of perverted maternity. Repeatedly seduced, or raped, by Zeus, Lamia is driven mad by the deaths of her children and takes to haunting lonely roads, sucking the blood of unfortunate travellers. Instead of giving suck, she sucks. 'Christabel' confuses not only bad and good mothers, but virtually all social and psychological boundaries, repeatedly transgressed and never re-established.

Throughout the century there is no established sexual hierarchy among vampires. This agent of 'corporeal pleasure and destruction' appears as either male or female. Sheridan LeFanu's 'Carmilla' (1871), influenced by Coleridge's Geraldine, preys on motherless girls, implicitly a substitute for the lost parent. Furthermore the sexual attraction between female vampire and female victim is also consistent with the pre-Oedipal origins of the fantasy. Bram Stoker wrote a chapter about Jonathan Harker's encounter with a female vampire before he reaches Transylvania, but omitted it from *Dracula* (1897). Perhaps made uneasy by the increasingly public discourse on homosexuality in work by writers such as Havelock Ellis, his relentlessly heterosexual Count attacks women, but his powerful male monster embodies the culturally 'female': blood, madness, death, soulless materiality (Williams 1995: 121–40). Bram Dijkstra's *Idols of Perversity: Fictions of Feminine Evil in Fin-de-Siècle Culture* (1986) records the persistence of the female vampire, particularly in the visual arts, an association that would be popularised in the early days of silent film: Theda Bara, who specialised in playing the *femme fatale,* was nicknamed 'the Vamp'. According to Stoker's Van Helsing, the conquest of Dracula is necessary to preserve civilisation. He is quite right, for the vampire ignores the hierarchy of male over female, just as his coinage 'undead' is necessary to describe the vampire's escape from the ruling binary of alive/dead.

Luce Irigaray observes that:

> man only asks himself questions he can already answer using the supply of instruments he has available to assimilate even the disasters of his history ... The really urgent task is the colonisation of this new 'field', to force it, not without splintering, into the production of the same discourse. (Irigaray 1985: 137)

Stoker's vampire hunters gruesomely demonstrate this practice by driving a stake through the undead Lucy's heart, so that she becomes 'Lucy as we had seen her in life. True there were ... traces of care and pain and waste; but they were dear to us, for they marked her truth to *what we knew*' (Stoker 1997: 192; my emphasis). A 'mercy-bearing stake' is certainly one means of controlling female disruption of the categories, but confining her within the Law of the Father ironically facilitates its destruction from within.

Theologians would call Eloisa a heretic, the connoisseur of Gothic, a bad abbess; a psychoanalyst might define her as a 'castrating bitch'; but few readers readily place her within any of these categories, because Pope requires us to experience from within the pain inflicted by patriarchy. (How would the world of *Otranto* look through Hippolita's eyes, she who loses her son, her daughter, her husband and her house within a few days?) The birth of the Gothic coincided with an exponential rise in female literacy, and women writers soon took issue with Gothic tales that displace, or destroy, or demonise 'the female'. Clara Reeve's *The Old English Baron* (1778) challenged Walpole's supernaturalism, and

Ann Radcliffe's *The Italian* (1797) implicitly rebuked 'Monk' Lewis's scandalous improprieties.

But Ann Radcliffe's bestselling novels of the 1790s constitute a Copernican revolution in Gothic narrative technique. We share Emily St Aubert's fears and fantasies; we, too, burn to know what lurks behind the black veil. This perspective creates suspense and contributes to Radcliffe's atmospheric scene painting. But in making a female self the narrative centre, Radcliffe also laced a corset around her imagination. As Yael Shapira has argued, in appealing to a middle-class reader imbued with patriarchal ideology, the presence of the female body was problematic. Female sexuality had to be displaced to margins occupied by the likes of Laurentini di Udolpho or the Parisian aristocrat who temporarily seduces Valancourt. Emily worries about propriety, distressed that when she finally escapes Udolpho, she has no hat. Shapira analyses Radcliffe's strategies in avowing the embarrassments of the female body, and indeed speculates that she stopped publishing after *The Italian* because she felt so keenly the disapprobation arising from her very success: was it not 'wicked' for a woman writer to make so much money? (Shapira 2006: 453–75).

Five decades later Charlotte Brontë would allow Jane Eyre to write her own story in her own words – though herself publishing under a male pseudonym. Discovery of the author's sex, however, predictably led to attacks that she was 'unfeminine': she got the food wrong and the clothes wrong; Jane should not have stayed to hear Mr Rochester's amorous adventures. Furthermore, as Elizabeth Rigby wrote, 'Jane Eyre is proud and therefore ungrateful, too'. This hostile reader understood that female rebelliousness threatens culture itself. Jane voices:

> A proud and perpetual assertion of the rights of man, for which we find no authority in either God's word or God's providence ... We do not hesitate to say that the tone of mind and thought which has overthrown authority and violated every code human and divine abroad ... is the same which has also written *Jane Eyre*. (Brontë 1971: 442)

As the active threat of Catholicism ceased to loom so darkly, the debauched nun receded from the Gothic imagination. But the wicked woman's uncanny fusion of 'masculine' and 'feminine' continued. Charlotte Brontë first describes Bertha Mason as an asexual wild animal ('The clothed hyena rose up, and stood tall on its hind feet'); but if human, she seems more male than female: 'She was a big woman, in stature almost equalling her husband, and corpulent besides: she showed virile force in the contest – more than once she almost throttled him, athletic though he was' (Brontë 1971: 258).

Nearly a century later, Daphne du Maurier's *Rebecca* is also disconcertingly masculine:

> The real Rebecca took shape and form before me, stepping from her shadow world like a living figure from a picture frame. Rebecca slashing at her horse: Rebecca seizing life with her two hands; Rebecca triumphant, leaning down from the minstrels' gallery with a smile on her lips. (du Maurier 1971: 272)

Her last provocation challenges her husband Maxim's identity as master of Manderley: "'If I had a child, Max,' she said, 'neither you, nor anyone in the world, would ever prove that it was not yours ... The property's entailed'" (du Maurier 1971: 279). In the plot's most powerful twist, we learn that she was not only infertile but dying of uterine cancer.

However, the novel's most uncanny events demonstrate the power of Rebecca's body to reappear: her temporary 'rebirth' when Mrs Danvers persuades the second Mrs de Winter to repeat her masquerade as the portrait of the ancestress Caroline, and the literal reappearance of her drowned body on her boat, the *'Je reviens'*. But telling Gothic tales from a woman's point of view facilitated the transformation of the wicked woman's story into a medical case history: Maxim remarks that Rebecca 'was not even normal' (1971: 271). Just as Pope implies a potentially sympathetic diagnosis of Eloisa as a hysteric, that 'female malady', Radcliffe discloses how Laurentini di Udolpho became a murderess and a madwoman. Her parents had 'indulged her with weakness and reprehended her with violence (Radcliffe 1998: 654). She falls in love with the Marquis de Villeroi, who first promises marriage and then makes her his mistress. After they conspire to poison his virtuous wife, he demands that she remove herself to a convent, no doubt despising her as an embodiment of his own guilt. She obeys, and lives out her life as Sister Agnes, a *nouvelle* Eloisa, bitterly unreconciled to her fate and eventually lapsing into madness. Emily learns that the murdered woman was her aunt, and inherits a third of Laurentini's estate, nominally a happy ending but for the grim implication that in this world, 'good' women flourish when 'bad' women die.

Throughout the nineteenth century, Gothic villainesses increasingly appear as pathological specimens; Bertha Mason and Lady Audley inherit their madness. Meanwhile, the disruptions of the madwoman in the attic became increasingly interesting to men of science. In 1895 Freud and Breuer published *Studies in Hysteria,* which analyses some women's bizarre nonconformity to the standards of female propriety. They realised that that their patients' physical symptoms expressed their unspeakable frustration and rage. They were, in effect, speaking for themselves in a bodily language that circumvented the patriarchal symbolic order. Not that this medical project was consciously feminist. As Adam Phillips remarks, 'What [Freud and Breuer] had in common was an ambitious interest in the treatment of certain kinds of disturbed women (though their question was, what can you do with the women who disturb you?) (Phillips 2014: 108). But in learning to read this new language, Freud theorised the existence of the unconscious, demonstrating that man is not the master in his own house, an idea that wicked Gothic women had been acting out for more than a century.

Scientific sophistication about female hysteria enabled Freud's contemporary Henry James to create his supremely uncanny Gothic, *The Turn of the Screw* (1898). (What reader has not feared to see Peter Quint staring through her window?) Framed as a ghost story, it concerns a nameless governess hired to care for two orphaned children, Miles and Flora, at Bly, an idyllic country house, with the stipulation that she is entirely responsible for their welfare. She soon learns from the housekeeper that the two mysterious figures she sees about the estate are the valet Peter Quint, and the former governess, Miss Jessel – both dead. Convinced that the 'ghosts' will corrupt the children and certain that it is her sacred duty to save them, she becomes increasingly desperate to confirm her view of reality. In the end, Miles dies as she tries to force him to admit that he also sees Peter Quint.

James called the story 'An amusette to catch those not easily caught' (James 2010: 228). It has caught a seemingly innumerable number of literary critics in a debate as to whether the ghosts are real or the product of the governess's hysteria. James probably had not read Freud on hysteria, but his brother William was a distinguished psychologist and Henry was aware of the scientific investigations into the paranormal fashionable at the time. Although the governess remembers *Udolpho* by name, and alludes to *Jane Eyre* shortly after she arrives at Bly, there has not been much analysis of the tale's Gothic roots. Only six of the 458 titles concerning this story link it with 'Gothic' in the *MLA International Bibliography*. But James's chief source of the uncanny is undoubtedly Gothic: he makes it impossible for the reader to determine whether his women are 'wicked' or not. The governess, Mrs Grose, and Miss Jessel are obviously familiar to readers of the genre. Little Flora is not yet a type, but anticipates the twentieth-century convention of the wicked child, including sociopathic Rhoda in William Marsh's *The Bad Seed* (1954) and Shirley Jackson's Merricat in *We Have Always Lived in the Castle* (1962). James's frame narrative presents the governess as unambiguously good, but her frantic attempts to 'save' the children from an ambiguous threat results in Miles's death. Mrs Grose the housekeeper appears benign, like Mrs Fairfax in *Jane Eyre* (who nevertheless hides the truth about Bertha); but she may be as manipulative as Rebecca's Mrs Danvers. The governess assumes that Miss Jessel is 'evil', but may have been seduced (by Peter or the Master?); she may have given birth; and she may have committed suicide. Flora may be an innocent flower, but she can seem unnaturally knowing and lies fluently.

James's late prose style is an ideal medium for this exercise in ambiguity. Like 'Christabel', the story remains stubbornly resistant to interpretation, a 'hysterical' text. James was neurotically careful of his language, making some 500 revisions between his first and second published versions (James 2010: 121). But in adapting the form to the content, James was also participating in the Gothic tradition that shows how the nature of the tale determines how it must be told. From *Jane Eyre* onwards it seemed that the good woman's story demanded the comic marriage plot, a formula enthusiastically rediscovered in the mass-market Gothic of the 1960s. But what happens when the old stories lose their magic? What happens to the house of fiction when the madwoman escapes?

One solution is to tell the tale from the wicked woman's point of view, as in Jean Rhys's revision of *Jane Eyre*, *Wide Sargasso Sea* (1966) or Gregory Maguire's *Wicked* (1995), which revisits Oz. Two novels by Margaret Atwood, however, answer this question from within the specific constraints of the female Gothic formula. *Lady Oracle* (1976) is the history of Joan Foster, who fakes suicide to escape the unbearable contradictions among her separate and mostly secret lives. Her husband Arthur, a philosophy student involved in ineffectual left-wing causes, does not know about her former life as a fat woman, her past affair with a Polish count in London, or her present one in Toronto with avant-garde artist Chuck Brewer, aka 'The Royal Porcupine'. Nor does he know that she writes 'Costume Gothics' for the money, reproducing the mass-market, nineteenth-century formula offering women romantic escape and reassuring them that women cannot only survive but thrive within patriarchy. Arthur is uneasily aware that his wife has published a celebrated volume of Gothic prose poems, *Lady Oracle*, but not that she dredged them from her unconscious by means of automatic writing.

Various facets of Joan's dissociated lives foreground the realities of experience that the Gothic formula represses, such as inadequate parenting: her remote father, now an anaesthetist, was once a secret agent behind enemy lines, but his only emotional outlet is listening to Metropolitan Opera broadcasts; Joan's unhappy mother is unkind to her, desperate to inculcate 'feminine' conformity by means of Brownies and dance class; her spinster aunt works in public relations for a sanitary napkin company and also dabbles in spiritualism. Joan's early marriage to Arthur does not automatically bring 'happily ever after'. When she unconsciously echoes the fate of the 'poetess' in an apparent suicide, she goes to Italy, where she struggles to complete her 'Costume Gothic' in progress. But she discovers that her characters are refusing to play their assigned roles. Felicia is the beautiful, sophisticated, and wealthy wife of Redmond, Lord of the Manor, fated to fall in love with the heroine Charlotte; thus wicked Felicia must die. But Joan complains, 'I couldn't seem to get rid of her' (Atwood 1976: 316). She has a will of her own. '*Felicia was lying in the shrubbery of the maze ... She'd been making love with Otterly,* [the gardener] *who lay exhausted beside her ... Redmond suspected nothing ...*' (317; emphasis in original). Felicia, in short, is claiming her own story:

> I opened my eyes, got up from the typewriter ... Sympathy for Felicia was out of the question, it was against the rules, it would foul up the plot completely ... If she'd been a mistress instead of a wife, her life could have been spared; as it was, she had to die ... But what had she ever done to deserve it? (Atwood 1976: 319)

The truth, which negates the myth promulgated in Costume Gothics, is 'nothing'.

In *The Blind Assassin* (2000) Atwood again rewrites the female Gothic formula from the 'wicked' woman's point of view. The narrative form is complex. It includes a series of newspaper articles giving the public facts about the lives of Iris and Laura, daughters of a wealthy button manufacturer growing up in Ontario in the 1930s. The first announces the death of Laura, who has driven Iris's car over a bridge under construction. But Laura was subsequently celebrated as author of a posthumous 'post-modern' novel, *The Blind Assassin,* a science-fiction fantasy ostensibly being composed by a pair of anonymous lovers meeting furtively in seedy hotels. Iris tells two stories: one concerning the present indignities of her old age, and the other a confession about the past that gradually divulges the true history of Laura and herself. Atwood shatters the female Gothic formula and reconstructs it as a mosaic. Iris and Laura grow up in a decaying Victorian mansion, 'Avilion', named from Tennyson by their culturally ambitious grandmother and famous for its stained-glass windows portraying Tristan and Iseult. Their young mother dies in childbirth, and their father becomes an arbitrary, sometimes cruel patriarch, drinking more and more as his button factory begins to fail during the Great Depression. Both sisters fall in love with Alex Thomas, a Byronic figure of mysterious origins and Marxist politics. They are cared for by Reenie, the housekeeper, who keeps family secrets and dispenses Old Wives' Tales as wisdom.

Laura is blonde, pretty and naïve, but unlike the conventional Gothic heroine, destroyed by life; Iris lives to be a very old woman, quite candid about her failures as wife, mother and grandmother. Her unsympathetic sister-in-law has even legally deprived her of her granddaughter Sabrina. But every choice Iris has made was constrained by the difficulties of her situation. Her father arranged her marriage at eighteen to a wealthy, pompous business colleague; her sister-in-law insists she live the life of the indulged, but powerless, society lady. Eventually Iris realises that her husband, who had insisted on incarcerating Laura in a home for the mentally disturbed, has in fact seduced her, and forced her to have an abortion. She tries to save Laura and Alex and fails at both. After fighting in the Spanish Civil War, Alex joins the army and is killed in battle. Laura kills herself after learning of Iris's affair with Alex, and his death.

But Iris's most disruptive, rebellious and successful act of defiance is her success in resurrecting Laura as author of an unconventional fiction excoriated for its sexual candour. It was she and Alex who had fantasised the tale of *The Blind Assassin,* a 'science fiction' still incorporating earthly patriarchy's cruel social practices. Publishing it as Laura's work provides both a pseudonym for herself and resurrects her sister as a feminist icon. But at the end, she tells the reader why she has done what she did – and of her own most material subversion of patriarchy:

> When I began this account of Laura's life – of my own life – I had no idea why I was writing it ... But it's clear to me now, I was writing for you, dearest Sabrina.
>
> Since Laura is no longer who you thought she was, you're no longer who you think you are, either. That can be a shock, but it can also be a relief ... Your real grandfather was Alex Thomas, and as to who his father was, well, the sky's the limit ... Your legacy from him is the realm of infinite speculation. You're free to reinvent yourself at will. (Atwood 2000: 513)

Iris's story, like her novel, partially frees at least three women from the 'cages and prisons of patriarchal patterns' (Daly 1987: 3). Although she masquerades as her dead sister – the tragic embodiment of the Gothic heroine – she dies a natural death. Unlike the fictional Corinne or L.E.L. (1802–38), the creative Iris is not required to die young. She removed at least some walls within the house of fiction. For the woman who writes is also a witch; she has the power to change the ways we think and feel. She is patriarchy's most formidable *femme fatale.*

Bibliography

Atwood, Margaret (2000), *The Blind Assassin,* New York: Nan A. Talese.

Atwood, Margaret (1976), *Lady Oracle,* New York: Simon and Schuster.

Brontë, Charlotte [1847] (1971), *Jane Eyre,* ed. Richard J. Dunn, New York: W. W. Norton.

Byron, Lord (1986), *Byron: A Critical Edition of the Major Works,* ed. Jerome J. McGann, Oxford and New York: Oxford University Press.

Coleridge, S. T. (1985), *Samuel Taylor Coleridge,* ed. H. J. Jackson. Oxford and New York: Oxford University Press.

Craciun, Adriana (2003), *Fatal Women of Romanticism,* Cambridge and New York: Cambridge University Press.

Daly, Mary and Jane Caputi (1987), *Websters' First New Intergalactic Wickedary of the English Language,* Boston, MA: Beacon Press.

Dijkstra, Bram (1986), *Idols of Perversity: Fantasies of Feminine Evil in Fin-de-Siècle Culture,* Oxford and New York: Oxford University Press.

du Maurier, Daphne [1938] (1971), *Rebecca,* New York: Avon Books.

Hilton, Nelson (1992), 'Keats, Teats, and the Fane of Poesy' in Deirdre Coleman and Peter Otto (eds), *Imagining Romanticism: Essays on English and Australian Romanticisms.* West Cornwall, CT: Locust Hill Press, pp. 49-72.

Hoeveler, Diane Long (2014), *The Gothic Ideology: Religious Hysteria and Anti-Catholicism in British Popular Fiction 1780-1880,* Cardiff: University of Wales Press.

Irigaray, Luce (1985), *Speculum of the Other Woman,* trans. Gillian C. Gill, Ithaca and London: Cornell University Press.

James, Henry [1898] (2010), *The Turn of the Screw,* ed. Peter G. Beidler, Boston and New York: Bedford/St. Martin's.

Kraemer, Heinrich and Jakob Sprenger (2013), *The Malleus Maleficarum* [1486], trans. Montague Summers. Create Space Independent Publishing Platform.

Lewis, W. S. (ed.) (1960), *The Yale Edition of Horace Walpole's Correspondence,* Vol. 20, New Haven, CT, and London: Yale University Press.

Mitchell, Juliet (2000), *Mad Men and Medusas: Reclaiming Hysteria,* New York: Basic Books.

Phillips, Adam (2014), *Becoming Freud: The Making of a Psychoanalyst,* New Haven, CT, and London: Yale University Press.

Radcliffe, Ann [1794] (1998), *The Mysteries of Udolpho,* Oxford and New York: Oxford University Press.

Royle, Nicholas (2003), *The Uncanny,* Manchester: Manchester University Press.

Shapira, Yael (2006), 'Where the Bodies Are Hidden: Ann Radcliffe's "Delicate" Gothic', *Eighteenth-Century Fiction*: 18(4): 453–76.

Stoker, Bram [1897] (1997), *Dracula,* ed. Nina Auerbach and David J. Skal, New York: W.W. Norton.

Tracy, Ann B. (1976), *The Gothic Novel 1790–1830: Plot Summaries and Index to Motifs*, Lexington: University Press of Kentucky.

Williams, Anne (1995), *Art of Darkness: A Poetics of Gothic*, Chicago and London: University of Chicago Press.

Chapter 7

The Female Gothic Body
Marie Mulvey-Roberts

Women have been identified primarily through the body which, throughout history, has been associated with monstrosity. This representation persists within the Gothic in various forms, from the gorgon to the vampire. For Aristotle, the female was a monster, an aberration from the normative male and, in the words of Luce Irigaray's book title, *The Sex Which Is Not One* (1977) (Battersby 1998: 49). As a departure from the male, the very notion of the female body has proved troublesome. The demonisation of woman as succubus, harpy, witch and any number of supernatural beings has located the female outside nature and beyond the natural order of things. In Western religious, philosophical and psychological traditions, the alignment of the female with the monstrous or animal body has helped demote the category of woman in social and political hierarchies. Within patriarchal ideology, monstrosity has been regarded as quintessential to the construction of femininity. Going back to the classical mythology of the Ancient Greeks, the snaky-haired Medusa, with her deadly paralysing gaze, allegorises the *femme fatale*, who encodes the perils of sexual autonomy and aberration. Originally the most beautiful of the three Gorgon sisters, she was turned into a monster by Athena for violating her temple, where she was either seduced or ravished by Poseidon. According to the Christian creation myth, the first woman originated from a male body part, Adam's rib, which aptly illustrates the ancillary nature of her role as help-mate or mere adjunct to the male. Through the fallen figure of Eve, woman has been represented as a temptress and the feminine identified with the serpent, a creature associated with evil, poison and lowliness as it slithers along the earth.

This representation continued into the theological misogyny of the Middle Ages, typified by Bishop Marbod of Rennes (c.1035–1123), who pronounced: 'Woman [is] the unhappy source, evil root, and corrupt offshoot, who brings to birth every sort of outrage throughout the world

... Woman subverts the world; woman the sweet evil, compound of honeycomb and poison' (Gilmore 2001: 86). These sensual and deadly metaphors point to female flesh as a corrupting and poisonous influence. During the Renaissance, the sexual nihilism of Christian Europe equated reproduction with sin and demonised the pregnant female body as a fecund house of horrors and woman as a 'two-legged she-beast' (88), shunned by the church. As Mikhail Bakhtin indicates, 'The combination of human and animal traits is [...] one of the most ancient grotesque forms' (Bakhtin 1984: 316) and at that time women were seen as 'naturally grotesque' (Stallybrass 1986: 126). Earth and the reproductive body have an obvious synergy with the feminine, which Bakhtin incorporates into his concept of grotesque realism, for like 'the fruitful earth', 'it is always conceiving' (Vice 1997: 156). Because of this proliferation and the metamorphic physicality linked to the female body, it has also been associated with excess. Conversely, at a later period, women were perceived as an embodiment of lack. In her analysis of the 'monstrous-feminine', Barbara Creed draws attention to the absence of a phallus, as a marker of sexual difference (Creed 1993: 1). This lack had been applied by Sigmund Freud to his theory of castration, which signified the female body as characterised by loss. Mainly on the grounds of sexuality and reproduction, the female body has been stigmatised by patriarchal controls, both systematically and institutionally, as in the Freudian Law of the Father and institution of marriage. Driving forces have been power, possession and patrimony. These manifest as a policing of the female body and its constituent parts, particularly the open mouth and vulva, as well as the threshold of the house (Stallybrass 1986: 126). The domestic space has been seen as an extension of the female body and, in his essay, 'The Uncanny' (1919), Freud regards the womb as *'unheimlich'* or uncanny, which, for men, is unfamiliar, as well as familiar in signifying the return home. The classical female body, as opposed to the unruly or transgressive female Gothic body, is represented by the closed mouth, enclosed body and locked household door. These synecdoches of enclosure personify the mute virginal woman obliged to 'suffer and be silent', the mantra of the repressed Victorian woman (see Vicinus 1972). The idealised Victorian wife is eulogised in Coventry Patmore's poem, *The Angel in the House* (1854), on the courtship of his first wife, while Bram Dijkstra conceptualises such a woman as a household nun in *Idols of Perversity: Fantasies of Feminine Evil in Fin-de-Siècle Culture* (Dijkstra 1986: 12–24).

Since the earliest days of humanity, negative stereotypes of women have been culturally absorbed, evolving into a widespread cultural misogyny in most societies. These have been reflected within Gothic literature, which has sometimes critiqued or even reinforced this distorted view of the feminine through representations of female monstrosity, feminine evil or enhanced passivity. Within the eighteenth-century Gothic novel, female powerlessness is epitomised by ways in which the property and inheritance rights of the Gothic heroine could be seized by control of her body, whether through marriage, domestic violence or imprisonment. As this chapter will demonstrate, the female Gothic body has developed through the Madonna/whore duality, incarceration, fragmentation, hybridity and sexuality, while femininity itself has been demonised in Gothic literature by way of the *femme fatale*, man-made monster, vampire and Medusa. This chapter will explore how Gothic fictions embody a dialogue between an unquestioning representation of the female body as threatening and an awareness of how such images work to sustain a misogynistic patriarchal inheritance.

The dichotomy between Madonna and whore is fundamental to numerous readings of the female body within Gothic writing, which encompasses a world of binary oppositions. In Charlotte Dacre's *Zofloya, or The Moor* (1806), the wicked heroine Victoria de Loridani takes as her lover a satanic black African servant, who assists her in poisoning her husband. As Victoria's crimes multiply, she becomes increasingly less feminine, growing bigger, darker and more masculine. By contrast, her rival for the affections of another man is the fair, virtuous and 'fragile' Lilla. Victoria jealously stabs her with the masculinised murder weapon of a poniard and throws her 'fairy form' (Dacre 1997: 220) down a steep mountain. As a reincarnation of the Marquis de Sade's sadistic eponymous heroine in his novel *Juliette* (1796), Victoria effectively dismembers the stereotype of the passive Gothic heroine in a Sadean 'dissection of virtue' (Craciun 2003: 114). By murdering the Romantic equivalent of the Angel in the House, she anticipates Virginia Woolf, who expressed the longing in *A Room of One's Own* (1929) to assassinate this idealised woman, who threatened to throttle the creative impulses of the woman writer.

Robert Miles notes that Victoria is an obvious rewriting of the Bleeding Nun in Matthew Lewis's luridly sensational, *The Monk* (1796) (Miles 1993: 175).[1] This is Beatrice de las Cisternas, who renounces her monastic vows for a career of debauchery and is eventually stabbed to death by her lover. Her ghost bears the bleeding wound on her breast. While Lilla is the victim of multiple stab wounds, it is the one on her breast that haunts Victoria, for whom 'that lovely form, bounding from crag to crag, seemed at every turn to meet her view; – those fair tresses dyed in crimson gore, that bleeding bosom was before her' (Dacre 1997: 221). Victoria's lust is matched by that of the Bleeding Nun, who even refuses to allow her spectral body to get in the way of her yearning for carnal gratification. Beatrice's object of desire, Don Raymond, mistakes her for his bride, a runaway nun, who has disguised herself as the ghost of the Bleeding Nun in order to escape from her convent. Raymond's discovery that he has abducted a ghostly corpse strips away the veneer of any possible female temptation. Her flesh-eaten face is a symbol of her moral corruption, in contrast to the beautiful face of the equally corrupt Matilda, a demon witch who, like Eve, initially tempts Lewis's monk Ambrosio into re-enacting the Fall. She helps him ravish the virginal Antonia, who turns out to be his own sister. In *The Monk* criminality arises from concupiscence, which in most cases is a reaction against religious celibacy, a state which its Protestant author would have considered unnatural. The chief instigators of carnality are Matilda, initially disguised as the monk, Rosario, and the Bleeding Nun, who represent the insatiable demands of the female body, believed at that time to be inherently lustful. These women, along with Dacre's Victoria, can be read as case studies in nymphomania, in terms of M. D. T. de Bienville's *Nymphomania or, A Dissertation Concerning the Furor Uterinus* (1775), for as Adriana Craciun observes: 'The degeneration of the nymphomaniac's internal organs parallels the decay of the living corpse' (Craciun 2003: 128).

Unlike Dacre and Lewis, Ann Radcliffe's view of the female Gothic body is tempered by reason and sensibility, notwithstanding the tendency of her heroines to weep excessively or faint, when overcome by trauma. While the inert unconscious female body is an expression of passivity, whose ultimate expression is that of the corpse,[2] the swoon enables Radcliffe's heroines to gain some temporary respite from the horrors threatening to engulf them. In sentimental Female Gothic fiction, heroines confined within castles represent the containment of women within patriarchal social and legal structures. An ur-text is the Bluebeard legend, used by several male writers as a parable to stress the punishment due to a disobedient wife who, in this case, defies her husband's command not to enter the forbidden chamber, containing the murdered bodies of his former wives. Several female Gothic novelists have rewritten the legend to bring out the triumph of the final wife, who survives her husband's attempt to chop off her head. In *Mysteries of Udolpho* (1794), Radcliffe replays the mystery lying behind the locked door, through the wax effigy of a decomposing body concealed by an enigmatic black veil. This is satirised by Jane Austen when her heroine, Catherine Morland, discovers a humble laundry list in a mysterious cabinet in *Northanger Abbey* (1818).[3] The forbidden room of the Bluebeard legend is recreated in the modern-looking bedroom, where Catherine wrongly suspects that her host General Tilney murdered his wife. More recent versions include Elizabeth Gaskell's 'The Grey Lady' (1861), whose Bluebeard wife acquires a female 'husband', and Elizabeth Bowen's short story and black comedy, 'The Cat Jumps' (1934), in which a husband turns the marital home into a bloody chamber, by leaving parts of his wife's body in different rooms and depositing her heart in a hat-box, as the place where he decides it most truly belongs. In Fritz Lang's film, *Secret Beyond the Door* (1948), the Bluebeard husband, Mark Lamphere, an architect and war veteran, reconstructs rooms in his house to recreate the sites of murdered women. He conducts tours of six of his rooms, but the seventh remains private. When Celia his wife enters this forbidden room, she discovers a replica of her own bedroom. The truth finally dawns on her that this is going to be the scene of the next crime, her murder.

Bluebeard was a popular pantomime during the Victorian period, a time when the punishment for an uncooperative or transgressive wife was not the forbidden room or bloody chamber, but the authorised destination of the lunatic asylum. This is the fate of Mary Elizabeth Braddon's husband-killing heroine in *Lady Audley's Secret* (1862). Braddon was a friend of Edward Bulwer Lytton, whose eponymous villainess, Lucretia Dalibard, in his novel *Lucretia* (1846) ends up as a manacled maniac, after murdering two husbands. She is described as 'a grisly, squalid, ferocious mockery of a human being – more appalling and more fallen than Dante ever fabled in his spectres' and whose 'red devouring eye' (Bulwer Lytton 1874: 427) never seems to close. Lucretia Dalibard has a fictional kinship with Bertha Mason in Charlotte Brontë's *Jane Eyre* (1847), the mad wife of Edward Rochester, who has been confined by him within the family home. Described as a 'clothed hyena' standing 'tall on its hind feet' (Brontë 1966: 328), Bertha is compared to 'the foul German spectre – the Vampyre' (317). In 1858, Bulwer Lytton placed his own wife, the novelist Rosina Bulwer Lytton, in a private asylum, even though she was sane, as punishment for publicly exposing his adultery and marital violence. He also intended to thwart her surveillance of him, by effectively closing her 'red devouring eye'. Edward feared that his estranged wife's revelations concerning his private and public life would destroy his political career. Rosina was wrongly diagnosed with dementia, probably because at that time it was associated more with delusional states, rather than a degenerative age-related disease. A more common diagnosis for women refusing to conform to the straitjacket of traditional femininity was hysteria, a malady affecting both mind and body, which was often connected to sexuality. Gothic heroines presenting symptoms of hysteria include Catherine Earnshaw in Emily Brontë's *Wuthering Heights*

(1847) and Lucy Westenra in Bram Stoker's *Dracula* (1897). Stoker's contemporary and Freud's mentor, Jean-Martin Charcot, treated hysterics at his Salpêtrière Hospital in Paris, which provided him with a kind of living museum of pathology. Under his orchestration, they 'performed' their illnesses in a lecture theatre for an audience of doctors and medical students. The body of the hysteric was believed to be so sensitive that it was susceptible to dermographism or skin-writing by doctors and, around 1893, one woman was photographed, not entirely untypically, with the word 'SATAN' inscribed upon her back (Beizer 1994: 25), in what can be seen as a modern form of witch-pricking. According to Beizer, 'Doctors fascinated by dermographism often used the sign of the devil in their writing experiments' (1994: 25).

During the Middle Ages, witches were believed to copulate with demons and generate hybrid offspring. This was a projection of fears surrounding the reproductive female body, later expressed through the violent fragmenting of the female monster in Mary Shelley's *Frankenstein or The Modern Prometheus* (1818). From parts of dead bodies, Victor Frankenstein had begun creating a companion for his male creature or 'demon'. His fear was that if the monsters mated, they might produce a 'race of devils', which would terrorise mankind. Furthermore, the female might prove to be 'ten thousand times more malignant than her mate, and delight, for its own sake, in murder and wretchedness' (Shelley 2007: 170). This anxiety foreshadows Rudyard Kipling's refrain in his poem, 'The Female of the Species' (1911), in which he declares: 'For the female of the species is more deadly than the male' (Kipling 1945: 367, l.15). This is also the conclusion reached by both husband and hunter when comparing notes. Victor's solution is to tear into pieces his female creature, which he refers to as 'the thing' (Shelley 2007: 171). By using this neutering noun, he effectively de-sexes her, just as Mary Shelley's mother, Mary Wollstonecraft, had been de-sexed by Richard Polwhele, in his poem *The Unsex'd Females* (1798), for her transgressive love affairs and radical critique, *A Vindication of the Rights of Woman* (1792). In Shelley Jackson's feminist adaptation of *Frankenstein*, the hypertext *Patchwork Girl* (1995), the fractured female monster is pieced back together by the character Mary Shelley, while her body parts are given a voice, enabling them to tell their own story, thus providing a further layer of reintegration. Women have frequently been identified by parts of their bodies, whether it be mouth, breast or genitalia, which have all too often been separated from the whole in an erasure of individuality and denial of integral personhood. Fragmentation is conducive to hybridity, the stuff of monstrosity, particularly when seen as a collection of incongruent parts. The non-linearity of Jackson's digital and interactive novel allows the reader to unlock narratives contained within individual organs and limbs, which connect them back to their original owners, as well as to a collective women's history and greater sense of female unity. In another feminist novel, Elizabeth Hand rehabilitates the incinerated female monster, blown up by the male monster in the scientist's laboratory, at the end of James Whale's film, *Bride of Frankenstein* (1935). In this novel of that name, Hand celebrates the autonomous patchwork self, as well as her heroine's scarred and singed female body, in order to represent a painfully achieved female subjectivity. Her bride of Frankenstein names herself Pandora, as opposed to Shelley's unnamed female monster. She is given the opportunity to take control of the world by joining an all-female triumvirate, which includes the fembot from Fritz Lang's film *Metropolis* (1927). Not only does Pandora reject this dominant role, but she even saves the life of her creator who, in Shelley's novel, had destroyed her.[4] Conversely, the bride of Frankenstein figure in H. G. Wells's *The Island of Doctor Moreau* (1896) is a puma woman, 'scarred, red, and bandaged' (Wells 2005: 50), who does not hesitate to kill the scientist who recreated her from an animal. This is Dr Moreau, a sadistic father figure, whose experimental vivisections produce human and animal hybrids, which can be seen as a Gothicisation of miscegenation.

Another *fin-de-siècle* Gothic novel involving unspeakable scientific experiments is Florence Marryat's *The Blood of the Vampire* (1897), in which the mixing of race is addressed more directly. The heroine Harriet Brandt, who as a child was called 'the puma's cub' (Marryat 2009: 199), is the offspring of a mad scientist and an Obeah sorceress. Her father Henry trained in Switzerland with vivisectionists, who ostracised him for his barbarism. He continues his horrific experiments in Jamaica, until both he and his mistress are killed by locals, aghast at the atrocities carried out in his laboratory on humans and animals. His daughter Harriet has a draining and sickening effect on those she encounters, even though she does not actually drink blood. Her grandmother was a slave, who had been bitten by a vampire bat, while her mother is said to be not a woman but a fiend, who took sadistic pleasure in watching the dying agonies resulting from her 'brutal protector's' experiments. Harriet is also illegitimate, being the daughter of a man, 'cruel, dastardly [and] godless' and whose 'terrible mother' is described in a string of racist stereotypes, as 'a sensual, self-loving, crafty and bloodthirsty half-caste' (83–4). The verdict on her disastrous parentage is that she inherited a curse of 'black blood and of the vampire's blood which kills everything which it caresses' (188).

The novel was published in the same year as Bram Stoker's *Dracula*, in which the body of the female vampire is also racially inflected, only this time as the product of an unholy sexual alliance with an undesirable foreign aristocrat. Count Dracula's victims are transformed into blood-sucking *femmes fatales* with voluptuous red lips and white sharpened teeth. These include the three vampire women in his castle, who attempt to seduce the imprisoned Jonathan Harker and Lucy Westenra, the lascivious temptress whose eyes have become 'unclean and full of hell-fire, instead of the pure, gentle orbs we knew' (Stoker 1998: 249). Here she may be seen appropriating the male gaze, another attribute of the phallic or castrating woman. Metaphorically, the phallus is turned against these female vampires when destroyed by a stake through the heart. A further stage in the process of de-vampirisation, which can be read as de-sexualisation, is decapitation, identified by Freud with castration, while the stuffing of Lucy's mouth with garlic is metonymic for the stopping up of the marauding vagina. Before joining the ranks of the undead, she is treated with blood transfusions donated by the band of vampire hunters, including her former suitor Dr John Seward and fiancé Arthur Holmwood. As Professor Abraham Van Helsing, who masterminded the 'cure', insists: 'A brave man's blood is the best thing on this earth when a woman is in trouble' (186). This gendering of blood suggests that female blood is inferior to male and certainly it was tainted by its association with menstrual blood. The sanguinary losses experienced by Lucy have similarities with the draining effects of the menses.

Vampirism itself can be seen as a metaphor for menstruation. There was a time when menstruating women were banned from entering churches in England, and their reflection believed to dim mirrors (Walker 1983: 643). Similarly, churches have been beyond the pale for vampires, who, traditionally, have no reflection in a looking glass. In *Dracula* (1989), Liz Lochhead's adaptation of the novel for the stage, reference is made to menstrual cramps and the menarche as a visitor in the middle of the night, whose nocturnal visits resemble that of the vampire. The post-menopausal woman is represented as vampiric in Braddon's 'Good Lady Ducayne' (1896), where a mysterious old woman drains the blood of her young companions, which keeps her alive, even though she continues to age. More commonly, female vampires are equated with eternal youth. This offers a supernatural solution to the ever-changing female body in its passage from menarche to menopause or from puberty to old age. Yet the vampire body can go on to acquire new forms of mutability. In the case of Stoker's Lucy, she snarls like a cat and hunts for prey on Hampstead Heath. Facing her opponents, 'the brows were wrinkled as though the folds of the flesh were the coils of Medusa's snakes, and the lovely, blood-stained mouth grew to an open square' (Stoker 1998:

250). This may also be seen as a close encounter with menstrual taboo for, according to misogynist myth, the menstruating female could be lethal to the male (Walker 1983: 641–2). Having transmogrified into a powerful phallic woman, it is inevitable that Lucy will be vanquished by Professor Van Helsing and his band of 'good brave men' (Stoker 1998: 351). She brazenly displays the life and death power of the Gorgon, the ultimate *femme fatale*, for as Dr Seward observes: 'If ever a face meant death – if looks could kill – we saw it at that moment' (250).

During the twentieth century, literary representations of Medusa's castrating gaze have been extended through C. L. Moore's 'Shambleau' (1933), Susan Hill's *The Woman in Black* (1983) and Tanith Lee's 'The Gorgon' (1985). Moore's tale has a science-fiction setting, featuring the extra-terrestrial Shambleau, whom the narrator, Northwest Smith, finds sexually attractive. A cross between the Medusa and a vampire, she feeds on the life-force of others. Her hair is a crawling mass of slimy red tentacles and survival depends upon avoiding her gaze. Hill's version of the Medusa also crosses genres, this time into the ghost story, *The Woman in Black*, in which the malevolent ghost of Jennet Humfrye appears. Once beautiful, she is now a hideous spectre, whose appearance bears the marks of a disfiguring wasting disease so much so 'that it would not have been a kindness to gaze upon her' (32). Those who do look at her, soon discover that she is a presage of death, an evil born from the grief of having lost her son in a fatal accident. As he had been conceived out of wedlock, Jennet was forced to give him up to her sister and deny her own motherhood. Like the original Medusa, who turns into stone those who look directly at her, she has been punished for sexual transgression. In retaliation for her maternal deprivation, the woman in black embarks on an after-life vendetta by targeting other children. On first encountering her, the narrator is unaware that he is beholding a lethal ghost. As a result he loses not only his child but also, in an added twist, his wife. Tanith Lee's short story 'The Gorgon' is another variation on the theme of the classical Medusa. The legend is evoked through the story of a masked woman on a Greek island, who attracts the attentions of a male writer. His curiosity to see what lies behind her mask replays the Radcliffean heroine's desire to discover what is concealed behind the black veil. The woman is persuaded to remove the mask and reveals a face frozen in a rictus of horror, the sight of which has the power to render the writer's pen impotent. In his essay, 'Medusa's Head' (1922), Freud interprets the terror of Medusa as reflecting the castration complex for a young boy, on realising that the female has no penis and seeing her resemblance to a castrated male. The result can be a freezing or petrifying reaction, manifesting in a stiffening of the penis, as a powerful reminder of the vulnerability of the male. Even though Freud's castration complex is a danger emanating from the father, C. D. Daly has challenged his view by arguing that it is menstruation which ought to be seen as the real threat (see Mulvey-Roberts 2005).

Castration anxiety informs the misogynist myth of the *vagina dentata*, a horrific image conveying the dread that the female will eat or castrate the male during sexual intercourse. In Chinese patriarchy, the female genitals were regarded not only as a gateway to immortality but also as 'executioners of men' (Walker 1983: 1034). The collapse of the categories separating mouth and vagina is demonstrated by the Greek concept of the Lamiae, 'lustful she-demons, born of the Libyan snake-goddess Lamia', whose name means either 'lecherous vaginas' or 'gluttonous gullets' (1035).[5] The myth of the *vagina dentata* is deconstructed by Edgar Allan Poe and Angela Carter, who demonstrate how fears of the feminine continue to be articulated through the female body and its constituent parts. Poe's story 'Berenice' (1835) displaces the anxieties and fascination surrounding the fanged vagina. Egaeus has a fetishist fixation with 'the white and ghastly spectrum of the teeth' of his cousin and fiancée Berenice, who dies of epilepsy: 'The teeth! – the teeth! they were here, and there, and everywhere, and visibly and palpably before me' (Poe 1982: 646). After her death and burial, a servant informs Egaeus that Berenice is still alive and that her coffin has been disturbed. In the library on his desk sits an ivory box containing instruments of dental surgery and extracted teeth along with an open book, in which a line of poetry has been underscored. Tellingly, it expresses the comfort in visiting the grave of a beloved.

In Angela Carter's 'The Lady of the House of Love' (1979), the *vagina dentata* is synonymous with the rose. The heroine is the 'queen of the vampires' (Carter 1986: 93) and mistress of disintegration, whose beauty is an abnormality, because it is so unnaturally perfect. From between her thighs, she plucks a 'dark, fanged rose', which is 'like a flower laid on a grave' (107) and leaves it for a young man who has visited her castle. Her intended conflation of sex and death was to have been enacted through taking this surrogate bridegroom to her bed and to his death but, as it transpires, he drinks her blood instead, thus ending her unnatural existence. After her death, he goes to his barracks, shortly before his regiment leaves for France, and attempts to revive the rose by placing it in water. When the 'monstrous flower' blooms with 'corrupt, brilliant, baleful splendour' (108), the destructive power of the *vagina dentata* it represents points to the red poppy of the battlefield, which has come to signify the bloodshed of the First World War. Fear of the toothed vagina is almost literalised in Carter's novel, *The Passion of*

New Eve (1977) by Zero, the cult leader of a band of women, who has their incisor teeth removed to protect himself from castration when they are performing fellatio on him. The cult members invade the glass-and-mirrors house of the reclusive screen goddess, Tristessa, who turns out to be a male-to-female transvestite. The house is a museum of life-size waxwork effigies of movie stars, which they dismember, rearranging body parts and jumbling up gender differences in a demonstration of Judith Butler's theory of gender as performance, which had already been exemplified by Tristessa (see Butler 1990; 1993). Zero and his women parody Charles Manson and his harem, known as 'the family', who carried out the murder of Hollywood actress Sharon Tate. She appeared in several horror films including *Eye of the Devil* (1966), *Rosemary's Baby* (1968) and the comic horror, *The Fearless Vampire Killers* (1967), directed by her husband Roman Polanski. What remains particularly horrific about the killing is the fact that Tate was eight-and-a-half months pregnant.

Giving birth used to be far more hazardous for women than nowadays, especially since in certain families and religions, the life of the baby could be prioritised over that of the mother. Stephenie Meyer, author of the *Twilight* tetralogy, evokes such sacrificial motherhood, alongside the perils of childbirth. Her heroine Bella Swan is pregnant and the baby, fathered by vampire Edward Cullen, threatens to destroy her body from the inside out, causing considerable pain. Despite the mother's life being endangered, Bella refuses to terminate the pregnancy. It is likely that she had calculated, correctly as it turns out, that Edward will turn her into a vampire, rather than let her die. In Meyer's fictional world, vampires have their own specific supernatural skills and once Bella joins this elite, her post-maternal body becomes an almost invincible shield, with which she protects others. The simpering love-struck girl has been transformed into the most powerful member of the Cullen vampire family. In the final novel, *Breaking Dawn* (2008), Bella demonstrates her powers against the Volturi, a vampire coven based in Volterra in Tuscany. They resemble a latter-day Italian Inquisition, and recruit members with special powers, including Jane, who, in being able to convey the illusion of agonising pain, effectively substitutes for a dungeon of torture instruments.

Bella's vampire transformation changes her body into that of a powerful maternal figure, who is also wealthy and stunningly beautiful. Her resemblance to a super-model sends out a message to women today, pointing to the material and corporeal rewards of motherhood, which incorporates the ideals of youth and beauty. In the world of *Twilight*, these attributes are acquired through the risky and painful transition from human to vampire. A parallel may be drawn with current procedures for cosmetic rejuvenation, some of which sound like a recipe for Gothic horror. These include: the paralysing poison of Botox; the Vampire Facelift, involving a blood transfusion for smoothing out wrinkles; the burning or abrasion of the facial epidermis with a laser, to improve the complexion; and the wielding of a surgeon's knife. Fay Weldon in *The Life and Loves of a She Devil* (1983) draws on the techniques of cosmetic surgery to empower one woman to wreak revenge upon another, as happens when Ruth Pratchett's husband Bobbo is stolen by the successful romance novelist Mary Fisher. The big, dark and ugly Ruth recreates herself in the image of her petite, fair and pretty rival, for the purpose of destroying her. This doubling is a modern version of Victoria's destruction of her doppelgänger Lilla in Dacre's *Zofloya*.

The eroticisation of women's bodies whether modestly covered or glaringly exposed is evident from the female Gothic body in Lewis's *The Monk*. Near the start of the novel, the virtuous churchgoing Antonia is veiled, arousing Lorenzo's passionate desire to unveil her.[6] On becoming the victim of religious corruption, Antonia is secretly observed undressing with the help of a magic mirror for the voyeuristic delectation of the monk, Ambrosio, as a prelude to her rape and murder. Similarly today, at one extreme, is the fully veiled woman wearing the niqab, whose body is denied to the world, and at the other is the denuded and debased female body that has been rendered pornographic. As a kind of living death of the female body, they conjoin in conveying fears of the feminine. Both have a curious dependency on the Other, sustained by the Male Gaze. Ideally the Gothic female body functions as an ongoing critique of such gender inequalities, though it can still reinforce the monstrosity of these figurations. The misogyny to be found in Gothicised literary representation is a permeable membrane to the outside world. This mirrors in myriad ways the violations perpetrated against the female body which continue unabated today in the form of domestic violence, femicide, sex slavery, the trafficking of women and girls, female genital mutilation, child brides, honour killings, bride burning, female infanticide, rape as a weapon of war, and other such everyday horrors.

Notes

I would like to thank Andrew Smith for introducing me to Shambleau, and Nigel Biggs, Zoe Brennan and Marion Glastonbury for commenting on my draft.

1. Dacre wrote poetry under the name of 'Rosa Matilda' in a blatant homage to Lewis's *The Monk*, in which Matilda disguises herself as the novice Rosario.
2. Edgar Allan Poe's controversial statement, 'the death of a beautiful woman is, unquestionably, the most poetical topic in the world' is seen by Elisabeth Bronfen to have a perversely logical significance for Western cultural myth. See Bronfen 1992: 59–75.
3. The novel was actually published posthumously in December 1817, though 1818 appears on the title page.
4. This is the benign Dr Pretorius. Pandora is the brain-child of two scientists, the other being the malevolent Dr Henry Frankenstein. For a discussion of the novel, see Mulvey-Roberts 2011.
5. John Keats's narrative poem, Lamia (1820) concerns Lycius, a young man from Corinth, who falls in love with Lamia without realising that she is a serpent inhabiting the body of a beautiful woman.
6. The veil as Gothic trope is explored in Sedgwick 1986: 140–75.

Bibliography

Bakhtin, Mikhail [1965] (1984), *Rabelais and his World*, trans. Helene Iswolsky, Bloomington: Indiana University Press.

Battersby, Christine (1998), *The Phenomenal Woman: Feminist Metaphysics and the Patterns of Identity*, London: Polity Press.

Beizer, Janet (1994), *Ventriloquized Bodies: Narratives of Hysteria in Nineteenth-Century France*, Ithaca, NY, and London: Cornell University Press.

Bronfen, Elisabeth (1992), *Over Her Dead Body: Death, Femininity and the Aesthetic*, Manchester: Manchester University Press.

Brontë, Charlotte [1847] (1966), *Jane Eyre*, ed. Michael Mason, London: Penguin.

Bulwer Lytton, Edward [1846] (1874), *Lucretia; or The Children of Night*, London: Routledge.

Butler, Judith (1990), *Gender Trouble: Feminism and the Subversion of Identity*, New York: Routledge.

Butler, Judith (1993), *Bodies that Matter: On the Discursive Limits of Sex*, New York: Routledge.

Carter, Angela (1977), *The Passion of New Eve*, London: Gollancz.

Carter, Angela [1979] (1986), 'The Lady of the House of Love', in *The Bloody Chamber*, Harmondsworth: Penguin, pp. 93–107.

Craciun, Adriana (2003), *Fatal Women of Romanticism*, Cambridge: Cambridge University Press.

Creed, Barbara (1993), *The Monstrous-Feminine: Film, Feminism, Psychoanalysis*, London and New York: Routledge.

Dacre, Charlotte [1806] (1997), *Zofloya; or, The Moor: A Romance of the Fifteenth Century*, ed. Adriana Craciun, Peterborough, ON: Broadview Press.

Dijkstra, Bram (1986), *Idols of Perversity: Fantasies of Feminine Evil in Fin-de-Siècle Culture*, New York and Oxford: Oxford University Press.

Gilmore, David D. (2001), *Misogyny: The Male Malady*, Philadelphia: University of Pennsylvania Press.

Hill, Susan [1983] (1989), *The Woman in Black*, Harlow: Vintage/Longman.

Jackson, Shelley (1995), *Patchwork Girl*, Watertown, MA: Eastgate Systems.

Kipling, Rudyard [1911] (1945), 'The Female of the Species', in *The Definitive Edition of Rudyard Kipling's Verse*, London: Hodder and Stoughton, pp. 367–9.

Lee, Tanith (1985), 'The Gorgon', in *The Gorgon and Other Beastly Tales*, New York: DAW Books.

Marryat, Florence [1897] (2009), *The Blood of the Vampire*, ed. Brenda Hammack, Kansas City, MO: Valancourt Books.

Miles, Robert (1993), *Gothic Writing 1750–1820: A Genealogy*, London: Routledge.

Moore, C. L. [1933] (1953), 'Shambleau', in Moore, *Shambleau and Others*, New York: Gnome Press.

Mulvey-Roberts, M. (2005), 'Menstrual Misogyny and Taboo: The Medusa, Vampire and the Female Stigmatic', in Andrew Shail and Gillian Howie (eds), *Menstruation: A Cultural History*, Basingstoke: Palgrave Macmillan, pp. 149–61.

Mulvey-Roberts, Marie (2011), 'Cinematic Femmes Fatales and Weimar Germany in Elizabeth Hand's *The Bride of Frankenstein: Pandora's Bride*', in *Twenty-First Century Gothic: Great Gothic Novels Since 2000*, ed. Danel Olson, Lanham, MD: The Scarecrow Press, pp. 50–9.

Poe, Edgar Allan [1835] (1982), 'Berenice', in *The Complete Tales and Poems of Edgar Allan Poe*, London: Penguin, pp. 642–8.

Sedgwick, Eve Kosofsky [1980] (1986), *The Coherence of Gothic Conventions*, New York and London: Methuen.

Shelley, Mary [1818] (2007), *Frankenstein or The Modern Prometheus*, ed. Maurice Hindle, London: Penguin.

Stallybrass, Peter (1986), 'Patriarchal Territories: The Body Enclosed', in Margaret W. Ferguson, Maureen Quilligan and Nancy J. Vickers (eds), *Rewriting the Renaissance: The Discourse of Sexual Difference in Early Modern Europe*, Chicago and London: University of Chicago Press, pp. 123–42.

Stoker, Bram [1897] (1998), *Dracula*, ed. Glennis Byron, Peterborough, ON: Broadview Press.

Vice, Sue (1997), *Introducing Bakhtin*, Manchester: Manchester University Press.

Vicinus, Martha (ed.) (1972), *Suffer and Be Silent: Women in the Victorian Age*, Bloomington and Indianapolis: Indiana University Press.

Walker, Barbara, G. (1983*)*, *The Woman's Encyclopedia of Myths and Secrets*, New York: HarperSanFrancisco.

Weldon, Fay (1983), *The Life and Loves of a She Devil*, London: Hodder and Stoughton.

Wells, H. G. [1896] (2005), *The Island of Doctor Moreau*, ed. Patrick Parrinder, London: Penguin.

Chapter 8

Spectral Femininity
Rebecca Munford

> The ghost ... is a paradox. Though non-existent, it nonetheless *appears*.
>
> (Terry Castle, *The Apparitional Lesbian*, p. 46)

Spectres are the lifeblood of the Gothic. Ghosts, phantoms, apparitions and revenants return to the Gothic scene again and again, giving expression to its preoccupation with the fragile thresholds of mind and body and the phantasmatic aspects of language. Owing to its cultural associations with the territories of irrationality, otherness and corporeal excess, femininity has been particularly and peculiarly susceptible to 'spectralisation'. From the 'spectral presence' of the 'dead-undead mother, archaic and all-encompassing' (Kahane 1985: 336) that haunts the Radcliffean Gothic heroine and the feminist critical imagination alike, to the female revenants and ghoulish women conjured in the macabre writings of those such as Edgar Allan Poe and Charles Baudelaire, the Gothic brings into view the troubling movements of wraithlike women.

Etymologically related as much to the sphere of vision as to the realm of phantoms, the 'spectre' (from the Latin *specere*, meaning 'to look, see') signifies both that which is looked at and the act of looking. It is owing to this connection between the spectacle and the specular, suggest María de Pilar Blanco and Esther Peeren, that the spectre is especially suitable 'for exploring and illuminating phenomena other than the putative return of the dead' (2013: 2). In *Specters of Marx* (1993), a text that insistently ghosts discussions of spectrality, Jacques Derrida offers 'hauntology', with its evocation and radical unsettling of 'ontology', as a new way of thinking about being (with ghosts). According to Derrida, learning to live with ghosts would be to live 'otherwise' and, crucially, 'more justly'; for 'being-with specters would also be, not only but also, a *politics* of memory, of inheritance and generations' (Derrida 1994:

xviii). A way of living 'between all of the "two's" one likes' (1994: xvii), Derrida's hauntology attributes to the ghost a paradoxical status as neither being nor non-being that brings into view the spectrality of identity. Most particularly for this discussion, Derrida's account of the spectre emphasises its uncertain status as 'a furtive and ungraspable visibility, or an invisibility of a visible X ... the tangible intangibility of a proper body without flesh, but still the body of some*one* or some*one* other' (1994: 6). Neither fully present nor fully absent, material nor immaterial, the spectre not only troubles the stability of the subject but renders categories of identity – including gender and sexuality – uncertain and undecidable.

In *The Female Thermometer* (1995), Terry Castle argues that the late eighteenth century saw the disappearance of 'old-fashioned' ghosts and the emergence of an altogether different kind of apparition, one that belongs to the inner world of the mind (Castle 1995: 123). Castle avers that a crucial feature of this new post-Enlightenment sensibility, which becomes naturalised in the twentieth century, is 'a growing sense of the ghostliness of other people' – a tendency to 'spectralise' the other that rendered his or her corporeality 'strangely insubstantial and indistinct' (1995: 125). For Castle, this new model of consciousness (the Gothic underside of romantic individualism) is heralded in the work of Ann Radcliffe, and particularly the apparitional language of *The Mysteries of Udolpho* (1794), which makes ambiguous the boundary between life and death, the present and the absent. It is with Castle's anatomisation of the 'the uncanny Radcliffean metaphor of haunted consciousness' (1995: 137) in mind that this chapter turns its attention to the relationship between female subjectivity and spectralisation in three Gothic texts – Daphne du Maurier's *Rebecca* (1938), Shirley Jackson's *The Haunting of Hill House* (1959) and Ali Smith's *Hotel World* (2001) – in which ghostly representations and narrative effects make present experiences of social invisibility and historical dispossession, as well as anxieties about the 'visibility' of new models of 'femininity' emerging in the twentieth century. Foregrounding its status as a kind of 'spectrality effect' (Derrida 1994: 48), this discussion considers how 'femininity', constructed through the insistent repetition and return of corporeal gestures and impressions, might share the ghost's paradoxical position – as something that is 'non-existent' but which 'nonetheless *appears*' (Castle 1993: 46).

'You can't possibly not appear':
Daphne du Maurier's *Rebecca*

There has scarcely been a more emphatic example of spectral femininity than that of Daphne du Maurier's *Rebecca*, both in terms of the novel's complex reiterations of spectrality and spectralisation, and its haunting presence, its ghostly visitations and returns, in subsequent Gothic writing by women. Allan Lloyd Smith points out that the very name 'Rebecca' includes 'the suggestion of a revenant: *Rebecca*, who comes again, who *beckons* again' (Smith 1992: 304). Certainly, the novel's preoccupation with revenance, repetition and return is embodied (or, rather, disembodied) by Rebecca, whose ghostly presence in Manderley becomes the focus for the nameless narrator's anxieties about her own social visibility and presence. *Rebecca* is haunted by a Gothic tradition concerned with the troubling figure of the 'other woman', most notably the representation of Bertha Mason, 'the foul German spectre' in *Jane Eyre* (1847), who, as Avril Horner and Sue Zlosnik point out, is 'Otherised' through the supernatural (Horner and Zlosnik 2000: 212). Rebecca has thus been cast in the spectral guises of uncanny double, ghost, vampire and phantom. For Neil Badmington, discussing Alfred Hitchcock's film adaptation of the novel, it is precisely Rebecca's undecidability that suggests her status as a spectre (or 'SpectRebecca' in his coinage) who 'is neither perfectly present nor absolutely absent, neither wholly alive nor definitely dead' (Badmington 2011: 207). Yet, Rebecca is not the only ghostly presence in du Maurier's novel. If Manderley is a haunted house, and Rebecca its revenant, they are so because of the novel's spectralising first-person narration.

From her arrival in Manderley, the nameless narrator is spooked by various 'ghostly yet corporeal trace[s]' (Horner and Zlosnik 2000: 209) of her predecessor, the first Mrs de Winter. Sitting in the library, she becomes conscious that she 'was not the first one to lounge there in possession of the chair' (2003: 86); she feels herself to be occupying the 'imprint' on the cushions and the arm rest of Rebecca's bodily contours, and to be touching the silver coffee pot and cup once caressed by Rebecca's hands and lips. The narrator's experience of Rebecca's ghostly presence is heightened by the supernatural vocabulary of 'possession' that marks her narration; her spectralised language makes present the absent other woman as a chilling corporeal effect when she 'unconsciously' shivers 'as though someone had opened the door ... and let a draught into the room' (du Maurier 2003: 87). Horner and Zlosnik argue that it is Rebecca's handwriting that most powerfully 'constitutes the metonymic representation of her body through the text, indelibly inscribing her presence' (2000: 215). In stark contrast to the narrator's 'cramped and unformed' scrawl (du Maurier 2003: 98), Rebecca's script appears to be vibrant and vital: 'How alive was her writing ... how full of force. Those curious, sloping letters. The blob of ink. Done yesterday. It was just as if it had been written yesterday' (63). If her reading of Rebecca's inky, permeable script is an act of spectralisation – a way of summoning a living image of the 'other woman' – it is one that the narrator attributes to the urgent whispers of a 'demon', placing herself in dialogue with the otherworldly. While Rebecca, the 'ghost', becomes animate, it is the narrator who is 'Otherised' through her association with the supernatural.

Rebecca's palpable absence is not only felt in the disquieting spectral effects of her handwriting but in the ghostliness of her clothing, the garments and accessories that she has left behind, in which traces of her body and, more particularly for the narrator, her embodied femininity remain. Elizabeth Wilson highlights the uncanniness of garments that have had 'an intimate relationship with human beings long since gone to their graves', arguing that they 'are so much part of our living, moving selves ... that they hint at something only half understood, sinister, threatening; the atrophy of the body, and the evanescence of life' (Wilson 2003: 1). Touched by bodies that are no longer present, uninhabited clothing has a peculiarly spectral quality, offering a tangible reminder of the otherwise intangible, absent body. Dressed in her predecessor's old mackintosh, which is too large for her, the nameless narrator imagines Rebecca wearing it 'over her shoulders like a cape, or ... loose, hanging open, her hands deep in the pockets' (du Maurier 2003: 133). Appearing in the garb of the other woman, the nameless narrator herself feels diminished and insubstantial. Uncomfortable and awkward in her dowdy and 'ill-fitting' clothes (30), she sees in Rebecca an at once enthralling and unsettling image of accomplished 'femininity' and, most particularly, of the sexually confident and fashionable 'modern' woman, that she is unable to inhabit. The narrator is captivated by the fashionable dresses and accessories in Rebecca's wardrobe, from which wafts a 'breath' of azalea scent. But this 'breath' of Rebecca does not animate her. Rather, with the appearance of Mrs Danvers, whose 'skull's face, parchment-white, set on a skeleton's frame' (74), makes her (from the spectralising perspective of the narrator at least) a peculiarly otherworldly figure, she finds herself 'like a dumb thing' (189). Indeed, images of dumbness and dummies run throughout the narrative. While Rebecca's clothes are a reminder/remainder of her embodied femininity, time and again the narrator envisages herself as a 'dummy' or a 'dumb thing' – as a spectral 'body without flesh' and a subject without words. Ethereal, insubstantial and nameless, she too haunts Manderley like a living ghost whose 'own dull self did not exist' (225). Rebecca's phantasmal status in the text might thus be read as a symptom of the narrator's self-spectralisation; the haunting threat that the body of the other (woman) might materialise finds its reflection in the narrator's anxiety about her own disembodiment – and her ability, like that of the ghost, to 'appear' in her proper role as Mrs de Winter.

The narrator's disquiet about the appearance (the 'look' and 'presence') of her 'femininity' is crystallised at the fancy-dress ball that takes place at Manderley. Inveigled by Mrs Danvers to dress as Caroline de Winter, a 'famous London beauty' (227) and sister of Maxim's great-great-grandfather, whose portrait hangs over the staircase, the narrator feels revitalised by the possibility of masquerading in an image of femininity drawn from the past, one that is previous to Rebecca's modern and sexually ambiguous femininity (she bemoans, for example, degrading the house 'with our modern jig-tunes, so out-of-place and unromantic' (237)). It is thus by making of herself an anachronism, and dressing in a copy (repetition) of Caroline's white dress with puffed sleeves and a small bodice, that the narrator hopes to body herself forth at a distance from Rebecca. In this anachronistic garb, she feels 'different already, no longer hampered by my appearance' (236). However, if the narrator is finally able to 'appear', she can do so only *as a ghost*, masquerading, unknowingly, as her own predecessor, the first Mrs de Winter (who dressed as Caroline at the previous Manderley ball). As Peter Buse and Andrew Stott suggest, 'anachronism might well be the defining features of ghosts, now and in the past, because haunting, by its very structure, implies a deformation of linear temporality (Buse and Stott 1999: 1). Caught up in a ghostly cycle of repetitions and returns, the narrator is left once again without language; like a 'dummy' she is unable to speak. Sent by Maxim to dress instead in 'an ordinary evening frock' (240), she is urged too by Beatrice to return to the ball because she 'can't possibly not appear' (243). The narrator is compelled to assume the clothes of conventionality that will once again make visible her proper femininity. Yet, in so doing she remains a strangely anachronistic figure. 'Appearing' in her 'ordinary' evening dress at the fancy dress ball, where others are dressed as 'romantic figure[s] of the past' (250), she remains a temporal anomaly. Watching 'the swaying couples' dancing like 'bobbing marionettes' she experiences herself as disembodied and ghostly: 'it was not I who watched them at all, not someone with feelings, made of flesh and blood, but a dummy-stick of a person' (252). Anachronism thus works here to make visible the model of ordinary, acquiescent femininity as itself a masquerade, as a 'fancy dress' ensemble.

What the narrator's ghostly presence in *Rebecca* reveals, then, is the apparitional nature of femininity, its status as a spectrality effect. When Rebecca's fleshless corpse is eventually returned to the narrative shorn of its clothes (including the boyish trousers that signal her ambivalent 'modern' femininity), the nameless narrator appears to inhabit more fully her position as Mrs de Winter, identifying with the old-fashioned paternal authority of her husband, Maxim, who has confessed to killing his first wife. But she remains an anachronism that returns to and from the past. From its famous first sentence, the narrator's present-day account of her dreamed return to Manderley is couched in an idiom of ghostliness: 'I was possessed of a sudden with supernatural powers and passed through the barrier before me' (1). Like all spectres, the nameless narrator *'begins by coming back'* (Derrida 1994: 11). Far more than a novel about a ghost, *Rebecca* is a ghost-written novel; spectrality is the very condition of its narration.

The Spectre That Has No Name: Shirley Jackson's *The Haunting of Hill House*

Shirley Jackson's *The Haunting of Hill House* also belongs to a tradition of Gothic fiction about 'women who just can't seem to get out of the house' (DeLamotte 1990: 10). Published in 1959, and concerned with the spectralising effects of domestic entrapment, Jackson's text might be read more specifically as anticipating some of the concerns articulated in Betty Friedan's seminal work of Second-Wave feminism, *The Feminine Mystique* (1963). A peculiarly Gothic phenomenon, the feminine mystique, Friedan proposes, 'has succeeded in burying millions of American women alive' (Friedan 1965: 293); it represents a turning-away from the educational and intellectual rights won by an earlier generation of feminists and a return to the home and the trappings of domestic femininity. Friedan's analysis illuminates the ghostlike situation of 1950s American housewives, whose feelings of 'emptiness, non-existence, nothingness' prevent them from feeling 'truly alive' (264) and, in so doing, makes visible what she famously describes as 'the problem that has no name' – that is, the problem that 'lay buried, unspoken, for many years in the minds of American women' (13). By calling attention to the indeterminate animism of the housewife, Friedan gives expression to a model of spectral femininity that is profoundly affiliated to the uncanny space of the home.

'Haunting', writes Julian Wolfreys, 'is nothing other than the destabilisation of the domestic scene, as that place where we apparently confirm our identity, our sense of being, where we feel most at home with ourselves' (Wolfreys 2002: 5). In Jackson's *The Haunting of Hill House*, the home is inextricably connected to constructions of female subjectivity in its most ghostly articulations. For Eleanor Vance, who is confined to the house looking after her invalid mother, home is not a space in which she can feel 'truly alive'; neither is it a space where she experiences a clear sense of her identity. Rather, she inhabits a ghostlike state of weariness and despair, unable even to talk 'to another person without self-consciousness and an awkward inability to find words' (Jackson 2009: 7). While looking after her mother, she sets out 'endless little trays' of food and steels herself to the 'filthy laundry', like Friedan's spectral housewife, in the hope that 'someday something would happen' (7–8). When Eleanor's mother dies (after Eleanor fails to hear, or neglects to respond to, her mother's knocking on the wall for her medicine), she is further denied a full adult subjectivity by her infantilising sister and brother-in-law with whom she lives, sleeping in the nursery. It is during her subsequent time at Hill House, however, that she comes to be 'walled up alive' (240) in a yet more disturbing enactment of the domestic scene.[7]

Eleanor is invited to the 'honestly haunted' Hill House as one of three 'research assistants' (along with Luke Sanderson, a member of the family who own the house, and the bohemian Theodora, who has had a violent quarrel with her flatmate) assembled by the ghost hunter Dr Montague to investigate 'supernatural manifestations' (4). At first she sees in this invitation an opportunity to confirm her identity and sense of being outside of her daughterly role of domestic duty. But the exhilaration of expectation soon gives way to anxiety and uncertainty when she arrives at the startlingly animate Hill House, the hauntedness of which is associated with maternal possession. In the words of Luke, Hill House is a 'Mother house ... a house mother, a headmistress, a housemistress' (211). Indeed, the very walls of the house become a site for the spectral projection of Eleanor's guilt about her mother's death when they mysteriously bear the message 'HELP ELEANOR COME HOME'. When Eleanor sees the writing on the wall and realises that the ghost 'knows [her] name' (146), she experiences a moment of corporeal estrangement that accelerates her feelings of dispersal and dissolution: 'It's my own dear name, and it belongs to me, and something is using it and writing it and calling me with it and my own *name* ... I *hate* seeing myself dissolve and slip and separate' (160). Insofar as Eleanor's spectrality lies in her indeterminate presence and sense of being, it resonates with Derrida's notion of the spectre as 'something that one does not know, precisely, and one does not know if precisely it is, if it exists, if it responds to a name and corresponds to an essence' (Derrida 1994: 5). Hill House appears at times to offer a space in which Eleanor can feel 'at home' with herself as '[a]n Eleanor who belongs, who is talking easily' (Jackson 2009: 61). She is able too to know herself more fully as an independent being: 'what a complete and separate thing I am, she thought, going from my red toes to the top of my head, individually an I, possessed of attributes belonging only to me' (83). Although Eleanor's sense of selfhood is rooted here in her understanding of the tangibility of her body, the detached tone and use of indefinite articles ('an Eleanor', 'an I') marking her focalised narrative suggest that her presence and self-possession are rather more fragile. Indeed, these spectralising linguistic gestures work to unsettle and destabilise her sense of self by calling into question the ability of a name to correspond 'to an essence' and blurring the boundary between mind and body.

In *The Haunting of Hill House*, the spectrality of the body is linked in particular to the ghostly image of the hand (writing on the wall) that at once inscribes and makes it absent. Contemplating the ontological status of hands in the act of writing, Judith Butler argues that:

> There is no writing without the body, but no body fully appears along with the writing that it produces ... the text quite literally leaves the authorial body behind, and yet there one is, on the page, strange to oneself. (Butler 1997: 11)

The ghostly status of hands in Jackson's novel is initially intimated by Luke's spooky allusion to the 'disembodied hand in the soup' (Jackson 2009: 69), which gestures to the Old Testament story of King Belshazzar's banquet and the appearance of a disembodied hand writing a message on the wall portending the end of the Babylonian Kingdom (Daniel 5: 5–7). The writing on the wall in Hill House (of which Eleanor is the suspected author) similarly becomes an ominous sign of Eleanor's impending estrangement and dissolution. Hand imagery returns again and again in the narrative, most notably when the tangibility of the body (and its relation to the body of the Other) is being called into question. Eleanor and Theodora hold one another's hands frequently at moments of fear and uncertainty, on occasion 'so hard that each of them could feel the other's bones' (161); and, in one of the novel's most chilling moments, Eleanor asks in an exclamation of terror 'God God – whose hand was I holding?' (163), evoking the image of the disembodied hand to render uncertain (and ghostly) the presence of Theodora lying in the bed beside her.

If the ghostly happenings in Hill House are linked to Eleanor's projected feelings of guilt at her mother's death, they also illuminate her ambivalent desire for Theodora, to whom she is immediately drawn and quickly comes to think of as 'close and vital' (49). Like Rebecca (whose apparitional status and ambiguous relationship with the ghostly Mrs Danvers, or 'Danny', invites an interpretation in terms of same-sex desire), Theodora represents the modern and sexually confident woman who exists outside of patriarchal familial structures. In *The Apparitional Lesbian* , Terry Castle illuminates and explores the longstanding association between ghostliness and lesbianism, drawing attention to the ways in which the lesbian has been repeatedly 'ghosted' or made to 'seem invisible' by culture (Castle 1993: 5); lesbianism, she proposes, is the 'repressed idea' at the heart of patriarchal culture (61–2). Eleanor and Theodora are, from the beginning of Jackson's novel, identified with the supernatural. Dr Montague explains that he selected the two women for his study because 'Theodora has shown herself possessed of some telepathic ability, and Eleanor has in the past been intimately involved in poltergeist phenomena' (Jackson 2009: 73); and, on their first meeting, Luke Sanderson addresses them as 'the ghostly inhabitants of Hill House' (57) emphasising further their affinities with the otherworldly.

In one respect, then, the text uses the spectral metaphor to explore cultural anxieties about 'aberrant' female sexuality, the spectralisation of lesbian desire gesturing towards the prospect of its exorcism. The suspicion that Eleanor, a spinster with a privileged relationship to the supernatural, might require some kind of investigation and diagnosis is intimated early in the narrative in her sister's whispered speculation that she has been invited to Hill House to take part in *'experiments'* (8).[8] When pressed by Luke about how he would define Hill House, Dr Montague replies: '"People ... are always so anxious to get things out into the open where they can put a name on them, even a meaningless name, so long as it has a scientific ring"' (69). Given Eleanor's peculiar identification with Hill House, and the text's feminisation of spectrality, the doctor's description of the house as 'disturbed', 'leprous', 'sick' and 'insane' (70) uses a medical register that pathologises aberrant femininity and works to, in Castle's terms, 'derealise' or 'disembody' the lesbian by making her a deathly and ghostly figure (Castle 1993: 34).

Nevertheless, if Jackson's novel never quite brings into view the ghost, what its spectral register does make visible is intimacy between women – exemplified by Theodora's bold promise to Eleanor that 'the two of us will be *visible* from one end of Hill House to the other' in their bright sweaters (Jackson 2009: 47; my emphasis). Time and again, as already suggested, their intimacy is expressed through their bodily proximity and in particular through acts of touching one another's hands. Walking 'side by side' together 'in the most extreme intimacy of expectation', they move too 'along the outskirts of an open question, and once spoken, such a question – as "Do you love me?" – could never be answered or forgotten' (174). This question thought but unspoken by both women echoes Castle's imagining of the 'kiss that doesn't happen, the kiss that can't happen, because one of the women has become a ghost' (Castle 1993: 30) as a crucial metaphor in the apparitional articulation of lesbian desire. Indeed, it is in such moments, when their bodies are touching, when the boundaries between them are uncertain, that Theodora is rendered most ghostly to Eleanor (she notes, for example, that Theodora's 'hand was pale and luminous' (Jackson 2009: 175)). If, in Hill House, the identities of 'ghost' and 'girl-lover' become interchangeable (Castle 1993: 246 n.15), the 'problem that has no name' appearing, ghostlike, at the heart of the patriarchal domestic scene, is lesbian desire.

'Remember you must live': Ali Smith's *Hotel World*

Published in 2001, in the shadows of the 'spectral turn', Ali Smith's *Hotel World* conjures images of spectral femininity as part of its broader exploration of experiences of social invisibility and dereliction in the context of patriarchal global capitalism. Here the haunted house is reconfigured as the multinational Global Hotel that becomes a site for the interconnected spectral narratives of dislocated, liminal women. Indebted to Second-Wave feminist analysis of the female subject's entrapment in imprisoning structures, *Hotel World* resonates too with a third-wave feminist critique of the dispersed modes of power that characterise postmodern culture. While *Rebecca* and *The Haunting of Hill House* are 'ghost-written' by living ghosts seeking to inhabit more fully their subjectivity, in *Hotel World* spectrality is the typical condition of the postmodern subject. The text opens with the ghoulish holler – 'Wooooooooo-hoooooooo' (Smith 2001: 3) – of the already deceased Sara Wilby, a teenage chambermaid who crams herself into a dumb waiter at the hotel and plummets to her death when the cord snaps transforming her into a '[d]ead I' (4). Sara's spectral narrative offers a point of connection for the other (barely) living characters in the text, whose own narratives intersect, fleetingly, across the space of a single night: Else, a homeless woman who sleeps on the street against the hotel walls and who, having lost her vowels, is reduced to uttering guttural noises; Lise, the hotel receptionist whose indeterminate illness means she can no longer find her words; Penny, a hotel reviewer whose appropriation of vacuous corporate language reveals her own emptiness; and Clare, who returns to the hotel dressed in her sister Sara's uniform, hoping to fill in the gaps about her death.

Returning to tell the story of her untimely death, Sara slips in and out of language as both her memory and her words begin to fall away: 'This is how it ended. I climbed into the, the' (Smith 2001: 6). The 'dumb waiter' that is the absent presence in this sentence thus comes to represent both the aporia (the impassable passage) at the centre of the corporate body (the 'nothing that ran the length of this hotel' (145)) and the bodiless spectral subject's precarious relationship to language as she is left 'hanging falling breaking between this word and the next' (31). Marked by absence and loss, Sara's aphasic narrative draws attention to the spectrality of language, which in turn underpins the text's exploration of the relationship between female subjectivity and temporality, of being and time – and, as the verb tenses that furnish the titles of the chapters suggest, of being *in* time. Divided into five parts ('past', 'present historic', 'future conditional', 'perfect', 'future in the past'), connected by the untimely death of Sara Wilby, the spectral structure of *Hotel World* draws attention to the desynchronising gestures of the ghost. 'Furtive and untimely', writes Derrida, 'the apparition of the specter does not belong to that time, it does not give time, not that one' (1994: xix). Troubling temporal boundaries and disordering the chronology of the past, present and future, the spectre signals that, in the words of Derrida quoting Hamlet, '"[t]he time is out of joint": time is *disarticulated*, dislocated, dislodged, time is run down, on the run and run down [*traqué et détraqué*], *deranged*, both out of order and mad' (20). For Derrida, the present is not simply haunted by the ghosts of the past but also by those ghosts that are yet to come (back). To speak about ghosts, he suggests, is to speak about 'inheritance, and generations, and generations of ghosts, which is to say about certain others who are not present, nor presently living, either to us, in us, or outside us' (xviii).

In Smith's novel, the ghost is a similarly anachronistic figure who does not 'belong to that time', but whose return makes visible the ethical bearing of the spectre. Even Sara Wilby's name, as Monica Germanà points out, is 'suggestive of the ghost's permanent anachrony: a repetition of the French "*sera*" and English "will be"' (Germanà 2010: 164). Here Sara's spectral visitation casts lines of connection between the barely 'visible' others of the past, present and the future. While the Global Hotel shares the uniform interior décor repeated throughout its international branches, this particular building was once a house with servants' quarters and, after that, a brothel, 'where the cheap girls, the more diseased or ageing girls, were put to sell their wares' (6). Although the hotel's sterile and homogenising corporate surfaces make invisible this history, the affinity between the servant, the prostitute and the chambermaid in Sara's ghostly narration transforms the architecture of the hotel into a palimpsest, which makes visible once again the spectralising bodily labour of previous generations of women who have been 'put to sell their wares' but are not 'presently living'. Highlighting the women's shared etymological connection to '*corps*', the spectrality effect here reveals that the 'corporate' body cannot fully erase the 'corporeality' of the subjects who inhabit and have inhabited its alienating structures.

Unlike *Rebecca*, where spectral effects emerge from the conspicuous absence of a corpse, Smith's novel returns the ghost to its body. Suspended between worlds and fast slipping away, Sara's ghost longs for the tangibility of bodily matter to give meaning to her nothingness.

> A mouthful of dust would be something ... The rolled-up hairs and dried stuff and specks of what-once-was-skin, all the glamorous leavings of breathing creatures ground to essence and glued together ... Beautiful dirt, grey and vintage, the grime left by life, sticking to the bony roof of a mouth and tasting of next to nothing, which is always better than nothing. (Smith 2001: 5)

In Smith's reimagining of the narrative of spectral visitation, it is the ghost who, in the face of nothingness, is left with nothing but 'words, words, words' (6). Through its multiple echoes of Shakespeare's *Hamlet* (the 'ghost story' on which Derrida's *Specters of Marx* hinges and a text that shares *Hotel World*'s preoccupation with the insides of the body), Sara's spectral narration reconfigures the opposition of being and not-being in terms of nothing and not-nothing. Seeking meaning, she thus moves downwards, travelling through the sodden earth and passing through the 'lid of the wooden room' to commune with her somnolent and taciturn corpse; unable to slip fully back into her 'broken and rotting' body she lies 'half-in, half-out of her under the ruched frills of the room's innards' (14, 15) pressing her to fill in the gaps of her story. The ghost's encounter with her corpse throws into sharp relief the ways in which spectrality highlights the precarious relationship between presence and absence, the material and the immaterial, the corporeal and the ethereal. Although the separation and union of the corpse/spirit (conveyed through the shifting use of pronouns I, she, we) dramatises Cartesian separation, it is the body, with its broken bones and heart jammed in its mouth, that offers a moment, albeit a transitory one, of certainty – 'It's my story, this is it' (17) – for the spirit's aporetic narrative.

In another of its recorporealising gestures, *Hotel World* returns the lesbian body to the text as the corpse narrates the romantic 'fall' and sexual awakening that precedes Sara's fatal descent in the dumb waiter: 'I had expected all my life to fall for some boy, or some man or other, and I had been waiting and watching for him. Then one day my watch stopped' (17). Playing also with the homonym 'watch', the body's story establishes an interconnection between temporality and visibility that centres on Sara's encounter with the girl in the watch shop. Surrounded by 'watches in cabinets, watches in cases, watches all up and down the walls' and wearing the 'only working watch in the shop ... ticking into the warm underside of her wrist' (18), the girl in the shop presents as a timely and embodied subject. Sara, in contrast, is rendered ghostly by her desire as the beautiful watch girl looks 'straight through' her as if she 'wasn't there': 'Falling for her had made me invisible' (23). The spectralising effects of Sara's desire here prefigure her death; her mortal experience is that of the 'apparitional lesbian' who remains a figure of invisibility and 'not-thereness', her story 'a non-concept, a nothingness, a gap in the meaning of things – anything but a story there to be read' (Castle 1993: 67). In *Hotel World*, however, the apparitional metaphor is reimagined (and, to use Castle's term, 'repossessed') through the return of the lesbian body to the narrative scene.[9] In the final section of the novel, 'Present', the title of which captures both narrative tense and the idea of material presence, an omniscient narrator casts her eye up and down the landscape making visible the various ghosts who are 'out and about' (Smith 2001: 226). She reveals that the girl in the watch shop, who is now wearing Sara Wilby's repaired watch and awaiting her return, 'had pretended not to notice S. Wilby ... The timing was wrong' (235). Now feeling the 'small wings moving against the inside of her chest, or something in there anyway, turning, tightened, working' (235), the girl gives belated corporeal expression to lesbian desire as the body reappears to redress the spectralising effects of untimeliness. In turn, her watchful wait for Sara's return gives the spectre a presence that allows her to take leave from the wor(l)d. The reanimation of the Muriel Spark epigraph ('Remember you must die') that reappears at the close of the text – 'remember you must live remember you most love remainder you mist leaf' (237) – suggests how, through its repetitions and returns, the spectre makes visible the possibilities of being (of living and loving) in time.

In du Maurier's *Rebecca* and Jackson's *The Haunting of Hill House*, the power of spectrality lies foremost in its expository and analytical possibilities, its ability to 'explore' and 'illuminate' the category of femininity by making visible its instabilities and contingencies – its 'apparitional' status in patriarchal domestic structures that work to render invisible female agency and desire. In the transitory 'hotel world' of Smith's novel, however, the haunted house motif is used less to make visible the plight of the middle-class woman possessed by the home, as it is to bring into view those whose dispossession leaves them homeless and displaced in a late capitalist culture that dehumanises and spectral-ises its subjects. While the spectral femininity of the nameless narrator and Eleanor condemns them to perennial incompleteness, unable to present fully as embodied subjects, in *Hotel World* the spectre's undecid-ability and indeterminacy become a resource for change and regenera-tion. By bringing the body back to the wor(l)d, and by materialising the affinities between women in the present, past and future, *Hotel World* 'repossesses' the trope of spectrality. Here the absent presence, or invis-ible visibility, of the spectre becomes the site from which new embodied subjectivities and connections are forged in a time that might be – or 'wilby' – (ghost-)written differently.

Notes

1. Eleanor's imprisonment within the ghostly spaces of Hill House is brought to a conclusion at the end of the novel when she drives into a tree and kills herself in its grounds.
2. In light of its publication at the height of the Cold War, the atmosphere of suspicion that haunts Hill House can be interpreted in the context of wider cultural anxieties about the infiltration of the social and political spheres by communists and homosexuals.
3. Castle argues that if used 'imaginatively – repossessed, so to speak – the very trope that evaporates can also solidify. In the strangest turn of all, perhaps, the lesbian body itself returns' (1993: 47).

Bibliography

Badmington, Neil (2011), *Hitchock's Magic*, Cardiff: University of Wales Press.
Blanco, María del Pilar and Esther Peeren (2013), 'Introduction: Conceptualising Spectralities', in María del Pilar Blanco and Esther Peeren (eds), *The Spectralities Reader: Ghosts and Haunting in Contemporary Cultural Theory*, London: Bloomsbury, pp. 1–27.
Buse, Peter and Andrew Stott (1999), 'Introduction: A Future for Haunting', in Peter Buse and Andrew Stott (eds), *Ghosts: Deconstruction, Psychoanalysis, History*, Basingstoke: Palgrave, pp. 1–20.
Butler, Judith (1997), 'How Can I Deny That These Hands and This Body Are Mine?', *Qui Parle,* 11(1): 1–20.
Castle, Terry (1993), *The Apparitional Lesbian: Female Homosexuality and Modern Culture*, New York: Columbia University Press.

Castle, Terry (1995), *The Female Thermometer: Eighteenth-Century Culture and the Invention of the Uncanny*, New York: Oxford University Press.

DeLamotte, Eugenia C. (1990), *Perils of the Night: A Feminist Study of Nineteenth-Century Gothic*, New York: Oxford University Press.

Derrida, Jacques [1993] (1994), *Specters of Marx*, New York: Routledge.

du Maurier, Daphne [1938] (2003), *Rebecca*, London: Virago.

Friedan, Betty [1963] (1965), *The Feminine Mystique*, London: Penguin.

Germanà, Monica (2010), *Scottish Women's Gothic and Fantastic Writing*, Edinburgh: Edinburgh University Press.

Horner, Avril, and Sue Zlosnik (2000), 'Daphne du Maurier and Gothic Signatures: Rebecca as Vamp(ire)', in Avril Horner and Angela Keane (eds), *Body Matters: Feminism, Textuality, Corporeality*, Manchester: Manchester University Press, pp. 209–22.

Jackson, Shirley [1959] (2009), *The Haunting of Hill House*, London: Penguin.

Kahane, Clare (1985), 'The Gothic Mirror', in Shirley Nelson Garner, Claire Kahane and Madelon Sprengnether (eds), *The (M)other Tongue: Essays in Feminist Psychoanalytic Interpretation*, Ithaca, NY: Cornell University Press, pp. 334–51.

Smith, Ali (2001), *Hotel World*, London: Penguin.

Smith, Allan Lloyd (1992), 'The Phantoms of *Drood* and *Rebecca*: The Uncanny Reencountered through Abraham and Torok's "Cryptonymy"', *Poetics Today* 13(2): 285–308.

Wilson, Elizabeth [1985] (2003), *Adorned in Dreams: Fashion and Modernity*, London: I. B. Tauris.

Wolfreys, Julian (2002), *Victorian Hauntings: Spectrality, Gothic, the Uncanny and Literature*, Basingstoke: Palgrave.

Chapter 9

Female Gothic and the Law
Sue Chaplin

Introduction

This chapter offers an analysis of the complex nexus between Female Gothic and law as it has developed over at least two centuries. From its point of origin in the late-eighteenth century, the extent to which the Female Gothic mode has foregrounded, and often sharply interrogated, the position of women in relation to patriarchal legal systems could be regarded as one of its structuring thematic principles. Even in its most conservative forms (see, for instance, the fictions of Eliza Parsons discussed below), Female Gothic repeatedly deploys the conventions of Gothic fiction in order to represent the extent to which the law in various ways facilitates the incapacitation and maltreatment of the female subject.

As it developed in the 1780s and 1790s, Female Gothic came to establish certain precedents in terms of the ways in which later Female Gothic fictions were to conceptualise and critique the rule of law. This chapter examines the juridical and literary contexts out of which Female Gothic emerged and developed. It considers aspects of eighteenth-century English civil law that began tentatively to construct a certain civil legal identity for women in response to modern democratic ideals, only to render this new mode of female juridical subjectivity exceptionally problematic in so far as it conflicted with well-established patriarchal juridical norms. Certain connections also emerge in this period between developments in literary theory and literary culture, and shifts in juridical theory and practice from the mid-eighteenth century onwards. Legal and literary theory begin to converge upon questions to do with verisimilitude, authenticity and authority, and both discourses came to posit the 'feminine' as inimical to questions of truth and reason in literature and law. This had significant implications for the production and reception of Female Gothic fiction and the manner of its engagement with eighteenth- and nineteenth-century legal and literary contexts. The second section of the chapter considers these early Female Gothic negotiations of textuality, female identity and law, particularly in terms of the complex figurations of Gothic space that emerge in the fictions of Sophia Lee, Ann Radcliffe and Eliza Parsons.

Moving from nineteenth-century Female Gothic through to the new millennium, this chapter seeks finally to establish a connection between early Female Gothic and the most popular contemporary form of Female Gothic fiction in the early-twenty-first century – vampire romance. This point of contact can be analysed productively in and through women's encounters with, and contestations of, the law.

Female Gothic and the 'Romance' of Law

One of the most famous representations of English law in the eighteenth century is found in William Blackstone's *Commentaries on the Laws of England*:

> We inherit an old Gothic castle, erected in the days of chivalry, but fitted up for a modern inhabitant. The moated ramparts, the embattled towers, and the trophied halls, are magnificent and venerable, but useless. The inferior apartments, now converted into rooms of conveyance, are cheerful and commodious, thought their approaches are winding and difficult. (Blackstone 1966: 51)

As Diana Wallace observes, and as this chapter discusses below, Female Gothic fiction later in this period was to use the figure of the law as a 'Gothic castle' in order to articulate the terrors visited upon the female subject through legal practices and institutions that subjected women to a kind of 'civil death' (Wallace 2009: 31). In mid-eighteenth-century jurisprudence, however, Blackstone's formulation served an important nationalistic ideological function: to represent the English juridical system in almost mythic terms as a powerful, ancient construction that guaranteed the rights and duties of free English *men*. Blackstone draws upon the popular contemporary idea that the English nation was descended not from the Norman conquerors of 1066, but from Germanic 'Gothic' warrior tribes which included the Anglo-Saxon forebears of the English. What emerges here is something akin to a national masculine and militaristic 'Gothic romance' of juridical and political origin.

The term 'Gothic', however, had a range of conflicting meanings in early-modern legal discourse beyond its deployment to validate a certain version of the nation's past. The status of English law as peculiarly 'Gothic' – as a labyrinth of often contradictory principles with no central reference point – was a source of anxiety to legal philosophers concerned to codify the nature and function of the nation's constitution. As early as 1628, Richard Burton characterised English law as 'the general mischief of our time, an unsensible plague' (Goodrich 1995: 5). In the late eighteenth century, this hostility towards the perceived absurdities of an uncodified juridical system found its most coherent and influential philosophical expression in Jeremy Bentham's *A Fragment on Government* (1776). Bentham wrote this essay at least in part as a response to Blackstone's celebration of the 'Gothic castle' of English law. Blackstone's affirmation of an archaic 'romance'' of national identity and origin was, in Bentham's estimation, irrational and dangerous. What is most interesting about Bentham's argument for my purposes is the extent to which his castigation of Blackstone's *Commentaries* deploys a certain conceptualisation of the feminine which relates Bentham's legal philosophy directly to contemporary literary debates concerning Gothic romance and its status as an incoherent and pernicious mode of fiction. Bentham takes particular issue with Blackstone's flights of legal fancy, and especially his recourse to romantic Gothic metaphors which ought to have no place within a modern, rational Enlightenment discourse of English law. Moreover, Bentham associates Blackstone's conceptualisation of English law with a dangerous and degenerate femininity, with a 'capricious mistress' and Adam's 'crooked rib' that breeds 'out of the bed of metaphor' a series of 'pernicious' legal fictions (Bentham 1967: 5).

Bentham's aim was to rationalise English law and rid it entirely of its romance elements. A parallel can be drawn here between his endeavours and the emergence from the mid-eighteenth century onwards of a literary hegemony that sought to privilege a new form of fiction – the novel – over its historical antecedent, the romance. The development of the Gothic in general, and of the Female Gothic in particular, cannot be divorced from this wider ideological matrix within which a highly gendered conceptualisation of 'romance' conflicts with Enlightenment assumptions concerning the proper parameters of juridical and literary discourse. In the 1790s, the decade in which female authors of Gothic romance were numbered among the best-selling writers of their time, critics frequently lamented the pernicious moral and aesthetic influence of a mode of fiction perceived as abhorrently and aberrantly feminine. This was in spite of the fact that men were just as avid consumers and producers of Gothic romance as women (see Clery 1995; Wright 2007).

What is at issue here is not historical veracity, but ideological spin. As Botting observes:

> Popular romances, sentimental love stories and romantic fictions find themselves in the same bracket as gothic forms ... fixed in a devalued cultural sphere and possessing limited aesthetic or moral value. Both genres, moreover, have been feminised: since the eighteenth century the notion that tales of love and adventure were produced and consumed, in the main, by female writers and readers has remained a persistent, if pernicious, cultural fiction. Gothic romance, a subordinate type of romance, was subordinated again almost as soon as it appeared. (Botting 2008: 10)

At the moment of its inception, then, Female Gothic is aligned with a pernicious feminine textuality that, in the words of the conservative contemporary critic Thomas Matthias, could only serve to lead the reader along 'fatal paths' and into 'mental darkness' (Botting 1996: 84–5). Female Gothic fiction was subordinated to a mode of writing deemed more rational and more moral: the realist novel. In the legal sphere, Bentham's attempt to develop a quasi-scientific codification of law replicated this gesture: the 'romance' of law would be replaced with a form of legal 'realism', through which juridical truths would be expressed transparently within the statutes of modern English law. In juridical and literary discourse, Gothic romance (gendered 'feminine') emerged as inimical to reason. This further inscribes within the legal and literary hegemony of this period the sense that femininity itself is inimical to reason. The rational subject of Enlightenment thought is implicitly masculine and, in particular, the political and juridical subject, whose rights are guaranteed by Enlightenment models of contractual, consensual governance, is implicitly masculine. In so far as femininity is constructed as inimical to reason, then the very notion of a coherent female juridical subjectivity is a contradiction in terms. Radical women writers of the 1790s were beginning to discern this painful reality, and this political, juridical and literary context provides a vital access point into Female Gothic fiction of the 1790s.

Woman, the Law and the Law's Gothic Space

Under the influence of Enlightenment political philosophy, especially the social contract theory of John Locke (see Wootton 1993), English law in the eighteenth century underwent a process of systemisation designed to bring it into conformity with the new economic realities of a rapidly developing capitalist, imperialist nation. Contract law in particular was

rapidly expanded so as to stabilise and regulate new financial and pro-
prietary interests in stocks, shares, land and commodities. What mattered above all within this often highly volatile economic climate was
that all forms of property be capable of exchange as freely and as widely
as possible. To some degree, this contractarian principle began in the
early eighteenth century to extend certain rights to women, who, as
potential consumers within this new free-market economy, acquired in
various contexts new forms of juridical agency. In 1710, for instance,
a wife's personal allowance was held to be unencumbered by her husband's debts; it could not therefore be claimed as a part of his estate. In
1725, a wife inheriting property from her family was deemed capable
of holding that property separately from her husband (see Staves 1980).
These developments, however, conflicted with the long-standing legal
principle that a married woman's legal identity was subsumed entirely
by her husband's. Thus, in order to find in favour of women without
jeopardising the patriarchal basis of marriage and inheritance laws, the
courts had to generate what Lord Hardwicke in 1750 termed a legal
'fiction': namely, that a married woman could be treated as a single
female (a 'femme sole') if the equitable management of her property
demanded it. The legal agency afforded to women was thus highly
ambivalent; it lacked the solid philosophical foundation provided for
the adult male legal subject by Enlightenment social contract theory (see
Staves 1980; Pateman 1988). Moreover, by the 1790s, such gains as had
been made by women were largely halted, and in many cases repealed.
In the reactionary, post-revolutionary period, the juridical and economic
independence of women, however limited, was found 'to be intolerable'
(Staves 1980: 152) by the English civil courts.

The 1790s was the decade in which Female Gothic fiction emerged as
a distinct mode of literary Gothicism and its subject was often the precarious juridical position of women. As Diana Wallace makes clear, the
Female Gothic became a means whereby women could explore metaphorically what often amounted to the 'civil death' of the female subject
before the law. It was in this context, moreover, that Blackstone's notion
of English law as an 'old Gothic castle' acquired a significant symbolic
twist in the work of Female Gothic writers. Gothic spaces became potent
symbols of juridical institutions that closed down the possibility of
female juridical self-representation.

Critics have observed that Female Gothic writing places great emphasis on configurations of space (Ellis 1989; Williams 1995; Wright 2007).
Gothic spaces depicted frequently in the work of Ann Radcliffe, Sophia
Lee, Eliza Parsons and others include castles, crypts, caverns and labyrinthine corridors in which women are imprisoned or forced to hide.

These subterranean spaces symbolise the dangerous, confined and marginalised position occupied by women within patriarchal structures of power – the place of woman is hidden within, or secreted beneath the 'Gothic castle' of paternal law. One might consider here the mythic figure of Sophocles's Antigone entombed within the walls of the city as punishment for her transgression against the law of the father. One significant detail here links the fate of Antigone with that of the Female Gothic heroine: she is not *exiled* from the city, but rather *buried within* its borders, within the boundary that delineates the space of the community and its laws. The Gothic heroine likewise often occupies the recesses and crypts of the law's own Gothic space.

A case in point here is Sophia Lee's 1785 *The Recess*. This novel presents itself as a historical account (through the Gothic device of the 'discovered manuscript') of the lives of the two daughters of Mary Queen of Scots. The novel establishes from the outset an alternative female genealogy that poses a challenge to patriarchal, monarchical governance. Paternal law depends upon lines of male succession that guarantee its continuity and legitimacy, and the very existence of these marginalised royal sisters threaten this juridical hegemony. They are thus hidden away in the 'recess' of the novel's title. The physical and symbolic relation of these young women to centres of power within the novel reveals the deeply problematic status of female juridical subjectivity. The women are posited as legal subjects; indeed, their royal status guarantees them a degree of juridical agency that is nevertheless profoundly disruptive of the legal and political order. Their blood-line (evoked repeatedly in the novel's early stages by the royal portraits that surround them in their hiding place) connects them irrevocably to the source of English juridical authority. Their inheritance of an illegitimate, Catholic and feminine genealogy, on the other hand, exiles them from that locus of power and constitutes a kind of haunting of the patriarchal, Protestant line of succession. The physical location and origin of the recess evokes this process of exile and haunting that both defines and disrupts paternal law. The space, the novel discloses, was constructed as a Catholic hiding place in the years immediately following the Reformation. A series of secret doors and passages connect the recess to a modern country house; the only external sign of the presence of this cryptic space is a bolted door within a ruined monument around which lie 'vast heaps of stone … wild and awful to excess' (Lee 2000: 37). The sisters' illegitimate maternal inheritance is contained and confined within this cryptic space, a space that signifies the law's violent, yet precarious attempt to repudiate its past and reconstitute its legitimacy through the abjection of an impure feminine influence.

In Ann Radcliffe's Gothic fiction, beginning with *The Castles of Athlin and Dunbayne* in 1789, the motif of the lost and/or imprisoned mother recurs frequently and it is invariably implicated in disputes pertaining to the legitimacy or otherwise of male governance. In the 1789 text, for instance, the Baroness of Dunbayne is imprisoned within a secret chamber in order to facilitate an illegitimate usurpation of power. Her liberation accompanies the restoration of the legitimate ruler to Dunbayne, but one must acknowledge that the recovery of the mother is hardly *necessary* to this reconstitution of rightful paternal rule. The revelation of her identity consolidates this transference of power, but the substance and legitimacy of the new juridical authority depends entirely upon the restoration of the male line of succession. A similar dynamic emerges in *A Sicilian Romance*, in which a mother, Louisa, is again incarcerated, this time to facilitate her husband's illegitimate second marriage. Once more, an abjected feminine presence haunts a deeply dysfunctional system of paternal governance, and indeed the early signs of Louisa's presence (the lights that flicker, for instance, in the chamber that connects the castle to her subterranean prison) are mistaken for evidence of supernatural activity. *A Sicilian Romance* goes beyond Radcliffe's first novel, however, in prioritising the maternal genealogy that connects Louisa to her daughters, Julia and Emilia. Julia's apartment provides a point of access into the disused quarter of the castle that leads eventually to Louisa's cell. It is Julia (as opposed to the son, Osbert, in *Athlin and Dunbayne*) who descends into this cryptic, feminine space in order to find her mother and set right the abuse of power perpetrated by her tyrannical father. Although the ultimate logic of paternal rule remains undisturbed here – the restored order reinstates the legitimacy of the proper male line of succession, as in the earlier text – this novel introduces a theme that was to become central to Radcliffe's later fictions, and to the Female Gothic more generally: the centrality of female relationships and genealogies to the symbolic and thematic structure of women's Gothic fiction.

One of the most widely read Gothic fictions of the early 1790s was Eliza Parsons's *The Castle of Wolfenbach* (1793), famous also for its inclusion in Austen's list of 'Horrid Novels' in *Northanger Abbey*. Austen's satirical treatment of writers such as Parsons points again to the generic impropriety associated with Female Gothic romance in this period. Through the voice of her hero Henry Tilney (the voice of patriarchal reason, of legal and literary respectability), Austen positions Radcliffe as a writer worthy of serious consideration, while novelists such as Parsons are condemned as the purveyors of exactly that variety of romance likely to lead the female reader into 'mental darkness'.

As Diane Hoeveler observes, however, Parsons's text conforms to the Gothic formula already established by Radcliffe's highly successful first three Gothic romances (Parsons 2006: x). Parsons's work belongs firmly within the emerging tradition of Female Gothic that Radcliffe helped initiate. Indeed, it is Parsons's deployment of the Radcliffean Gothic mode, and its interrogation of paternal models of power, that gives the text its potency (in spite of its often overt nationalism and social conservatism) in terms of articulating the dire predicament of alienated, disempowered female subjects.

Parsons's novel begins with a typical Radcliffean gesture: a young woman of refined sensibility is in peril and finds herself in a Gothic space that appears to be haunted, or at least to have been the site of extraordinary violence in the past. Like the Radcliffean heroine, she refuses to give in to superstitious fears as she hears 'a clanking of chains followed by two or three heavy groans' (Parsons 2006: 7). This apparent 'haunting' indicates that the castle is a repository of past violence that is shortly to return, and the explanation offered for the spectral sounds generates a parallel between the predicament of the heroine (who is escaping persecution at the hands of her uncle) and an imprisoned, persecuted wife and her dead child who now haunt the site of their incarceration and death. The narrative of the 'haunting' returns again later in the text, when it almost exactly parallels the account by the Countess of Wolfenbach of her disastrous, violent marriage. Female experiences of trauma are thus mirrored back and forth across the generations, and women rely upon the support of other women to narrate and expose these injustices. At the centre of these narratives is an abused woman lacking any capacity to protect herself legally against the machinations of vengeful men. This is Gothic 'virtue in distress' very much in the Radcliffean mould, but what distinguishes Parsons from her predecessor is that the abuse of women is violently enacted in this text – intimations of assault become bodies bruised and bathed in blood. Parsons's more shocking, less respectable mode of Gothicism thus allows her to materialise fully the extent of violence to which the female subject, lacking any form of coherent civil identity, can be made to suffer. Patriarchal, aristocratic systems of law (although ultimately rehabilitated, as they invariably are in Radcliffe) are thoroughly 'Gothicised', and what they inflict on the various female protagonists of the novel's parallel narratives might be read as a vivid Female Gothic representation of the law's brutalisation of woman.

Love, Law and the Female Gothic – From the Nineteenth Century to the New Millennium

In 1854, Lady Caroline Norton wrote a powerful and moving account of her disastrous marriage in an attempt to encourage the reform of English divorce and child custody laws. Lady Norton was married to a brutal man from whom, as the law stood, she could hope to obtain no redress. Her case exemplifies the position of the woman who suffers 'civil death' before the law and her text begins with a highly Gothic evocation of the plight of married women:

> In arguing my case from my own example, I am not ignorant that there are persons who think such argument blameable on other grounds; who deem a husband's right so indefeasible, and his title so sacred, that even a wronged wife should keep silence. How far will they carry that principle? A few years ago, a French nobleman, the Duc de Praslin, assassinated his wife in the midst of her slumbering household. When morning broke, she was dead; but many a proof remained of the desperate resistance and agonised efforts to escape, made by that wretched woman before her doom was completed. Do the advocates of the doctrine of non-resistance consider that her duty would have been to submit tranquilly to the fate pre-determined for her? If not, let them waive judgment in my case; for if choice were allowed me, I would rather be murdered and remembered by friends and children with love and regret than have the slanders believed, which my husband has invented of me. It is he, who has made silence impossible. With HIM rests the breaking of those seals which keep the history of each man's home sacred from indifferent eyes. He has declared himself my deadliest foe, whose dagger has too near an aim to miss my heart, – and, of the two, I hold his stab to be worse than that of the Duc de Praslin, for he would assassinate even my memory. (Norton 1854)

Following precedents set in earlier decades by writers such as Lee, Radcliffe and Parsons, Female Gothic authors throughout the nineteenth century continued to deploy key Gothic tropes and conventions in order to interrogate the position of women before the law. Charlotte Brontë's 1847 *Jane Eyre*, for instance, follows the trajectory of earlier Female Gothic fiction in critiquing the impact on married and unmarried women of a law that denied them a fully functioning juridical agency. To cite another example from the late-nineteenth-century American context, Charlotte Perkins Gilman's *The Yellow Wallpaper* (1892) posits a former nursery (ostensibly the ultimate in safe domestic space) as an increasingly surreal and deadly prison for a young wife who has no authority to resist the devastating 'rest cure' imposed upon her by her husband and her doctor. Moving towards a more contemporary context, this Female Gothic tradition of interrogating the juridical position of women continues, I want to argue, in postmillennial modes of Female Gothic fiction: most notably, vampire romance. These texts are, of course, responding to an entirely different juridical context in so far as paternal law, at least as it existed in the era of Radcliffe and Parsons, has virtually expired in the West. It can be argued, though, that systems of law and governance that have replaced it continue in various ways to complicate and compromise female juridical agency.

The work of Juliet MacCannell is especially useful, I want to suggest, in accounting for the demise of paternal authority in modern Western juridical systems and the impact of this upon women. Late modernity, she argues, has witnessed a shift from the order of the father to what she terms 'the regime of the brother'. The move towards modernity has replaced the principle of paternity with that of fraternity: power is democratised and dispersed among 'brothers'. The 'brother' becomes the universal citizen in whom civic rights and responsibilities are vested. This democratic, egalitarian ideal, however, masks the fact that the regime of the brother rests upon ritualised forms of group bonding that repudiate difference in order to maintain a sexually and racially homogenous regime of the Same. In a revision of the Freudian model, MacCannell contends that this is an economy governed not by Oedipus, not by an identification with the paternal principle, but by Narcissus, by an identification with homogenous, interchangeable subjects – the 'brothers'. The fraternal principle becomes a means 'for enforcing identicality and identification'; it is marked by a rigid conformity to the homogenous group and underscored by 'an unlimited, aggressive narcissism' (MacCannell 1991: 34).

MacCannell argues that for this fraternal regime to function, it must assert the ideological importance of equal rights within a neutral, liberal legal framework. Nevertheless, marginalised groups within this regime remain deeply vulnerable to outbreaks of violence designed to assert the supremacy of the dominant group against the 'other', whose difference cannot be articulated or accepted on its own terms. Within this regime, MacCannell contends that the older, Oedipal model of paternal rule might actually begin to look attractive to and protective of women compared to a culture which insists upon the value of gender equality while simultaneously denying women status and security. This insight offers a valuable point of access into postmillennial female Gothic fictions, which often seems to display an intense nostalgia for a patriarchal order perceived as benevolent and protective from the perspective of the contemporary female subject.

For Anne Silver, and many other feminist critics of *Twilight*, 'the novel's gender ideology is unapologetically patriarchal' (Silver 2010:

122; see also Dietz 2011, and Whitton 2011). The model of subjectivity the series offers to Bella is resolutely self-sacrificing and although she is by no means entirely passive, her choices tend to work to confirm her dependency on Edward. Her agency is deeply compromised within an order of power that validates the judgements and actions of men over women. In the first book, for instance, Bella finds herself surrounded by a violent gang of rapacious men while walking alone through Port Angeles in search of a book store. Edward's car speeds up to her and he orders her to get in. Having read the minds and the violent sexual intent of these men, he is furious and he takes his anger out on Bella, as if she is to blame for making herself vulnerable by exercising her right of free movement around this city. Later, her insistence on experiencing sex with Edward while she is still human results in her fatal pregnancy and the fact she achieves her dream of vampiric transformation does not alter the fact that it is the 'God-like' Edward's blood that must confer eternal life upon a female subject whose attempts at self-determination would otherwise have destroyed her; he is her 'perpetual savior', 'terrible and glorious' as 'a young God' (Meyer 2005: 256, 166, 343). What I want to suggest, though, is that these female Gothic fictions do not so much reaffirm the power of an *existing* system of strong patriarchal rule, but rather invest in a nostalgic fantasy of paternal law as constructing a safe place for women in a culture increasingly unable to sustain the cultural and juridical authority of the father. What the *Twilight Saga* negotiates, and this is true of much contemporary vampire romance, is the collapse of what MacCannell terms 'the regime of the father'.

Traditional paternal authority – the authority of the father within the conventional bourgeois nuclear family and the power of patriarchal law beyond the family – is shown as compromised, and at times entirely ineffectual, throughout *Twilight*. Bella begins the narrative as a marginalised figure moving to a new community, into which she never fully integrates. She leaves her mother in Arizona to live in Forks, Washington, with an ineffectual father who seems incapable of looking after himself, let alone his teenage daughter. The fact that Bella's father is a police officer is significant here; he lacks authority even as a representative of the public law, let alone as a father within his family. Bella becomes a surrogate wife to the man she invariably refers to as Charlie. The attention she receives from groups of men in and around Forks is posited as unwanted (in the case of her male class mates), or as dangerous (in the case of the gang that nearly attacks her in Port Angeles). Indeed, while the approaches of the various young men who compete for her attention at Forks High School are well-meaning enough, it is clear that Bella finds them irritating and at times intimidating, and the implicit threat posed by these young men is made real when one of them, Tyler, loses control of his van and nearly kills her. It is Edward whose supernatural strength saves her; he becomes a surrogate father to Bella in the absence of any other effective paternal authority. A similar complication of the role and rule of the father emerges through Bella's growing involvement with the Quileute werewolves at La Push. This is a hyper-masculine environment in which the power of the leader, Billy, is respected, but in practical terms relatively limited; he is quite elderly, diabetic, and uses a wheelchair. He can offer little protection to Bella against the aggression of his volatile adolescent 'sons'. As these young men make their transition, they rapidly acquire extraordinary height and musculature; the shift from boyhood to manhood is translated here into a change from human pre-pubescence to a supernatural hyper-masculinity that causes Jacob and his brothers initially to shun Bella. While Jacob's hostility to her is primarily due to her growing relationship with Edward, Bella's very presence at La Push appears to trigger conflict once the brothers have bonded through their werewolf transformation, and this conflict is something for which Bella herself is blamed. Jacob's volatile outbursts of temper are something for which she is implicitly held responsible and Jacob's shows of aggression towards her continue long after his initial transitional phase in the first book. He repeatedly scolds her for loving Edward instead of him; he insists that Edward is and always will be a predator, and yet Bella tends to suffer more direct violence from Jacob than the vampire. In *Eclipse*, for instance, a struggle over Bella ensues between Edward and Jacob, during which Jacob forcibly kisses Bella; she strikes out to defend herself and breaks her hand on his jaw. Her attempt to defend herself physically, like her attempts elsewhere to elude Edward's controlling behaviour and assert her own autonomy, backfires and appears to consolidate her status as a passive victim of violence between young males and against her. What saves her ultimately from this cycle of fraternal aggression is her transformation into a vampire through Edward's blood and her absorption into the patriarchal, bourgeois household of Carlisle Cullen. Bella's 'happy ever after' is a nostalgic, conservative evocation of stable paternal law that can only exist here within the phantasmic context of a vampire family.

Other vampire narratives of the postmillennial period are arguably less conservative than Meyer's texts. Contemporary Female Gothic fictions by Charlaine Harris, Lara Adrian and J. R. Ward attribute a reasonable degree of agency to women, even within the context of fairly traditional romance plots. This is especially true of Harris's fictions, in which Sookie Stackhouse earns her own living, manages her own household and enjoys considerable sexual freedom. At the same time, however, these fictions share with earlier female Gothic narratives a concern that the subjectivity of women before the law is deeply conflicted. Indeed, the 'regime of the brother' appears to have exacerbated some of the difficulties that have always beset women struggling to assert agency within the public sphere. Without the dubious protection of the paternal law (the order of governance invariably reinstated at the close of earlier Female Gothic fictions), women in this new mode of Gothic writing often struggle to protect themselves from violent men. The egalitarian legal ideal of Western modernity often appears to offer scant protection to women. In the vampire narratives of Ward and Adrian, for instance, it is often the human heroine's entrance into the vampire community that guarantees her a degree of safety and respect she cannot begin to enjoy in the supposedly egalitarian world outside. In Harris's *Southern Vampire Mysteries*, women are shown repeatedly to be vulnerable to male violence, in both the human and the supernatural communities, and the law is shown repeatedly to be incompetent or indifferent in the face of it. At one point, for instance, Sookie forms the rather melancholy resolution simply to try to avoid being beaten up and exploited by men. What MacCannell suggests in her study, and what these fictions bear out, is that men's violence against women is normalised by the culture they inhabit, and even by women themselves. This cultural reality undermines the law's claim successfully to have legislated for gender equality, for this is a culture in which convictions for sexual assault are notoriously low; in which women are routinely blamed for the violence directed against them; in which violent misogynistic abuse (for which women themselves are again often blamed) is commonplace across the new social media; in which the law's ostensible commitment to equality does not guarantee women equal pay, equal prospects, freedom from sexual harassment, or freedom from sexual shaming. As Helene Meyers observes, the cultural reality that underlies Western juridical constructions of gender equality raises pressing questions concerning 'the theoretical status and limits of the female subject' (Meyers 2001: 2).

Meyers has argued that much contemporary Female Gothic narrative is comprised of what she terms 'femicidal plots' – plots that narrate the actual or symbolic annihilation of women. These plots (like those of earlier Female Gothic fictions) turn upon fraught questions concerning female agency and the female body that do not seem capable of resolution through the intervention of law. Indeed, these questions appear to have become even more vexed in light of the fact that advances *have* indeed been made in legislating for gender equality during the twentieth century (in terms of marriage and property law, employment rights, reproductive rights, and so on). As Meyers suggests, there appears to be a gap between the ideal legal subject – posited as the inviolable, inalienable, rational self – and the continuing reality of the 'economic, psychological and physical vulnerability' of women (Meyers 2001: 18). Contemporary Female Gothic in the form of popular vampire romance is not necessarily radical (and I agree with Silver that *Twilight* is an overtly sexually conservative narrative), but it continues to exemplify the female Gothic's preoccupation with the violence, authority and limits of law.

Bibliography

Bentham, Jeremy [1776] (1967), *A Fragment on Government*, Oxford: Blackwell Press.

Blackstone, William [1765–9] (1966) *Commentaries on the Laws of England*, Oxford: Clarendon Press.

Botting, Fred (1996), *Gothic*, London: Routledge.

Botting, Fred (2008) *Gothic Romanced: Consumption, Gender and Technology in Contemporary Fictions*, London: Routledge.

Clery, E. J. (1995), *The Rise of Supernatural Fiction*, Cambridge: Cambridge University Press.

Dietz, Tammy (2011), 'Wake up Bella! A Personal Essay on Mormonism, Feminism and Happiness', in Liza Anatol (ed.), *Bringing Light to Twilight: Perspectives on the Pop Culture Phenomenon*, London: Palgrave.

Ellis, Kate Ferguson (1989), *The Contested Castle: Gothic Novels and the Subversion of Domestic Ideology*, Chicago: University of Illinois Press.

Goodrich, Peter (1995), *Oedipus Lex: Psychoanalysis, History, Law*, Berkeley: University of California Press.

Harris, Charlaine (2001–13), *The Southern Vampire Mysteries*, London: Orion Books.

Hoeveler, Diane (1993), 'Introduction' to Ann Radcliffe, *A Sicilian Romance*, Oxford: Oxford University Press.

Lee, Sophia [1785] (2000), *The Recess*, Lexington: University Press of Kentucky.

MacCannell, Juliet Flower (1991), *The Regime of the Brother: After the Patriarchy*, London: Routledge.

Meyer, Stephenie (2005), *Twilight*, London: Atom.

Meyer, Stephenie (2006), *New Moon*, London: Atom.

Meyer, Stephenie (2007), *Eclipse*, London: Atom.

Meyer, Stephenie (2008), *Breaking Dawn*, London: Atom.

Meyers, Helene (2001), *Femicidal Plots: Narratives of the Female Gothic Experience*, New York: SUNY Press.

Norton, Caroline (1854) *English Laws for Women in the Nineteenth Century*. Available at: http://digital.library.upenn.edu/women/norton/elfw/elfw.html (accessed 1 September 2015).

Parsons, Eliza [1793] (2006), *The Castle of Wolfenbach*, ed. Diane Hoeveler, Richmond, VA: Valancourt Books.

Pateman, Carol (1988), *The Sexual Contract*, Cambridge: Polity Press.

Radcliffe, Ann [1789] (1995), *The Castles of Athlin and Dunbayne*, Oxford: Oxford University Press.

Radcliffe, Ann [1790] (1993), *A Sicilian Romance*, ed. Diane Hoeveler, Oxford: Oxford University Press.

Silver, Anne (2010), 'Twilight is not good for Maidens', *Studies in the Novel*, 42(1–2): 121–38.

Staves, Susan (1980), *Married Women's Separate Property in England, 1660–1893*, Cambridge, MA: Harvard University Press.

Wallace, Diana (2009), '"The Haunting Idea": Female Gothic Metaphors and Feminist Theory', in Diana Wallace and Andrew Smith (eds), *The Female Gothic: New Directions*, London: Palgrave, pp. 26–41.

Whitton, Merrine (2011), 'One is not born a vampire, but becomes one: Motherhood and Masochism in *Twilight*', in Giselle Liza Anatol (ed.), *Bringing Light to Twilight: Perspectives on the Pop Culture Phenomenon*, London: Palgrave.

Williams, Anne (1995), *Art of Darkness*, Chicago: University of Chicago Press.

Wootton, David (ed.) (1993), 'Introduction' to John Locke, *Political Writings*, London: Penguin.

Wright, Angela (2007), *Gothic Fiction*, Basingstoke: Palgrave Macmillan.

Chapter 10

Female Vampirism
Gina Wisker

Vampires were supposed to menace women, but to me at least,
they promised protection against a destiny of girdles, spike
heels and approval.
(Nina Auerbach, *Our Vampires Ourselves*, p. 4)

Disruptive and troublesome, female vampires are an embodied oxymo-
ron, a thrilling contradiction, fundamentally problematising received
notions of women's passivity, nurturing and social conformity. Female
vampires destabilise such comfortable, culturally inflected investments
and complacencies and reveal them as aspects of constructed gender
identity resulting from social and cultural hierarchies. This chapter
explores this destabilisation in Gothic fiction, arguing that performativity, abjection and carnival lie at the heart of the construction and representation of female vampires, so that there is a constant tension between
punishment and celebration of their transgressive nature. The exciting
threat offered by female vampires in Victorian texts such as Le Fanu's
'Carmilla' (1872) and Stoker's *Dracula* (1897) is terrifying, punished,
but lingers, re-read as disturbing potential. The fiction of Angela Carter,
Anne Rice, Poppy Z. Brite, Jewelle Gomez, shows female vampires at
the height of their representation as liberating, sexually transgressive
feminist figures, provoking questioning and undermining received certainties of identity, family and hierarchies based on gender, sexuality
and ethnicity. Recent texts such as Nalo Hopkinson's culturally inflected
'Greedy Choke Puppy' (2001) and Charlaine Harris's ethnicity-focused,
neighbourhood novels refocus the female vampire in a more socially
engaged role. The popularity of Stephenie Meyer's *Twilight* series
(2005–8) suggests that the female vampire, at least in the United States,
has been reclaimed for neo-conservatism as her Young Adult vampire
romance endorses both eternal (quite chaste) romantic love and family
values. There are, however, encouraging signs that something more

topical and subversive has emerged to challenge the imaginative impasse of the vacuously flamboyant or merely mundane female vampire. This may be seen in two fascinating texts, each filmed: *Byzantium* (2013), a twenty-first-century tale of survival, and *A Girl Walks Home Alone at Night* (2014), an Iranian feminist vampire tale written in comic vein. So, contemporary women's vampires have arisen energetic and crusading, indicating a new feminist energy.

The Emergence of the Female Vampire

The vampire is everything we love about sex and the night and the dark dream-side of ourselves: adventure on the edge of pain, the thrill to be had from breaking taboos.

(Poppy Z. Brite, *Love in Vein 1*, p. vii)

The Gothic revisits, replays and returns, rewriting itself like something occasionally annoying or, for lovers of vampire fiction, something delightfully invigorating, an exciting return of the familiar and the repressed. It is hardly surprising then that the undead, transgressive figure of the female vampire should be considered a suitable receptacle for and actor in narratives which Otherise, demonise, abject and punish in order to manage wayward energies. In culture and literature, women are frequently constructed as bearers of moral good and represent the conventional securities of family, home, nation, purity, heredity, economic security, health. When women reject this template of goodness, the forces of order offload social, bodily and spiritual terrors onto the demonised figure of woman. Each of these – the conventional order and the demonised Other – are fictional constructs. The Gothic exposes the tensions between them, the juxtaposition between conformity and deeply disturbing deformity acted out in the figure of the female vampire, whose liminal being represents terror at everything in flux, unfixed. It unsettles certainties expressed in the neat polarities of life/ death, male/ female, dead /undead. Vampires, creatures of myth and cultural metamorphosis, a metaphor for disruption, enable a critique of what is feared and desired at different times: women's sexuality, foreign invasion, cultural difference, homosexuality, fear of blood-borne disease, AIDS. Psychoanalytically, they represent the abject, that which must be rejected to develop identity (Kristeva 1982).

The first fictional woman vampires were based on women with blood-thirsty reputations for vampire-like behaviour, in particular, Elizabeth Bathory (1560–1614), near-contemporary and almost neighbour to

Vlad the Impaler (1431–6), who was rumoured to retain her youthful looks by drinking and bathing in the blood of virgins. The best-known early fictional female vampires are Sheridan Le Fanu's eponymous Carmilla (1872), probably the first lesbian vampire, who preyed on and seduced young women; the protagonist of 'The Good Lady Ducayne', by sensation novelist Mary Elizabeth Braddon (1896); Harriet Brandt, a first female colonial vampire in Florence Marryat's *The Blood of the Vampire* (1897) and Mary E. Wilkins Freeman's 'Luella Miller' (1903), possibly the first American fictional female vampire. These last two exemplify the vampire who drains life energies rather than blood. With the exception of Harriet Brandt, who does not understand the fatal effect she has on those she loves until it is explained to her by a doctor, these female vampires are self-centred, duplicitous, voracious and desperate for longevity and eternal youth, depicting stereotypically negative female traits. The threat of each is highly sexualised, invasive, non-conformist; each is demonised for her active sexuality and desire for eternal youth. Some drain babies and men of their lifeblood, some drain anyone available of their life force. In this period, their various sexualities would have no doubt caused frissons of delight and disgust. The demands of the day closed down and punished those sexual energies, which in later years were to be celebrated as radical, positive, challenges to a dull, conforming status quo. What was terrifying and disgusting can be recognised as repression of restrained emotions, hidden Victorian and Edwardian desires.

The Gothic figure of the female vampire exposes contradictions and constructions formed from fear and a refusal to accept flexibility, change, difference, challenge; in this respect, those earlier fictional women vampires are often read by contemporary critics as exposing deep uncertainties in the societies which produced them, particularly in terms of the representation of women. We read them now as markers of a lack of ease, as gaps, fissures in social certainties, projected nightmares emanating from imperial, patriarchal comfort zones.

Victorian Female Vampires

The lascivious vampire women in *Dracula* (1897) terrify and attract staid Jonathan Harker not merely because they hold him spellbound, but because of their radical behaviour, which is lustful and predatory. When not seducing him in a delightful dream, they devour babies, a behaviour contrasting strongly with the daytime conformity of nurturing Victorian women back home. These three voluptuous blood-sucking sirens threaten Jonathan Harker's marriage, sanity and life, their bodies expressing threats to women's chastity, purity and maternal instincts and through them, a danger to male sexual self-management, heredity and blood purity. Harker nearly succumbs; later he and Van Helsing's Crew of Light soon show, through the example of staking the child-devouring, non-maternal Lucy, that potential promiscuity and non-maternal behaviours must be surgically exorcised: stake through the heart, cut off her head, coffin her perpetually.

Influenced by 'Carmilla' (Riquelme 2002: 8–12) and possibly reflecting Stoker's own issues with women and sexuality (Signorotti 1996: 619–21), the original first chapter (shortened by the editor) included close references to Le Fanu's story. As Sian Macfie has demonstrated (1991), reactions against the freedom-seeking 'New Woman' of the late nineteenth century demonised energetic women. Threats of impurity also appear in imagery that demonises women, portraying them as half snake, half-human, product of a fear of contagious diseases and a continued failure to suppress unlicensed lust: the *fin-de-siècle femme fatale* (Dijkstra 1986). If vampire women were clearly a threat to everything British, male, imperial, conventional, traditional, safe, how much more dangerous and terrifying was Carmilla, the invasive sexual predator, a lesbian, whose very being challenges maintenance of norms of sexual behaviour? Or Harriet Brandt, a colonial vampire threatening miscegenation and sorcery?

'Carmilla', narrated by Laura, the vampire's near-victim, takes place in Styria, Central Europe. Laura and her father entertain an unexpected visitor, a beautiful young woman who is in reality an ancient vampire. Carmilla's gender is already complicated. She possesses both those features typically figured as feminine for a Victorian audience: beauty, weakness, and a general languor, as well as those typically figured as masculine: sexual desire, strength and power over others. Laura's response is mixed: she feels 'a strange tumultuous excitement that was pleasurable, ever and anon, mingled with a vague sense of fear and disgust ... I was conscious of a love growing into adoration, and also of abhorrence' (Le Fanu 1872: 178). These contradictory responses of delight and disgust have prompted critics to see 'Carmilla' as an early lesbian tale, the abjection exacerbated by the lesbian overtones of this vampiric exchange. Carmilla's languor and fluidity are linked to witchcraft: she turns into a large black cat. So Botting notes: 'Feline, darkly sensual and threatening in its underlying, cruel violence, Carmilla's unnatural desires are signalled in her choice of females as her victims and the alluring as well as disturbing effects she has on them' (1995: 144–5).

While at one level representing women's sexual awakening as a disgusting supernatural event, the text leaves space for a more positive interpretation through the ambiguity of Laura's role: she is a quasi-active participant, both victim and lover. Karen F. Stein suggests:

> it is precisely this male disgust with woman's sexuality, male hatred and fear of woman's awful procreative power and her 'Otherness' which lies at the root of Female Gothic. A male strategy for alleviating this fear is to define woman as 'Other'. (Stein 1983: 124)

This is seeing 'woman' through a pattern of antitheses: saint/sinner, virgin/whore, nurturing mother/devouring stepmother, and angel/witch, binaries identified by Karen Horney as deriving from patriarchal thought (Horney 1967). Such binaries are the stuff of Gothic; dealing with male terrors, women writers reproduce them, ignore them, write back to them, celebrate the dualities. Stein continues, 'To win social acceptance many women have sought, consciously or unconsciously, to be the virgin, the angel, to hide or disown the traits which might be seen to threaten their acceptability' (1983: 125). One result is an investment in cosmetic beauty, physical manipulation into ideal shape, and an endless frustrated desire to ward off signs of ageing, of living.

Ellen Moers, who coined the term 'Female Gothic', argues that 'women's concern with their physical appearance colludes with their self-denigration' (1976: 90–1). Much lauded, much feted, much sought after, the body beautiful is both a celebration of woman's being in the world and contradicts the abject female body found in many Gothic horror works. Feminist theory of the body (Cixous, Kristeva, Irigaray) and much theory of horror concerning the monstrous feminine (Creed) help explain the seductions, delights, dangers and disgust engendered by worship of the body beautiful in horror by and about women. The female vampiric body is associated both with monstrosity and the desire for beauty. Mary Elizabeth Braddon's 'Good Lady Ducayne' (1896), successfully bleeding her young companions to retain her own youthful appearance, resembles Countess Elizabeth Bathory, retaining youth through bathing in the virginal blood. 'Good Lady Ducayne', first published in *The Strand* in 1896, has the familiar nineteenth-century heroine, an impoverished genteel woman, seeking employment as a companion. The employer accepting her without testimonial or training is Good Lady Ducayne, whose withered countenance suggests to avid readers of vampire narratives someone both ageing and on the lookout for young blood. Bella, the newly employed young companion, believes herself rescued in a 'fairy godmother's coach' (142), then notes:

Never had she seen anyone as old as the lady sitting by the Person's fire: ...
a face so wasted by age that it seemed only a pair of eyes and a peaked chin.
The nose was peaked too but between the sharply pointed chin and the great,
shining eyes, the small, aquiline nose was hardly visible. (Braddon 1989: 142)

Female vampires obviously resemble witches. Others who comment on
the lady and her waxen-faced foreign doctor, Parravicini, mention 'the
foul fiend' (48) and her slavish attachment to life as well as the untimely
deaths of all previous companions.

Bella starts to sicken, as did her predecessors, but luckily she is rescued
by friends, and paid off by Lady Ducayne for her silence with £100.
Braddon also played on contemporary images of dangerous women in
Lady Audley's Secret (1862), aware of how the rich used money for
self-preservation at the expense of the poor. This story reminds us of
the need to 'stay young and beautiful' when worth relies upon external
looks and survival upon wealth, a message current beyond *The Beauty
Myth* (Wolf 1990). Nalo Hopkinson's 'Greedy Choke Puppy' (2001)
revises problems of youth, beauty and selfish preservation with a soucri-
ant/soucouyant in a Caribbean setting.

A precursor of Hopkinson's narrative is Florence Marryat's *The Blood
of the Vampire* (1897), a novel in which the vampire drains life energy
rather than blood. Harriet Brandt, a social psychological soucriant (soucouyant), is an energy-draining, colonial vampire who links imperial
context and gender. Marryat's novel aligns with a contemporary focus
on women and hysteria and with issues concerning racial purity and
miscegenation, the foreign Other – also present in *Dracula* through the
shape-shifting Transylvanian Count. Harriet is from Jamaica, her looks
and behaviour suggesting a history of slavery, mixed-race relations, the
hidden shame of imperialism, Caribbean folklore, Obeah, spiritualism
and witchcraft. Her powers are probably more dangerous once she is
transposed to a middle-class watering hole in Belgium, among a range
of English ladies whose focus is on class distinction, aloofness and social
politeness, which leads them to accept her excessive friendliness because
she is a young woman travelling with a sick friend, otherwise alone in
the world. That politeness also makes them vulnerable to her invasive,
draining nature, which is on the one hand, a familiar social behaviour,
and on the other demonic. Harriet Brandt is a social vampire, bleeding the energies of men and women fascinated by her unusual beauty
and compelled by her to be close friends. A familiar, convincing figure
in social circles, Harriet is very beautiful, latching onto other women
and insisting on walking with them, holding hands, exhibiting all the
energetic and enthusiastic practices of girlfriends together. She is also

a soucriant. In Caribbean lore, soucriants are usually older women feeding mostly on babies and young children. Harriet does not seem to consume blood but the baby in the tale, unprotected by social inhibition like the adult women, falls prey to her allure, languishes and dies. Even a physician cannot save her.

Marryat constructs Harriet as Otherised, a product of lust and miscegenation. Today's readers might find disturbingly racist the portrayal of Harriet and her mother but it is a product of the time and context. We are reminded of Jean Rhys's descriptions of Christophine, the Obeah woman in *Wide Sargasso Sea* (1966) and the representation of the Creole mixed-race heiress Antoinette, a version of *Jane Eyre*'s madwoman in the attic, Bertha Mason. In representing Antoinette's desires through the eyes of the unnamed Rochester figure who finds her passionate embrace as unnatural, engulfing, vampiric, Rhys shows the sexual fascination and threat of what he sees as a voluptuous, hysterical madwoman from the tropics. We can read both Rhys and Marryat back through Gilbert and Gubar (1979), seeing Harriet as an example of female hysteria (see Depledge 2010), like Luella Miller (see Wilkins Freeman 1903). Women vampires are essentially unclean and the right to punish their behaviour is premised on versions of normativity, conventional modesty, purity, compliance and subordination. In early female vampire narratives, punishment comes from the forces of order, the right of men to define them as sick, hysterical, wrong, to be managed, constrained, locked up and destroyed. Elaine Showalter notes the resemblance of Lucy in *Dracula* to Freud's Dora case (1986: 99) while Marie Mulvey-Roberts argues 'Lucy's behaviour on both sides of the grave would have led many Victorian doctors to diagnose her as a classic hysteric' (1998: 86). Psychic draining, enervation and hysteria can be seen as constructed by a period and its problems with women's sexuality and energies.

Harriet is neither liberated nor celebratory, but she perhaps derives from earlier sensationalising errant women, like Lady Audley in Braddon's *Lady Audley's Secret* (1862). Both Lucy (*Dracula*) and Carmilla are destroyed by doctors: Van Helsing, Seward and the doctor called by Laura's father. Marryat and others aligned medical views on women and hysteria with the vampire myth (Heller 2000: 80) and she has Harriet Brandt commit suicide, having accepted a doctor's diagnosis that she has 'the blood of the vampire' in her (166). Heller traces the development of scientific/medical discourses on hysterical women, quoting American physician Weir Mitchell's (1877) assertion that a: 'hysterical girl is a vampire who sucks the blood of the healthy people about her ... surely where there is one hysterical girl there will be soon or late two sick women' (Heller 2000: 78).

Moment of Change – Angela Carter's Vampires

Pivotal texts in the reformation and re-representation of the female vampire are two short stories by Angela Carter who initiated a feminist Gothic revival, though she rarely used either of these terms (Wisker 1993). Carter's tales tell several stories, problematising the representation of the sexual woman in myth, fairy-tale and popular fictions, exposing vampire myths of eternal life and predation, and undercutting narratives in which women are rescued from static states by love. Her vampire women represent an active critique of such values and beliefs. In 'The Lady of the House of Love' (1979), Dracula's descendant waits for hapless male travellers. A reluctant vampire, the last of her kind, she falls in love with a bicycling British soldier on leave just before the outbreak of the First World War. Woken to the humanity of her nature, she is released from the vampire curse and dies, bequeathing him a rose grown in soil fertilised by the bones of her victims. This rose of 'Count Nosferatu' blooms in 'corrupt, brilliant, baleful splendour' (Carter 1979: 108) in his barracks on the eve of his regiment's departure for the slaughter of the French battlefields.

More active, agentic and a model for the vampire lesbian huntresses of the 1980s and 1990s, 'The Loves of Lady Purple' (1986) replays Pygmalion and Pinocchio with a marionette fashioned from the dark salacious dreams of the Asiatic Professor, to feed the hunger of local men who nightly watch her perform whorish acts. Lady Purple is the embodiment of Kristeva's notions that we construct that which we abhor and desire, in order to abject and Otherise it. This *femme fatale* marionette is manipulated to feed the lusts of her audience then punished for her behaviour. Carter exposes ways in which sexual desire and disgust are off-loaded onto constructs which are manipulated and Otherised. This literal treatment renders such performative transfers parodic. Lady Purple, feminist puppet, comes to life, drains the Professor and stalks off to the nearest village brothel, an active agent with her own sexual power. It is a tale both cautionary – about creating what you fear – and empowering. She is a model for the powerful women vampires in Anne Rice's *Queen of the Damned* (1988), in Poppy Brite's fictions and the short stories in *Nite Bites* (Brownworth 1996) and Pam Keesey's collections (1993; 1995).

Radical Lesbian Feminist Vampires

The vampire is the queer in its lesbian mode.
(Sue Ellen Case, 'Tracking the Vampire', p. 4)

In the 1980s and 1990s, the figure of the vampire was radically reappropriated by contemporary women horror writers, such as Anne Rice (*Interview with the Vampire,* 1976), Sherry Gottlieb (*Love Bite,* 1994), Poppy Z. Brite (*Lost Souls,* 1992) and Jewelle Gomez (*The Gilda Stories,* 1992). These authors reinterpreted the vampire for their own radical ends, investing the figure with all the disruptive power of the erotic and, through the troubling of gender roles, questioning conventional values and critiquing destructive relationships of power, inequalities based on racism, sexism, homophobia – both entertaining and forcing serious questioning of the logic and credibility of social conventions which enhance the rights of some over others. The lesbian vampire tale arrived, building on the work of predecessors, including the radical frissons of Carter and Brite's vampires as outsiders. *The Gilda Stories* has at its heart 'Girl', who escapes slavery, in Gomez's alternative African-American lesbian vampire sisterhood, which has evolved from a history of centuries of US inequality based on race and gender. In the Brownworth (1996) and Keesey collections (1993; 1995), tales of rock-and-roll lesbian vampire lovers, Pat Califia's S&M lesbian love (in 'The Vampire'), and sci-fi (in Katherine Forrest's 'O Captain, My Captain'), express lesbian relationships as central rather than marginal. The vampire, most particularly the boundary-breaking lesbian vampire, is liberated, refusing the constraints of gender, time, space and conventional power relationships. Paulina Palmer aligns lesbians and vampires in terms of lifestyle, pleasures and relationships. Indeed, she suggests that, from a social point of view, the lesbian, like the vampire, is generally regarded as both an independent loner and a member of a loosely knit network or group (Palmer 1998: 102).

Sue Ellen Case (1991) suggests the lesbian vampire can be read using queer theory foregrounding same-sex desire: it destabilises 'the borders of life and death', refusing 'the organicism which defines the living as the good' (Case 1991: 3). Ken Gelder takes her work further, arguing that 'queer' problematises stable notions of sexuality and of being, upsetting borders and binaries: 'In short the queer is the taboo-breaker, the monstrous, the uncanny' (Gelder 1994: 61). Lesbian and gay vampires undercut the divisions of life/death, male/female, self/Other, moving beyond the Freudian pre-Oedipal mother and child relationship to one which celebrates the in-betweenness enabled by destabilising those binaries. Case's arguments about the value of lesbian vampire exchange in the new economy of these fictions moves beyond the pre-symbolic re-reading of mother-and-child relations to imagine an 'in-between' state, 'between the familiar and the unfamiliar, the living and the dead, that Freud (and the Slovenian Lacanians) has left relatively untouched' (Gelder 1994: 62). In addition, as Case argues, since vampires have no reflection, they also undermine the symbolic order. Gelder glosses this as 'a political act, a revaluation of relations which refuses the symbolic/ pre-symbolic argument' (62).

In the texts of the 1990s and early twenty-first century, energies of revolt are often expressed through female vampires. In Sherry Gottlieb's *Love Bite* (1994) and Nancy Kirkpatrick's *Sunglasses After Dark* (1989), they stalk the streets seeking relationships with equals, draining the vulnerable, actively celebrating new modes of being and opportunities for eternal love, rescuing others, righting historical and endemic wrongs based on racial, gendered, sexual difference. In these and more contemporary texts (Buffini 2008 and *A Girl Walks Home Alone at Night,* dir. Ana Lily Amirpour, 2014), the themes and imagery of border-crossing open up new opportunities for agency. These liminal creatures, lesbian and/or heterosexual female vampires, choose whom they love from those whose sexuality is also unconventional. Context decides convention; lesbian vampires might well not be configured as radical in a context that does not demonise difference. Race equality and an ethical edge are characteristic of some lesbian vampire narratives. 'I hate blood, I hate the carnage. But I've learned to use it', says Victoria Brownworth's lesbian vampire, a reporter from New Orleans, who tells her friends how her lover, Dolores, initiated her into vampirism: 'She was Death itself. She fed me, and then she taught me how to feed' (Brownworth 1996: 210, 212). But, a sister of mercy, she turns her gift into a vampire rescue of destitute and dying young children in Rwanda, reporting the genocide of the Tutsis by the Hutu, becoming a vampire with a conscience.

Cosmetic Beauty and Ageing: 'Greedy Choke Puppy' (2001) and *Cereus Blooms at Night* (1996)

Two Caribbean soucouyants remind us of the problems of ageing and women seeking cosmetic beauty in cultures where a woman's worth depends on how she looks. Nalo Hopkinson's 'Greedy Choke Puppy' negotiates between false investment in cosmeticised beauty, and responsibility, individual and community freedoms, setting the wise grandmother against the selfish, wayward, reluctantly ageing grand-daughter. Responsibility, ageing and self-worth are differently dealt with in *Cereus Blooms at Night* (1996) where, characterised by the overwhelming, heady, freeing scent of the night-blooming cereus, Shani Mootoo's abused protagonist, the split self Mala/Poh Poh, can finally tell and have her tale told, and women's ageing is celebrated. This is a vampire without teeth: Mala/Poh Poh, is a non-invasive soucouyant who drains no one, but visits happy homes at night gaining from their positive energies. Postcolonial Gothic writers of vampire fictions recover hidden histories, enabling a re-embracing of the past and the value of the self in the present, turning the negative into positive and reclaiming voice and power.

'Greedy Choke Puppy' (2001) reprises and reverses issues in nine-teenth-century vampire narratives. Combining vampire lore with Caribbean myth, Hopkinson's Caribbean/Torontonian tale plays on concerns about women and knowledge, the community, values, ethics and cosmetic beauty. Jackie, an un-self-managed, selfish soucouyant, must drain vulnerable lives to maintain youthful looks and her 'sweet eye'. Ironically for Jackie the PhD student, study does not lead to self-worth and enlightenment; her research on 'Hurrucan' and Caribbean superstition only fuels her sense that she should be able to use the super-stitions and her own shape-shifting to maintain her youth and beauty confirmed by the male gaze:

> But I get to find out know how it is when the boys stop making sweet eye at you so much, and start watching after a next younger thing ... I know then I was a soucouyant, a hag-woman. I know what I had to do. When your youth start to leave you, you have to steal more from somebody who still have plenty. I fly out the window and start to search, search for a newborn baby. (Hopkinson 2001: 178)

She sheds her skin at night, flies like a blazing ball of fire, draining babies (preferably) to gain their blood and life. She does this without compunc-tion, killing her friend Carmen's baby. Daughter of a wayward vampire soucouyant, unaware of community ethics, Jackie is punished by her grandmother, a Caribbean wise woman.

Something Else at Last: *A Vampire Story* (Moira Buffini, 2008); *Byzantium* (dir. Neil Jordan, 2013); *A Girl Walks Home Alone at Night* (dir. Ana Lily Amirpour, 2014)

I want to end on two contemporary texts, one a play that was turned into a film and one a film which was then turned into a comic book series. Contemporary vampire fictions became mundane and conformist with *Twilight* (Meyer 2005–8), but more recently they have ventured into another space. The film *Byzantium* (dir. Neil Jordan, 2013) explores the edginess of homelessness and mutual support, the need to consume, the lack of safety and context in which to thrive. Ana Lily Amirpour's award-winning film, *A Girl Walks Home Alone at Night* (2014), later adapted as a comic-book series, features an Iranian feminist vampire who skateboards to avenge wrongs in contemporary Iran.

Moira Buffini's play, *A Vampire Story* (2008), commissioned by the National Theatre for New Connections and contemporary with *Twilight*, was turned into the film *Byzantium*. The play has been performed by young actors in schools and colleges and at the Lyric Theatre, Hammersmith, and as the film *Byzantium*, it offers an intriguing new take on what it might mean to be a woman vampire in the contemporary world. Claire/Clara and Eleanor are mother and daughter posing as sisters who survive because they stay close and fend for themselves, two women in a male-dominated world negotiating everyday behaviour. The film and play concern the need to consume and the transience of relationships; both represent some of the demands on twenty-first-century vampires. Clara /Claire and Eleanor's tale of abuse at the hands of violent legally protected aristocratic men 200 years earlier indicts hierarchies of gender and class. This new working of the myth does not celebrate vampire sexuality as radical freedom. Instead, it sees these women as survivors, imaginative, learning to change, living as they must according to how society constructs them, becoming agents in a depressingly seedy, continuously abusive cultural society – where Otherising and disempowerment are constant, morphing with time and place. Mother and daughter are homeless transients, a product of two centuries of rootlessness.

Byzantium, unlike the play, has a specific setting: Hastings on the English south coast. Clara/Claire had been forced into prostitution 200 years previously by a predatory, lascivious Captain and was rescued by becoming a vampire on a tropical island dominated by a soucriant. In Hastings, she befriends a bereaved man, sets up a brothel in his dead mother's run-down hotel, the 'Byzantium' of the title, offering safety and independence to local women. Clad in corsets and black fishnet tights, Clara enacts the routine predatory vampire, siren figure of men's heated imagination, to provide money so they can pay the rent, buy clothes and look normal, but she isn't a flamboyant flâneur. As men would prey on her, so she preys on them, only killing when abused; so a scene of her bleeding the violent pimp on the beach, in the early morning, as the sun rises, reminds us that her kind of new vampire has no difficulty with crosses and sunshine, unlike Anne Rice's Madeleine, Claudia and their predecessors. Clara's draining him, seen as a tender kiss by any onlooker, has a social and moral reason as well as one of survival of the fittest. Eleanor, forever condemned to stay the age at which she was turned into a vampire, visits hospitals and homes for the elderly, releasing into death the old who want to be set free. They see her as an angel. The mother/daughter morality recalls Hopkinson's 'Greedy Choke Puppy', which, like Marryat's novel *The Blood of the Vampire*, features soucouyants/soucriants, while the vampire gift is also used to rescue the dying (as in Brownworth, Gottlieb and Rice). The women are under threat from both social services and the patriarchal vampires whose lore regulates vampire-making, excluding them. But a pursuing male vampire sides with them, producing a happy ending. Buffini combines cultural myths, revitalising and re-energising the vampire female in an age of decaying social services, where the elderly are preserved beyond their own desires, so that vampires become angels of mercy, and women become self-sufficient despite poverty and vulnerability.

Most recently Ana Lily Amirpour's film *A Girl Walks Home Alone* (2014), shot in Farsi, offers a new slant on the female postcolonial vampire-turned-street avenger. Amirpour is a cosmopolitan figure – Iranian by origin, born in Britain, living in Los Angeles – whose film won awards at the Sundance Festival. An Iranian feminist film received with widespread enthusiasm, it contributes new energy to women's postcolonial vampire narratives, mixing the role of avenger and humanitarian. The protagonist, a fearless, skateboarding female vampire, suffers angst about living, refuses to drain her cat and launches full force into defending a young gay man about to be attacked by a burly homophobe. This single-minded Catwoman-like hero with a mission helps clean up the small Iranian dead-end town, its alleys and back streets, and sets out to eradicate poverty and violence. In a period in which women's rights are being drastically eroded in the Middle East, the hooded figure on a skateboard in the chador represents radical female energy and agency.

Conclusion

The representation of women as vampires acts as a weather vane or a cultural compass of changing values. While some historical vampire women were condemned as sexually voracious and socially disruptive, they have been reappropriated, re-read through the work of contemporary women vampire writers. Dracula's vampire women, Carmilla, Harriet Brandt, Luella Miller, and the Good Lady Ducayne are sexual predators, hysterics, dangerous colonial and foreign Others, exemplifying social constructions and concerns about women, including their desire to remain ever young and beautiful. Each characteristic is part of popular constructions of women taken to pathological extremes. Nineteenth-century writers, themselves confined within the dominant ideology, produced stereotypical constructions, often merely confirming the disadvantages suffered by women: lack of property ownership; denial of rights to control their own sexuality, whether heterosexual or lesbian; disempowerment; idealisation matched with demonisation; infantilisation, relating to representations of them as hysterics and parasites. Angela Carter exposed the 'mind-forged manacles', to use William Blake's phrase, which underpin the 'abject script' given to women and which they internalised and reproduced. She exploded the myths, the underpinning narratives of constraint. With the exception of the anodyne collusive YA vampire romances of Meyer and others, women's vampire fictions from the late twentieth century onwards use the ever-morphing figure to ask similar questions about women and society, in different cultural contexts, but offer more questions and different answers. Radical lesbian vampires celebrate sexual energies, relationships, sisterhood; their embrace of the freedoms to upset fixed polarities, assumptions and behaviours offer a social and psychological critique more fundamental than the often quite formulaic endings of vampire girl meets (vampire) girl. Contemporary women vampires question mothering, dependency, role collusion even if they risk punishment for doing so. Postcolonial women vampires problematise Otherising based on ethnicity, question the beauty myth and the demonisation of ageing. Some depict the vampire turn as a humanitarian act, avenging the wrongs arising from patriarchy and as celebrating sisterhood and agency.

Filmography

A Girl Walks Home Alone at Night, directed by Ana Lily Amirpour, USA: Logan Pictures, 2014.
Byzantium, directed by Neil Jordan, Ireland/UK/USA: StudioCanal, 2013.

Bibliography

Auerbach, Nina (1995), *Our Vampires Ourselves,* Chicago: University of Chicago Press.
Botting, Fred (1995), *The Gothic,* London: Routledge.
Braddon, Mary Elizabeth (1862), *Lady Audley's Secret,* London: William Tinsley.
Braddon, Mary Elizabeth [1896] (1989), 'Good Lady Ducayne', in Alan Ryan (ed.), *The Penguin Book of Vampire Stories,* London: Penguin, pp. 138–62.
Brite, Poppy Z. (ed.) (1994), *Love in Vein 1,* New York: Harper Prism.
Brownworth, Victoria, A. (1996), 'Twelfth Night', in Victoria A. Brownworth (ed.), *Nite Bites,* Berkeley, CA: Seal Press.
Buffini, Moira (2008), *A Vampire Story,* London: Faber & Faber.
Califia, Pat (1993), 'The Vampire', in Pam Keesey (ed.), *Daughters of Darkness,* San Francisco: Cleis Press, pp. 167–84.
Carter, Angela (1979), 'The Lady of the House of Love', in *The Bloody Chamber and Other Stories,* London: Gollancz.
Carter, Angela (1986), 'The Loves of Lady Purple', in *Wayward Girls and Wicked Women,* London: Virago.
Case, Sue Ellen (1991), 'Tracking the Vampire', *Differences: A Journal of Feminist Cultural Studies* 3(2): 1–20.
Depledge, Greta (2010), 'Introduction', in Florence Marryat, *Blood of the Vampire* [1897], Brighton: Victorian Secrets, pp. xi–xxxvi.
Dijkstra, Bram (1986), *Idols of Perversity: Fantasies of Feminine Evil in Fin-de-Siècle Culture,* Oxford: Oxford University Press.
Forrest, Katherine V. (2008), 'O Captain, My Captain', in *Dreams and Swords,* Ann Arbor, MI: Bywater Books.
Gelder, Ken (1994), *Reading the Vampire,* London: Routledge.
Gilbert, Sandra M. and Gubar, Susan (1979), *The Madwoman in the Attic: The Woman Writer and the Nineteenth-Century Literary Imagination,* New Haven, CT: Yale University Press.
Gomez, Jewelle (1992), *The Gilda Stories,* London: Sheba.
Heller, Tamar (2000), 'The Vampire in the House: Hysteria, Female Sexuality, and Feminist Knowledge in Le Fanu's "Carmilla" (1872)', in Barbara Leah Harman and Susan Meyer (eds), *The New Nineteenth Century: Feminist Readings of Under-read Victorian Fiction,* New York and London: Garland Publishing, pp. 77–96.
Hopkinson, Nalo (2001), 'Greedy Choke Puppy', in *Skin Folk,* New York: Warner Books Inc., pp. 167–82.

Horney, Karen (1967), *Feminine Psychology*, ed. Harold Kelman, New York: W.W. Norton.

Keesey, Pam (ed.) (1993), *Daughters of Darkness*, San Francisco: Cleis Press.

Keesey, Pam (ed.) (1995), *Dark Angels*, San Francisco: Cleis Press.

Kristeva, Julia (1982), *Powers of Horror: An Essay on Abjection*, trans. Leon Roudiez, New York: Columbia University Press.

Le Fanu, Sheridan (1872), 'Carmilla' in *In a Glass Darkly*, London: R. Bentley and Son.

Marryat, Florence [1897] (2009), *The Blood of the Vampire*, Richmond, VA: Valancourt Books.

Macfie, Sian (1991), '"They Suck Us Dry": A Study of Late Nineteenth-Century Projections of Vampiric Women', in Philip Shaw and Peter Stockwell (eds), *Subjectivity and Literature from the Romantics to the Present Day*, London and New York: Pinter Publishers, pp. 58–67.

Meyer, Stephenie (2005–8), *Twilight* Series, New York: Little, Brown.

Moers, Ellen (1976), *Literary Women*, New York: Doubleday.

Mootoo, Shani [1996] (2002), *Cereus Blooms at Night*, Toronto: M&S.

Mulvey-Roberts, Marie (1998), 'Dracula and the Doctors: Bad Blood, Menstrual Taboo and the New Woman' in William Hughes and Andrew Smith (eds), *Bram Stoker: History, Psychoanalysis and the Gothic*, London: Macmillan, pp. 78–95.

Palmer, Paulina (1998), *Lesbian Gothic Fiction: Transgressive Narratives*, London: Cassell.

Riquelme, P. (2002), *Dracula (Case Studies in Contemporary Criticism)*, London: Palgrave Macmillan.

Rhys, Jean (1966), *Wide Sargasso Sea*, London: Andre Deutsch.

Signorotti, Elizabeth (1996), 'Repossessing the Body: Transgressive Desire in "Carmilla" and *Dracula*', *Criticism* 38(4): 607–32.

Showalter, Elaine (1986), 'Syphilis, Sexuality and the Fiction of the *Fin de Siècle*', in Ruth Bernard Yeazell (ed.), *Sex, Politics, and Science in the Nineteenth-Century Novel*, Baltimore and London: Johns Hopkins University Press, pp. 88–103.

Stein, Karen, F. (1983), 'Monsters and Madmen: Changing Female Gothic', in Julian E. Fleenor (ed.), *The Female Gothic*, Montreal: Eden, pp. 123–37.

Stoker, Bram (1897), *Dracula*, London: Archibald Constable.

Wilkins Freeman, Mary E. (1903), 'Luella Miller', in *The Wind in the Rose-Bush and Other Stories of the Supernatural*, New York: Doubleday, Page & Company.

Wisker, Gina (1993), 'At Home All Was Blood and Feathers: The Werewolf in the Kitchen – Angela Carter and Horror', in Clive Bloom (ed.), *Creepers*, London: Pluto.

Wolf, Naomi (1990), *The Beauty Myth: How Images of Beauty Are Used Against Women*, New York: William Morrow and Company.

Part III

New Directions

Chapter 11

Queering the Female Gothic
Ardel Haefele-Thomas

All of us have a choice: We can stand on old ground, protecting 40-year-old borders, or we can throw open the gates and see what lies ahead in new thinking, new organising, new narratives, new intersections between political, cultural, economic, and gender-sex struggles. More than ever we have the tools for a deeper critique of gender both as a means of social control and as a promise of greater global freedom of gender and sexual expression.

(Joan Nestle, 'Genders on My Mind', p. 9)

Joan Nestle, an icon of Second-Wave Lesbian Feminism, calls for us to move forward beyond a gender binary to a place where feminism can and must embrace a multiplicity of intersecting identities.[1] While the border crossings and thrown-open gates she asks us to traverse offer new and expanding forms of feminist *as well as* queer theory and practice, Nestle could just as easily be pointing us toward new ways of theorising the Gothic. Indeed, 'queering' the Female Gothic just opens us all up to a broader understanding of historically marginalised authors in a historically marginalised genre. It is through its treble marginalisation that queer Female Gothic demands that we reconsider and question all of the social and cultural 'norms' that we have absorbed.

It has been well established that, for many women authors, Gothic has afforded a proverbial safe space in which to explore numerous and often overlapping social concerns. For women writers, often already dismissed simply because they are female, writing within a liminal genre like Gothic has enabled them to more honestly and thoroughly critique restrictive social and cultural conventions such as: patriarchal and heteronormative family structures; the medical pathologising of cisgender female and trans* bodies; and institutions of racism and sexism within various historic contexts, as well as in contemporary issues surrounding the intersections of sexuality, race, class, ability and gender identity.[2] The authors and their works explored in this chapter offer us an array of queer characters and queer situations – regardless of the author's own sexual orientation or gender identity. All these authors, ultimately, work within what I am calling a queer Gothic to render a much richer reading, *particularly* if we utilise a broadly defined and ever-changing feminist approach. Along the trajectories of feminist movements and feminist theories, queer Female Gothic (unlike queer women's romances) never adheres to any one essentialist formula because as a genre, Gothic thrives on complications and constantly throws what we think we know and believe into confusion, often with subversive and disturbing results.

Second-Wave Feminism and Queer Gothic: Chambers, Condé, Morrison and Gomez

Second-Wave Feminism's most important directive was to uncover, give voice to, and reclaim the largest marginalised group of people in history: women. Our academic institutions today include Women's Studies, Feminist Studies, Gender Studies and Queer Studies (LGBT Studies) thanks to Second-Wave Feminism. We need to acknowledge and give credit to the pioneering movement that demanded we interrogate women's inequality and gender as social constructs, while we simultaneously explore the ways in which the initial directives no longer are enough within Third-Wave, post-feminist, queer, and even post-queer theories.

As with any new political movement bent on quickly righting historic wrongs, some aspects of Second-Wave feminism became essentialist. For marginalised people, the overarching impulse – and usually a dangerous one – is to not only find the good first, but to re-silence that which might not fit into a specific political or theoretical agenda. In the early days of Second-Wave Feminism, for example, the focus was mainly on white middle-class heterosexual women creating all of the 'rules' of the new feminist movement. Of course, women – specifically white lesbians – outside the middle-class heterosexual 'in group' quickly demanded to be heard. Once a radical lesbian movement formed, however, that, too, became dogmatic. In April 1977, 'The Combahee River Collective Statement' penned by Black lesbian feminists explained precisely why they would *not* submit to a white lesbian agenda to become separatists and forget their Black brothers engaged in social and political struggles. In many cases, particularly for lesbian feminists of colour, there was a need to fight on multiple fronts: sexism, racism, classism and homophobia.

For women authors writing Gothic during and immediately follow-ing Second-Wave Feminism, one of the ways in which they utilised Gothic was to bring attention to historically important issues concern-ing women and women's history; however, they also helped illuminate a different vein of Second-Wave Feminism – one that was not essentialist, but rather full of complexity and competing, often disparate, demands. Queer and feminist themes in the Gothic of Jane Chambers's *Burning* (1978), Maryse Condé's *I, Tituba, Black Witch of Salem* (1986), Toni Morrison's *Beloved* (1987) and Jewelle Gomez's *The Gilda Stories* (1991) are surely products of Second-Wave Feminism, but at the same time, the authors' choice of the Gothic genre also allows them to break out of feminist and lesbian feminist essentialist strictures as they each re-examine historic moments in a queer Gothic light.

Jane Chambers and Maryse Condé employ queer feminist situations in their Gothic narratives to examine the 1690s witch trials of colo-nial Massachusetts. Toni Morrison and Jewelle Gomez focus on the American South in their explorations of the ramifications of slavery. These authors, two of whom are heterosexual women of colour, pub-lishing with mainstream presses, and two of whom are queer – one white and one African American and Native American – publishing with small independent presses, create queer Gothic situations that disrupt any sort of dogmatic Second-Wave Feminist approaches, even though the authors themselves are often thought of in terms of Second-Wave Feminism.

Jane Chambers's *Burning* takes two contemporary women – Cynthia and Angela – and, through the trope of the haunted house, forces them to relive the 300-year-old doomed lesbian relationship between Martha and Abigail. As the story unfolds, the reader learns that Martha and Abigail were in love but unable to have a full sexual relationship before Martha was burned at the stake for witchcraft. Chambers complicates this queer Gothic reimagining of misogyny run rampant in 1692 with her two contemporary characters: Cynthia is married to Dave and has two children; Angela, who is much younger, has only recently gradu-ated from college and has agreed to work for Cynthia as a nanny during the August respite from New York City's heat. Cynthia is heterosexual; Angela is only vaguely sensing that she might be a lesbian. The 300-year-old ghosts, however, have interesting plans for the two. It is as though Cynthia and Angela, whenever they each fall into a trance state caused by the one haunted room in the farmhouse, are puppets who will right the historic wrong. Part of Cynthia's horror about her specific haunting is that, through the eyes of Martha's spirit, she is able to watch the witch trials unfold, and she begins to comprehend that the ways women were treated in 1692 are not dissimilar to the ways women are treated in the late twentieth century. (This becomes clear at the end of the novel when she is nearly raped by two townsmen who want to teach the 'lesbian' a lesson. As Cynthia attempts to report the incident to the police, the male officer threatens to 'out' her affair with Angela to her husband.) But another part of Cynthia's horror is the realisation that she will, eventually, have to engage in sex with Angela in order to finally free the ghosts of Martha and Abigail. A reimagined lesbian utopia this is not.

Most lesbian feminist authors published by small presses in the 1970s and 1980s in the United States would have written this as a double-lesbian Gothic romance. Martha and Abigail, via Cynthia and Angela, would have finally been able to make love and set their own haunted souls free (this part of the stereotypic scenario does happen) and Cynthia would have discovered her 'true' lesbian self, left her husband and children and run off with Angela. Jane Chambers, however, keeps the tale more complex by giving voice to the often confusing and rich depth of situational queer relationships and bisexual possibilities as evidenced by Cynthia's realisation:

> Woman-woman was not the same as woman-man. There were no devices, no tactics, no ammunition that the other didn't have as well. No excuses served as camouflage; the battle for each other was fought unarmed, head-on. She expected more from a woman than from a man and, recognising this, Cynthia was stunned. (Chambers 1985: 95)

Chambers leaves Cynthia to work out her relationship with her husband and children; Angela, who has fully started to come out of the closet, heads back to New York and single life.

Like Chambers, Maryse Condé also turns her eye to the 1692 witch trials; however, in *I, Tituba, Black Witch of Salem*, rather than creating a purely fictional set of characters, she sets out to re-create the lost history of Tituba – the Black woman often blamed for bringing the contagion of witchcraft into the lives of the white residents of Salem, Massachusetts: 'I can look for my story among those of the witches of Salem, but it isn't there' (Condé 1992: 149). Condé's queer feminist Gothic allows her to explore patriarchal, capitalist, racist and Christian laws of the New World that victimised women and other marginalised people. A sort of Gothic time/space continuum takes over Condé's tale as she places the real historic figure of Tituba alongside Hester Prynne, Nathaniel Hawthorne's fictional heroine in *The Scarlet Letter* (1850).

Both women find themselves imprisoned because they have transgressed the Christian patriarchal laws of the land – Tituba is accused of witchcraft and Hester of adultery. These proud transgressors embody Second-Wave defiance as they fall in love with one another. Although Tituba is Black and Hester is white, she reminds Tituba, "'It's not my society. Aren't I an outcast like yourself? Locked up between these walls?'" (96). Moments later, Tituba writes, 'I was so moved [by Hester] I was bold enough to caress her face and whispered: "You, too, Hester, are lovely!"' (96). From this moment on, the pregnant Hester and Tituba become lovers until Tituba's release from prison. With the relationship between Hester and Tituba, Condé has created a mutual understanding within an interracial queer frame. It is an understanding and connection that 1970s white lesbian feminists and women from the Combahee River Collective only dreamed of having.

The fact of Tituba and Hester's relationship is only part of what makes Condé's Gothic tale queer. More than any sort of sexual act, it is Condé's collapse of time and space, indeed, the collapse of history itself that creates queer room in the novel. Tituba and Hester may be imprisoned in 1692 awaiting trial, but they hold each other and talk about feminism – and more specifically feminist separatism in those precise terms. Long after Hester has committed suicide and Tituba has died back in Barbados, her ghost writes:

> I have only one regret: it's having to be separated from Hester. We do communicate, of course. I can smell the dried almonds of her breath. I can hear the echo of her laugh. But each of us remains on her side of the ocean. I know that she is pursuing her dreams of creating a world of women that will be more just and humane. I myself have loved men too much and shall continue to do so. (Condé 1992: 178)

Condé's Tituba is queer beyond relations of the flesh, however. Like a ghost or a vampire, in death Tituba moves beyond being the lover of people of all genders and ethnicities to become a bird, a goat or even 'the sound of the wind as it whistles through the great trees on the hills' (179). Tituba's queerness and strength lies in her liminality and her ability to shapeshift.

While Maryse Condé takes Tituba's beginning slave narrative and turns it into a fantastical queer Gothic feminist tale meant to empower, Toni Morrison's feminist look at slavery becomes a queer Gothic nightmare. In her Pulitzer Prize-winning 1987 novel, *Beloved*, Morrison delivers a ghost story that underscores the devastation of the legacy of slavery that still marks culture in the United States today. The issue at the heart of Morrison's novel is the return of Beloved, a full-grown ghost of the 'crawling already?' baby girl whom Sethe, her mother, has murdered to keep out of the white slave owner's hands shortly after she has escaped across the river from Kentucky into Ohio. The question at the core of *Beloved* is 'what sort of society are we that makes killing our children a safer option than having them live in slavery?' Sethe can lay her dead toddler to rest and give her a human and humane burial; if she allows her little girl to live, though, it will only be to see her bought, sold and treated, as she had been treated, like an animal. *This* is the choice Sethe feels she has, and she chooses to take her one baby daughter's life as she breastfeeds her other newborn daughter, Denver: 'Beloved is my sister. I swallowed her blood right along with my mother's milk' (Morrison 1987: 205).

The slave system creates this inhumanity as it also, for Morrison, forges a queer incestuous space between a grieving mother and her two daughters as evidenced in the trio of voices:

Beloved
You are my sister
You are my daughter
You are my face; you are me
I have found you again; you have come back to me
You are my Beloved
You are mine
You are mine
You are mine ...
I drank your blood
I brought your milk ...
I loved you ...

(Morrison 1987: 216–17)

Morrison's use of Gothic helps illuminate the ways that a white, patriarchal and capitalist system at its absolutely most devastating metaphorically eats up African-American women and girls. The queer situations in Morrison's book are not meant to empower, but rather to horrify. This is not to say that Toni Morrison is coming at *Beloved* in a homophobic vein, but rather that she wants to underscore, through these incestuous queer elisions, the deep psychological trauma of the uncanny return of the prodigal daughter. In Beloved's case, she is the ghost of a murdered daughter. As the relations between the living and the dead and the mother and daughters devolve through the novel, so, too, does Morrison's language. From the beginning of *Beloved*, Morrison, like Condé, forces the reader out of the comfortable linear narrative style with her time/space disruptions and the sequence of events. As the novel progress, however, normative modes of storytelling break down, entirely underscoring, at the level of the word, the queer and ruined spaces left behind in the legacy of slavery: 'This is not a story to pass on' (275).

Jewelle Gomez's 1991 *The Gilda Stories* also envisions murder as the only solution to saving a young Black girl from slavery. However, in Gomez's queer Gothic world, the child is killed and then given eternal life as a vampire. Gomez's novel is comprised of several short stories that take place in the past, present and future and all feature the bisexual African-American vampire, Gilda. In the first chapter, 'Louisiana: 1850', we meet a young runaway slave who makes her way to the outskirts of New Orleans, hides in a barn, and then, in defending herself against a man intent on raping her, stabs him to death, only to be discovered – terrified and bloody – by an odd, elderly white woman named Gilda who speaks to her through her thoughts:

> She had heard of people who could talk without speaking but never expected a white to be able to do it. This one was a puzzlement to her: the dark eyes and pale skin ... she wore men's breeches and a heavy jacket. (Gomez 1991: 13)

Not only is Gilda's queerness marked by her cross-dressing, but her occupation as owner and operator of an illegal night-time speakeasy does not befit a proper Southern white lady. During the day, Gilda's speakeasy transforms into a homosocial women's commune. Gilda's partner, Bird, is a Lakota woman. Together, as a subversive interracial queer vampiric couple, they have created a safe space for women social outcasts of all ethnicities in an 1850s Southern American slave state.

Gilda, a 300-year-old vampire ready for a final eternal rest, is elated to find the young runaway girl in her barn, and much of the story in this chapter revolves around Gilda's tutoring the girl about the ways that vampirism and social justice can work together. In a touching scene at the chapter's conclusion, Gilda has given her own life and her name to the girl and has asked Bird to complete the exchange of blood: 'Bird pulled aside her woolen shirt and bared her breasts. She made a small incision beneath the right one and pressed the Girl's mouth to it' (48).[3] Jewelle Gomez has taken the negative stereotype of the lesbian vampire who sucks young women into 'the life' and turns it around as one of the ways that women can actually empower themselves and build community. The queer vampires that populate Gomez's *The Gilda Stories* are healers – not only of what ails physically, but politically and socially.

Post-Second-Wave Feminism and Queer Gothic: Waters, Heidt and Culpepper

Sarah Waters's haunting 1999 neo-Victorian *Affinity* benefits from an accumulated success of feminist and queer theory and politics. Waters, a mainstream queer Welsh novelist and recipient of numerous literary awards, employs a lesbian present to explore a fictionalised (albeit totally believable) lesbian past.

In *Affinity*, Sarah Waters renders imaginatively some of the insights achieved by contemporary Foucauldian, feminist and queer theories to breathe life into her dark novel that, ultimately, looks at the ways masculine heteronormative systems of power kill queer women. Waters revives the proper Victorian woman's mode of writing – the diary – to explore the suffocating social constraints placed upon upper-class women forced into the heterosexual economy of marriage. In a more radical twist, Waters not only gives voice to Margaret Prior, but also to the working-class spiritualist in prison, Selina Dawes. As their voices come together via their diary entries, we are treated to the inner workings of the Victorian home. In Margaret's case, the home is a completely heteronormative upper-class household, but in Selina's, it is one that illuminates more complicated class structures as they are experienced by the orphaned working-class spiritualist who is taken into the homes of wealthy, usually widowed, ladies, who demand her attentions both as a spiritualist and, quite possibly, as a lover. The hint of mother/daughter incest pervades Selina Dawes's diary entries as the reader learns that mothers quite often bring their daughters along with them to the queerly erotically charged séances in which Peter Quick (who is actually Ruth Vigers, Selina Dawes's maid and lover, dressed in drag) fondles the mothers and daughters. The conflation of Selina Dawes, an orphan, as lover and daughter also adds to the underlying Gothic trope of incest.

Affinity centres on Margaret Prior, a wealthy spinster, whose first love, Helen, has succumbed to societal pressures by marrying Margaret's brother, Stephen, thus complicating her relationship with Margaret. After a nervous breakdown and attempted suicide following Helen's marriage, Margaret decides to 'do good' in the community by visiting women at Millbank Prison, where she meets the enigmatic spiritualist, Selina Dawes. *Affinity* compares the dark and dank hallways and cells of Millbank Prison to the lavish homes that imprison Victorian ladies in much the same ways. In fact, by the novel's end, it becomes clear that women in prison might actually have more freedom to have special 'pals', i.e. women lovers, than 'respectable' English women. It is this analysis of the class system, along with the cross-class love affair between Selina Dawes and Margaret Prior, that gives this bleak novel an edge. The novel's final point is that systems of male power and domination have worked so well that men need no longer oppress women, rather they are quite capable of doing it to one another. Waters's novel is still feminist in that it gives voice to the Victorian lesbian – a figure whom the nineteenth-century British laws deemed insignificant and invisible enough to not even warrant an inclusion in the Criminal Law Amendment.[4]

On one hand, we can read Sarah Waters's success in mainstream publishing houses as a sign that, as queers and feminists, 'our work here is done'. Yet, what is the role of small queer presses if 'we' are now mainstream? Second-Wave lesbian feminists brought us independent lesbian publishing houses like Naiad Press and Firebrand Books in the United States and Sheba Feminist Press and the Women's Press in Great Britain. Just as it seemed that these smaller, independent publishing houses were going to become extinct, Bold Strokes Books in the United States became a huge publication house for LGBT books of all genres. I will now focus on two of this press's most recent books,which explore queer women in the Gothic mode: Yvonne Heidt's *Sometime Yesterday* (2012) and Cate Culpepper's *A Question of Ghosts* (2012). As Gothic queer romances, the stories all follow a typical romantic trajectory and actually, in some ways, harken back to a much more essentialist version of Second-Wave lesbian feminism – particularly in the case of Culpepper's *A Question of Ghosts*, which creates a lesbian feminist utopia populated by a group of friends desiring to create their own 'clan' modelled on that of the television heroine, *Xena: Warrior Princess*. Although there is humour and a hint of irony, this twenty-first-century imagining could just as easily have come out of 1970s visions of an American 'lesbian nation'.

Yvonne Heidt's *Sometime Yesterday* revisits the trope of the haunted house – and like Jane Chambers's *Burning*, features a contemporary female couple who must become lovers to reconcile and free nineteenth-century lesbian lovers who were murdered and buried on the property by the maniacal and abusive family patriarch. Natalie and Vanessa need to become lovers to work out the historical mess, but as the story unfolds, the two women also find that they are distant relatives of the murdered women.

In the haunted Victorian house on the Northern California coast, Natalie and Van are aided by Natalie's mother who comes to help cast the ghost of the sadistic Richard out of the house. In a nod to early queer Female Gothic from the 1980s that focused on feminist retellings of the Salem witch trials, Heidt informs the reader that Natalie's mother is a witch. Heidt's book can be read as a harkening back to the 1980s when lesbian feminists were trying to reclaim and create a history. However, what is different about this book – and where contemporary feminist and queer theory help our understanding – is that the characters who populate its pages (the heterosexual best friend and the blood relations) actively embrace the new relationship. Natalie is able simply and without angst to come out in the space of one paragraph. In essence, this twenty-first-century queer Gothic story utilises Second-Wave tropes and then moves forward into new, more liberated territory.

Cate Culpepper's *A Question of Ghosts* places the action in the centre of Seattle's LGBT district – Capitol Hill. Like Heidt's book, this too, is a ghost story about a mother who comes to save her queer daughter; however, in this case, the mother is the ghost. On her fifth birthday, thirty-four years before the main action of the novel, Becca Healy's mother, in a psychotic fit, shot and killed her husband and then herself as their daughter played in the adjoining room. At least this is the story Becca has been told. Ghostly voices transmitted by radio send her messages that lead her to right familial wrongs. On her sixteenth birthday, a ghost voice comes through the static of Becca's radio to tell her '*Not true*' (Culpepper 2012: 15). And then again, on her thirty-ninth birthday, she receives the same message. It is at this point that she decides to hire Dr Joanne Call, who studies Electronic Voice Phenomena (ghost voices). This, like other queer women's Gothic, sets out to rewrite a historic record. In this case, it is a personal one of righting a historic familial wrong – the one in which Becca's parents died at her mother's hand.

Although the novel is suffused with a sense of the supernatural, it also raises the possibility of Becca's 'haunting' being an early sign that she is, like her mother, becoming mentally ill. However, not only is the mother proven innocent, but the real murderer is one of Becca's most trusted friends: her mother's psychiatrist, Rachel, who has, since the night of the murders, kept a protective and watchful eye over Becca. Rachel did not kill Becca's parents in some sort of presumed heterosexual fit of jealous rage; she killed them because she was in love with Becca's mother. This extra queer twist at the end of the novel is important to note in relation to feminist writing and feminist Gothic we have moved beyond the point where 'typical' lesbian feminist romances, mysteries and Gothic (and this novel combines all of the above) feel the need to claim that all of the women – and more specifically, all of the queer women – are heroes. Rather, it is a more complex look at the ways that the closet kills and that women – queer women – are just as susceptible to murderous urges as anyone.

Trans* Feminism and Back to the Past: Lee, Marryat, McCullers

In the essay, 'Feminist Transmasculinities', reese simpkins writes the following:

> One of the strengths of feminism has been its ability to adapt and to wrestle with questions of identity. It has grown from a movement based upon the enfranchisement of upper-class white women to a movement that struggles to include a multiplicity of individuals with multiple and sometimes competing identities and realities of oppression. As feminism is forced to grapple with race, class, sexuality and gender/sex identification it reinvigorates itself, grows and remains relevant. (simpkins 2006: 79)

Like feminism, the Gothic has also continued to reconfigure itself and to keep itself relevant. The stories told may have changed in nuance and they certainly have moved, in many cases, away from some of the more essentialist Second-Wave ideals. What is really interesting about the more complex nuances of queer and trans* feminisms, is that these theoretical modes actually help us even better to understand authors like Vernon Lee, Florence Marryat and Carson McCullers, who pre-date Second-Wave Feminism – authors whom, to be exact, Second-Wave Feminism was not quite sure how to handle.

Vernon Lee's *fin-de-siècle* decadent Gothic, and indeed her works in general, were largely ignored throughout the first half of the twentieth century. Through Second-Wave Feminism, authors like Vernon Lee were resurrected. For feminist scholars and, more specifically, lesbian feminist scholars thirsty for historical figures, Vernon Lee proved to be a bit of a problem. The androgynous and reclusive Lee (who not only changed her name from Violet Paget for the purposes of publishing, but also, as an adult, asked to be referred to as Vernon Lee in everyday life), may or may not have had sexual relations with women. There are numerous stories of feminist and lesbian feminist historians travelling to rural Maine to sift through Vernon Lee's archived letters for that moment of truth – the 'proof' that she was a lesbian because she had sex with another woman.[5] When the researchers come away from the archive no less enlightened, they have often cast their eye toward her queer decadent Gothic tales. But even there, Lee causes us trouble. Many theorists bent on claiming Lee's works as examples of specifically female and lesbian Gothic have a hard time reconciling this desire with the reality of Lee's broadly queer Gothic stories that defy any one specific gender identity or sexual orientation. From 'A Wicked Voice' about a bisexual and trans* operatic ghost whose songs haunt and kill lovers, to 'Prince Alberic and the Snake Lady', in which a seemingly heterosexual affair is actually a decadent love story between an effeminate male prince and a beautiful snake woman, Vernon Lee's Gothic writing resists any specific categorisation beyond the broad definition of 'queer'.

Florence Marryat, another decadent *fin-de-siècle* author who has only recently been rediscovered (and thus has not undergone the same scrutiny as Lee) also writes queer Gothic scenarios layered with incredibly complicated racial and colonial themes. In her 1897 vampire novel, *The Blood of the Vampire*, Marryat creates an emotionally vampiric bisexual woman of Jamaican descent who feeds off of the emotions of British men, women and babies. Marryat's narrative ambivalence toward the queer biracial vampire actually invites the reader to rethink static Victorian notions about the nurturing, naive and heteronormative 'good English mother' (Margaret Pullen) as well as the older and 'kindly' male Western medical authority (Dr Phillips).

When the novel opens with a group of English tourists at a summer resort in Heyst, Belgium, we are introduced to the English spinster, Miss Leyton, and her friend, Margaret Pullen, who is there with her baby daughter waiting to be joined by her husband, a soldier (who never arrives). Harriet Brandt, the young Jamaican vampire, also arrives at the same resort on her way to England and immediately Margaret Pullen falls under her spell:

> [She] was struck by the look with which Harriet Brandt was regarding her – it was so full of yearning affection – almost of longing to approach her nearer, to hear her speak, to touch her hand! She had heard of cases, in which young unsophisticated girls had taken unaccountable affections for members of their own sex. (Marryat 2009: 27)

It is the married English mother – and *not*, stereotypically, the spinster – who recognises the tense moment as homoerotic. The Victorian reader (and perhaps the contemporary one as well) is in for a shock: the figure who should epitomise heterosexual and middle-class stability not only reads the flirtatious and homoerotic signals from the Jamaican woman, but she *participates* in the game.

In another instance of Marryat countering a Victorian stereotype, she juxtaposes the wise and intellectually 'sound' Dr Phillips, who speaks with the backing of years as a Western medical authority, with Anthony Pennell, the less-than-masculine socialist advocate for women, children and animals, who falls madly in love with Harriet. Dr Phillips's attempt to warn Pennell against the biracial and bisexual vampire falls on deaf ears. Pennell's outrage when he shouts '"Doctor Phillips be damned!"'

(201) flies in the face of Victorian convention just as the outburst signals that those 'solid' and 'normal' figures we could always trust to be proper, heteronormative and gendernormative will need to give way to rapidly changing ideas about empire, sexuality and gender roles in the fast-approaching twentieth century.

The conclusion to *The Blood of the Vampire* delivers to the reader the same outcome as the much more famous 1897 vampire novel, *Dracula*, since both monsters die. In Marryat's novel, however, it does not take an entire band of strong men to subdue the vampire. Rather, Harriet Brandt takes her own life the morning after she awakens to find her beloved husband dead in bed next to her. There is nothing triumphant about the suicide of this vampire; rather, we are left with a haunting scenario of a queer who has been told by 'authorities' that there is no place in society for anyone as grotesque and marginalised as she is.

Finally, Carson McCullers offers us another example of a pre-Second-Wave author. In her 1951 Southern Gothic novella, *The Ballad of the Sad Café*, McCullers explores a queer love triangle formed by the androgynous Miss Amelia, the hunchback Cousin Lymon and Miss Amelia's ex-husband, Marvin Macy. Miss Amelia is described as dark and tall and freakish; racial tensions underscore queer tensions and vice versa. Cousin Lymon is also portrayed as a 'freak' and gender transgressor. In fact, of the three, Marvin Macy is the only 'typically' gendered and normative person. In the end, Miss Amelia loses Cousin Lymon to her ex-husband.

Not only are the relationships in McCullers's grotesque story painted as queer, but the space of the cafe itself functions as both the town's sideshow *and* a safe space for social outcasts:

> But the new pride that the café brought to this town had an effect on almost everyone, even the children … There, for a few hours at least, the deep bitter knowing that you are not worth much in this world could be laid low. (McCullers 1981: 55)

The Sad Café functions much like its urban queer counterparts of 1950s America – underground gay bars populated by racial, gender and sexual outlaws. McCullers's odd story ends with a shift of the town's gathering space away from the cafe to a prison chain gang on the outskirts of town. Here, the sound of twelve mortal men – Black and white together – sings with one voice. The literal voice of an interracial and homosocial space rises up in the heated silence: 'And what kind of gang is it that can make such music? Just twelve mortal men, seven of them black and five of them white boys from this county. Just twelve mortal men who are together' (72).

Second-Wave Feminism, in its rush to give voice to the silent and the silenced, often glossed over the richness of varied voices. We needed Second-Wave Feminism to get where we are now – and as simpkins points out to us, feminism is still very much alive and relevant. In other words, we are continually developing new lenses through which to appreciate and explore the ways that these authors have written and utilised queer Gothic to critique systems of power – systems that are all still inherently wrapped into a white, bourgeois, patriarchal and capitalist gender ideology. The evolution of feminist thought is evidenced in the evolution of works by authors who have 'queered the Female Gothic'.

Notes

1. As one of the co-founders of the Lesbian Herstory Archives in New York, USA, Joan Nestle can often be identified with a very limited definition of Second-Wave lesbian feminism; however, it needs to be noted that Nestle, as an out and proud Jewish working-class fat femme, was on occasion barred from feminist conferences because her views – particularly on butch-femme identities outside a 1950s context in the US – were seen as 'politically incorrect' in many lesbian feminist circles. See Joyce Warshow's 2002 documentary film *Hand on the Pulse*.
2. For the purposes of this chapter, I am utilising trans* as it is currently evolving as an umbrella term for all genders that do not adhere to a 'cisgender' definition. 'Cisgender' refers to a person who identifies with their sex and gender assignment at birth.
3. Jewelle Gomez has gone back to J. Sheridan Le Fanu's initial site of the queer female vampiric bite – the breast.
4. In August 1885, the infamous La Bouchère Amendment to the Criminal Code was passed. Legally, it underscored sodomy as a criminal act punishable by at least two years in prison with the possibility of hard labour. Culturally, historians have noted that La Bouchère's amendment solidified the definition of sodomy as a homosexual and not a heterosexual act.
5. For a much more in-depth discussion about Vernon Lee and Florence Marryat, please see Ardel Haefele-Thomas's *Queer Others in Victorian Gothic: Transgressing Monstrosity* (2012: 96–148). Of course, one's sexual orientation does not necessarily need to hinge on the fact of sex. Many queer theorists have fallen into the trap of needing to 'prove' that someone had sexual encounters to be queer. We certainly do not ask that heterosexual identity be validated in the same way.

Bibliography

Chambers, Jane [1978] (1985), *Burning*, New York: JH Press.
Combahee River Collective, The (1977), 'The Combahee River Collective

Statement', in Deborah T. Meem, Michelle A. Gibson and Jonathan F. Alexander (eds), *Finding Out: An Introduction to LGBT Studies*, Los Angeles: Sage Press, pp. 110–17.

Condé, Maryse [1986] (1992), *I, Tituba, Black Witch of Salem*, trans. Richard Philcox, New York: Ballantine Books.

Culpepper, Cate (2012), *A Question of Ghosts*, Valley Falls, NY: Bold Strokes Books.

Gomez, Jewelle (1991), *The Gilda Stories*, New York: Firebrand Books.

Haefele-Thomas, Ardel (2012), *Queer Others in Victorian Gothic: Transgressing Monstrosity*, Cardiff: University of Wales Press.

Heidt, Yvonne (2012), *Sometime Yesterday*, Valley Falls, NY: Bold Strokes Books.

Lee, Vernon [1896] (1987), 'Prince Alberic and the Snake Lady', in I. Cooper Willis (ed.), *Supernatural Tales*, London: Peter Owen, pp. 19–72.

Lee, Vernon (1987), 'A Wicked Voice', in *Supernatural Tales*, pp. 127–58.

Marryat, Florence [1897] (2009), *The Blood of the Vampire*, Richmond, VA: Valancourt Books.

McCullers, Carson [1951] (1981), *The Ballad of the Sad Café and Other Stories*, Toronto and New York: Bantam Books.

Morrison, Toni (1987), *Beloved*, New York: Plume.

Nestle, Joan (2002), 'Genders on My Mind', in Joan Nestle, Clare Howell and Riki Wilchins (eds), *GENDERqUEER* , Los Angeles and New York: alyson books, pp. 3–10.

simpkins, reese (2006), 'Feminist Transmasculinities', in Krista Scott-Dixon (ed.), *Trans/Forming Feminisms: Trans-Feminist Voices Speak Out*, Toronto: Sumach Press, pp. 79–86.

Waters, Sarah (1999), *Affinity*, New York: Riverhead Books.

Chapter 12

No Country for Old Women: Gender, Age and the Gothic

Avril Horner and Sue Zlosnik

> People ought to be one of two things: young or dead.
> (Dorothy Parker, *The Portable Dorothy Parker,* p. 596)

Old Age, at least in the West, has recently become a pressing issue for several reasons. The 'demographic time bomb' ticks away inexorably, prompting new interest in researching the implications of an ageing population. The emergence of age studies in cultural studies, pioneered by thinkers such as Margaret Morganroth Gullette and Kathleen Woodward in the USA, designated pots of money in the UK's Arts and Humanities Research Council for research into age-related issues, the UK coalition government's decision to dedicate an extra £6 million to research into Alzheimer's Disease (2014): all of these signal that ageing needs 'dealing with', whether from a cultural, medical or social perspective. Although there have been initiatives to think about older people more positively and to get them back to work – or, one might say more cynically, exploit them as an economic resource – the sense that the aged are a 'problem' is still widespread, particularly in highly sophisticated technological societies driven by the young. As Simone de Beauvoir pointed out over forty years ago: 'Modern technocratic society thinks that knowledge does not accumulate with the years but grows out of date. Age brings disqualification with it: age is not an advantage' (de Beauvoir 1985: 210). As with women's internalisation of masculine values, so the internalisation of societal perspectives on the old can lead to a sense of dislocation and, at its most extreme, existential crisis, in even the most talented individual. W. B. Yeats wrote of himself as 'a tattered coat upon a stick',[6] for example, and Daphne du Maurier expressed horror at her appearance in photographs taken when she was 58 that made her look 'like an old peasant woman of ninety' ([1965] Malet 1993: 194). This 'Othering' of the self is due partly to the recognition of inevitable physical change and decay in one's own body and the sense of split subjectivity it can produce, and partly to the acceptance of social attitudes which see the old as irrelevant and an (increasingly heavy) economic burden.

It is clear that gender and age are both culturally inflected dimensions of subjectivity. Whereas medical science decrees 65 as the age at which senescence begins for both men and women, patriarchal societies tend to devalue women at a much younger age. Until well into the mid-twentieth century, for example, menopausal women were 'seen as standing on the brink of old age and degeneration' (King 2012: 8). Indeed Simone de Beauvoir argued that age and gender produce 'a "double jeopardy" for women: ageism on the one hand and sexism on the Other' (Yakir 2012: 29). The medical 'objective' judgement of when senescence begins might well change, of course, once living to be 100 becomes the norm rather than the exception, while the still widespread prejudice against older women is periodically challenged through the law.[7] As two ageing women authors, we are particularly interested in women and ageing. And as Gothic scholars, we have recently begun to think about the intersection between age and gender in the Gothic and how far age-related hegemonic misogyny is either endorsed and reinforced or challenged in Gothic texts. This chapter is the product of those reflections.

Gullette argues in her 2004 book *Aged by Culture* that one of her aims 'is to make "narrative ageing" a fruitful and unavoidable concept' in a time when age is being consistently foregrounded (Gullette 2004: 103). 'Age is a nice new devil', she asserts (192). Not so new in late capitalist societies (as de Beauvoir realised), nor in the Gothic, we might respond. Early Gothic was a youthful mode, spawning precocious writers such as Matthew 'Monk' Lewis and Mary Shelley who created young overreaching anti-heroes and besieged heroines. Their Gothic works – perhaps reflecting the mood of the Romantic Movement – associate age with the weight of history and the sins of earlier generations as they haunt lives in the present. Old decaying buildings and ancient family portraits are outward and visible signs of this oppressive past; older men are more often than not ill-intentioned patriarchal figures. Older women are for the most part entirely dispensable, as the fate of Walpole's Hippolita in *The Castle of Otranto* (1764) so woefully illustrates. In *The Monk* (1796), an older powerful woman in the shape of the Prioress is shown to behave with extreme cruelty towards a younger woman and is repaid for her sins by being torn apart by an angry mob (although we might bear in mind that things do not turn out so well for the more youthful male protagonist either). In Ann Radcliffe's *The Italian* (1797), the vigour and energy of the older woman, the Marchesa Vivaldi, are focused – via the wicked Schedoni

– on the murder of Ellena de Rosalba, the young woman loved by her son.

Ann Radcliffe's fiction features imperilled but resourceful young female protagonists. Yet the figure of the older woman lurks in the background, in the shape of the mother who is frequently absent, dead or thought to be dead. In *The Italian*, for example, the evil Marchesa is offset by a more benign older woman, Olivia (the long-lost mother of Ellena) but she is a rather passive figure and very much contained within her roles as an early victim of Schedoni's ruthlessness, subsequently as a nun of the Santa della Pieta convent, and finally as an idealised maternal presence.[8] Similarly benign is the surrogate mother figure in the earlier novel, *A Sicilian Romance* (1790), Madame de Menon. The determined heroine's discovery of her real mother, incarcerated for many years in an underground cavern, reveals 'a pale, emaciated figure' (Radcliffe 1993: 104). Weakened by age and imprisonment, a victim of a tyrannical husband, she is emblematic of disempowerment. As Carol Margaret Davison reminds us 'numerous analysts of the Female Gothic have suggested that fear of the mother lurks at the core' (Davison 2009: 95) For Davison, foremothers in the Female Gothic are often *memento mori* figures, their demise (like that of Radcliffe's Madame Montoni in *The Mysteries of Udolpho*, for example) 'dreadful reminders that transgressing the laws of patriarchy is often fatal to oneself and others' (102). This 'matrophobia', as Adrienne Rich calls it (Rich 1976: 235–6), is often signified symbolically in texts by absence through death or other causes (see Anolik 2003). For the French theorist Luce Irigaray, the symbolic order itself is predicated upon a repression of the mother, a failure of representation tantamount to 'cultural matricide' (Whitford 1994: 49–50).

Older childless women, on the other hand, figure prominently in folklore and literature. Second-Wave Feminist thinkers, in the wake of Mary Ellmann's influential *Thinking About Women*, published in 1968, would have recognised in Lewis's Prioress and the Marchesa of *The Italian* one of several negative stereotypes of older women: the witch figure. This stereotype of the malicious powerful older woman is reworked in later Gothic fictions; examples include the Countess Fosco in Wilkie Collins's *The Woman in White* (1860), Mme de la Rougierre in Le Fanu's *Uncle Silas* (1864), Madame Beck in Charlotte Brontë's *Villette* (1853), the 'good' Lady Ducayne in Mary Elizabeth Braddon's short story of 1896, and Mrs Danvers in du Maurier's *Rebecca* (1938). One of the most memorable figures from English nineteenth-century literature is Dickens's Miss Havisham in *Great Expectations* (1860–1), a withered and static presence, old in appearance if not years, exercising a poisonous influence on the young Estella and Pip. Variations on the witch figure are to be found in Gothic writing from different cultures. For example, one of the most famous texts of American Gothic, William Faulkner's 1930 short story 'A Rose for Emily', uses the eponymous Emily, an older woman recently deceased at the opening of the story, to stand for the remnants of the old South. Clinging to the past manifests itself here in gruesome Gothic terms: necrophilia is invoked as the long-dead corpse of a former suitor is discovered in her house. The conclusion of the story implies not only the abjection of the breaking of this taboo, but also the abject body of the older woman:

> Then we noticed that in the second pillow was the indentation of a head. One of us lifted something from it, and leaning forward, that faint and invisible dust dry and acrid in the nostrils, we saw a long strand of iron-gray hair. (Faulkner 1992: 330)

In Canadian literature, as Cynthia Sugars points out, ambivalence about the history of colonisation and contemporary Canadian identity coalesce round the figure of the early settler Susanna Moodie. While Margaret Atwood's poetry sequence, *The Journals of Susanna Moodie* (1970), Gothicises her into both monster and victim, Dennis Lee's long poem *Civil Elegies* (1968) embodies her as an everyday witching presence:

> I am the old woman
> Sitting across from you on the bus ...
> Hatpins, destroying
> The walls, the ceiling.
>
> (Sugars 2014: 155)

As these examples suggest, the figure of the old woman may function as a symbol of a burdensome historical legacy.

Without doubt, negative images of female age continue to assert themselves in spite of social progress made in the west in the wake of Second-Wave Feminism. Post-feminism – or Third-Wave Feminism – in its dismissal of Second-Wave Feminism as strident and in its embrace of plurality, diversity, performativity and individual choice, has been of little help to the older woman. As Rebecca Munford suggests, we seem to have embraced a politics – at least in the West – that construes 'women as consumers, for whom feminism is reduced from a political movement to a certain style that can be bought' (Munford 2007: 274). If, as Judith Butler argues, gender and politics can be performed, then so can youth. In contemporary western culture, as age critics are now clearly articulating, not only is it unfashionable to be old, it is unforgivable to *look* old, and the notion of surgical intervention is becoming normalised ('surgery can wait' says one advertisement for yet another rejuvenating cream). Sadly, in societies in which women are valued mainly for their youth and beauty, individual attempts to turn back the clock via plastic surgery sometimes result in a new form of the grotesque – as in Kim Novak's attempts to resurrect her younger self in her 81-year-old body – a 'make-over' that provoked widespread media derision in May 2014.

Such anxieties about youth and age are reflected in the immensely popular *Twilight* series. In these novels and their film adaptations, we see the male vampire resurrected as romantic hero with his female counterpart, the Gothic heroine, cast in traditional mode, suggesting that the success of the *Twilight* brand in both books and films owes something to a cultural nostalgia that, through a hyper-capitalist appropriation of Gothic devices, retrieves a reactionary agenda for gender. Disturbingly for feminist readers, Bella Swan's reasons for wishing to be transformed into a vampire herself include not only the desire to be with her vampire hero, Edward, forever, but also a terrible fear of ageing: her worst nightmare, described in the opening pages of *New Moon* (2006), is that she might see 'some sign of impending wrinkles in my ivory skin' (Meyer 2007: 7). As Diane Negra has commented, 'Post-feminism thrives on anxiety about aging and redistributes this anxiety among a variety of generational clusters while also always extending the promise/possibility of age evasion' (Negra 2008: 12).

Anxieties about age are powerfully expressed in the writing of one of the most successful women authors of the twentieth century, Daphne du Maurier. Her career preceded Second-Wave Feminism, but her fiction explores imaginatively the constraints of gender. Her later work represents both the anxieties of ageing and a search for a positive aged identity; her letters written in middle age indicate an anxiety about what it might mean to be old. Writing to Oriel Malet in 1965, when she was 58, she lamented her ageing looks and remarked jokingly:

> The only way to treat it is to think I'm a throwback to old glass-blowing provincial *aïeux* – you know how peasants etc. get very old and wrinkled by forty and bent, and in shawls, carrying pails of water to cows! (Malet 1993: 194)

Her last novel, a speculative fiction called *Rule Britannia* (1972), is defiant in tone with an old woman heroine leading the resistance movement in Cornwall against an invading American army. Yet it lacks the complexity of much of her other writing, abandons the Gothic mode and fails to convince. Her most famous late short story 'Don't Look Now' (1971), however, is haunted by ambivalence about age. John and

Laura are in Venice, trying to come to terms with the recent loss of their young daughter. They encounter two Scottish twin sisters of mature years, one of whom is blind and claims to be psychic: 'a couple of old girls' (du Maurier 1971: 9), 'two old fools' (16), 'frauds', 'a couple of freaks' (26) and 'those diabolical sisters' (42) John disparagingly calls them. His dismissal of the blind sister's visions leads eventually to the story's climax. Believing he is following a distressed child, he is lured into the labyrinthine alleys of Venice and is confronted by:

> not a child at all but a little thick-set woman dwarf, about three feet high, with a great square adult head too big for her body, grey locks hanging shoulder-length, and she wasn't sobbing any more, she was grinning at him, nodding her head up and down ... The creature fumbled in her sleeve, drawing a knife. (du Maurier 1971: 57)

The dwarf, like Venice itself, is a site of shifting meaning. She represents fear and terror as well as an avenging horror. For not only can she be read as the ultimate nightmare of patriarchy – the death-dealing figure of the avenging mother – but she may also be seen as a focus for masculine revulsion from the aged female body. The (natural) transition from youth to age is here grotesquely accelerated so as to become a sudden switch – or Gothic temporal metamorphosis – which conveys powerfully the cultural fear of the older woman.[9]

This device can be found in many texts, from the medieval tale of 'The Loathly Lady' (which reverses it) to Rider Haggard's *She* (1887) in which the narrator's horror at the dissolution of his beloved Ayesha is vividly conveyed:

> Smaller she grew, and smaller yet, till she was no larger than a baboon. Now the skin was puckered into a million wrinkles, and on the shapeless face was the stamp of unutterable age [...] At last she lay still, or only feebly moving. She, who but two minutes before had gazed upon us the loveliest, noblest, most splendid woman the world has ever seen, she lay still before us, near the masses of her own dark hair, no larger than a big monkey, and hideous – ah, too hideous for words. (Haggard 2007: 356)

However, just in case we read this as an expression of terror at the process of ageing in either sex, the narrator later qualifies his horror in a discreet footnote:

> What a terrifying reflection it is, by the way, that nearly all our deep love for women who are not our kindred depends – at any rate, in the first instance – upon their personal appearance. If we lost them, and found them again dreadful to look on, though otherwise they were the very same, should we still love them? (Haggard 2007: 362)

As Rider Haggard's novel illustrates so powerfully, whereas novels such as Vita Sackville West's *All Passion Spent* (1931) and Fay Weldon's *Rhode Island Blues* (2000) evoke admiration for the spirited independence of the older woman, Gothic texts often bring to the surface the cultural rejection and abjection of the older woman endemic to the Western world. This cultural prejudice had been internalised by du Maurier, who was 63 years old when she wrote 'Don't Look Now' (the same age as the twin sisters in the tale). What the story reveals so clearly is the paranoia inherent in patriarchy's misogyny and ageism and the price paid for it. On the other hand, the blind sister's visions perhaps suggest the white witch, or wise old crone[10] – another stereotype, but one that at least indicates that independence, insight and understanding might accompany the ageing process.[11] This figure can also be found in Sylvia Townsend Warner's *Lolly Willowes* (1926), in which the heroine leaves her position in her brother's house as a middle-aged 'spinster' aunt and, after making a pact with the devil, roams the countryside as a hedge witch. She justifies her drastic change of life to her brother by pointing out that in a patriarchal society the choice of meaningful roles for the older woman are pitifully few. Similarly, Margaret Drabble's *The Witch of Exmoor* (1996) features an older woman's decision to leave London and her three professional and rather smug adult children for an isolated life in a dilapidated house in Devon. Her defection to rural remoteness sets in motion a train of events which leaves them sadder but wiser; she has, in effect, worked a kind of painful white 'magic' on her family.

Acknowledging these more positive representations, our aim is to consider how some adaptations of the Gothic mode enable a different figuration of age and gender that challenges dominant narratives. Our project is related to recent scholarly interest in queering the Gothic. Ardel Haefele-Thomas's recent book *Queer Others in Victorian Gothic* (2012) finds instances of Gothic queering in unexpected places, including the ghost stories of Elizabeth Gaskell. Her persuasive reading of 'The Grey Woman' (1861), for example, examines Gaskell's use of cross-dressing in the rescue of a vulnerable young wife from the clutches of a murderous husband. For Haefele-Thomas, the masquerade of the woman servant Amante as a solicitous husband continues far longer than it needs to and creates what she calls a 'genderqueer' space that enables Gaskell to 'carry out her critique of women's roles as wives in Victorian culture' (Haefele-Thomas 2012: 69). There is another way of looking at this transgressive fiction, however. Amante is described as 'tall and handsome though upwards of forty' (Gaskell 2000: 265); in Gothic terms, she is old. However, Amante redefines her identity in relation to age as well as gender. Gaskell's 'genderqueer' fiction rewrites the Bluebeard narrative that underlies much Female Gothic by recuperating the mother figure through assigning to her the role of saviour – as, of course, does Angela Carter's 1970s tale, 'The Bloody Chamber', in which the vulnerable young wife is saved from imminent death by the arrival of her white-haired gun-wielding mother who, without a moment's hesitation, shoots her daughter's husband dead just as he is about to behead her. This, we might argue, is a valorisation of the power latent in older women. Not surprisingly, it emerges from the powerful groundswell of Second-Wave Feminism.

Even the transgressive figure of the witch has been recuperated by writers who challenge societal norms, especially those poised between cultures. Jean Rhys's revisiting of Charlotte Brontë's *Jane Eyre* in *Wide Sargasso Sea* (1966) is a case in point. In Brontë's novel, Rochester's wife (incarcerated for many years like the mother in Radcliffe's *A Sicilian Romance*) is rendered monstrous, a 'large, dark and terrifying' and sublime force, according to Donna Heiland (2004: 127). *Jane Eyre* is now often read as a work of colonial fiction in which the first Mrs Rochester represents the dirty secrets of colonisation and exploitation.[12] Rhys's novel changes the perspective of its source work by focusing on Antoinette, the Creole bride who is taken away from her native Dominica to a cold and dark England by her insecure young English husband. Like her own mother, she is rendered powerless by a patriarchal system in which men trade her like a commodity. The strongest figure in Rhys's novel is Christophine, Antoinette's former nurse, an independent woman with three children by different men but no husband: 'I thank my God I keep my money. I don't give it to no worthless man' (Rhys 1968: 91). 'An evil old woman' (120) the new husband describes her, as the marriage rapidly disintegrates and he hears whispers of her association with obeah and is warned that she is 'a very dangerous person' (118). Yet she is the only person who understands Antoinette's history and offers her sympathetic support, advising her to 'have spunks and do battle for yourself' (96). In the final showdown with the young husband, when Christophine tries to persuade him to dissolve the marriage and leave his wife in her care, she is threatened and defeated, however. Patriarchal power has its way and Antoinette leaves for England with her husband. Presciently, Christophine has earlier described Antoinette's distraught appearance as making her look like a 'coucriant', another word for a soucouyant (96). The soucouyant (also known as Ol' Hige [Old Higue], which is the Guyanese Creole expression for an old hag, or witch) (Rudd 2010: 32) is a figure from African and Caribbean folklore who has the power to transform herself into a ball of fire. However, it is the young woman, not the old, who at the end of this novel is associated with avenging fire; it is she who dreams of burning down the patriarchal house and who, it is intimated at the very end, will do so.

The soucouyant has been the subject of some critical debate in recent years. Giselle Anatol's influential work has prompted a recuperation of the soucouyant from its negative witching connotations into a transformative and empowering figure. The roots of 'this demonised folk figure', she believes, may lie in the relative longevity of women in times when life expectancy was much shorter. Already deemed 'Other', in patriarchal societies their survival into old age was attributed to mystical powers enabling the stealing of the life force from younger people (Anatol 2004: 33). It is perhaps not surprising that some postcolonial writers have used the soucouyant figure in their fiction, an appropriation into the Gothic mode to represent the contradictions of postcolonial identity. Two such examples are *White is for Witching* (2009) by Helen Oyeyeme, a Nigerian British novelist, and *Soucouyant* (2007) by David Chariandy, a Canadian of Caribbean descent.

White is for Witching is a complex tale of an uncanny house and a young female protagonist, Miranda, who is both haunted by her female ancestors and multiply monstrous in herself. The house in Dover where she lives, handed down through the female line for several generations, behaves as a living, or at least undead, entity. The spirits of her xenophobic foremothers coalesce in the malevolent figure of 'the goodlady', which becomes undistinguishable from the house itself. The novel melds elements of the European Gothic tradition, particularly the vampire, with African folklore. Miranda's university friend Ore, whose origins are Nigerian, is both horrified and fascinated by the figure of the soucouyant, 'that unnatural old lady' (Oyeyeme 2009: 147). When it becomes apparent that Miranda believes herself to be a soucouyant, Ore resists the idea (the soucouyant was the old lady: that was the rule [219]). Although for a moment it seems that Miranda has, like Antoinette at the end of *Wide Sargasso Sea*, absorbed the power of the soucouyant, the dream-like metamorphosis is fleeting and she is then lured in to self-destruction by the evil old 'goodlady'.

Although some critics have persistently tried to recuperate the figure of the soucouyant, it remains ambiguously both demon and victim. Fear of the supposed power of the old woman to transform into a fireball of destructive energy makes a scapegoat of her daylight counterpart. As the narrator of David Chariandy's *Soucouyant* reflects: 'In the morning, you'll only have to look for an old woman in the village who appears to have been beaten. Bruises upon her. Clearly the one to blame' (Chariandy 2007: 135). In this novel, David Chariandy uses the figure of the soucouyant to explore a trauma underlying diasporic identity in Canada. Adele, a prematurely old woman, is the focus for the competing discourses that characterise such hybridity. Presented through the eyes of her anxious son, she is a victim of pre-senile dementia, diagnosable in terms of the modern medicine of Canada, although not treatable by it. Yet as the novel progresses, a palimpsestic narrative emerges that eventually reveals a partially forgotten trauma that has resisted representation. Adele is insistent that she saw a soucouyant when a child in the West Indies, but the meaning of this claim is only revealed gradually. Stumbling around in the Toronto suburb where she lives, behaving anti-socially and babbling incoherently, Adele is clearly beyond any rational thinking about her own past. Instead, she is the medium through which her son achieves partial awareness of the trauma underlying history that has placed him where he is. However, his struggle to represent this indicates its resistance to containment. Nevertheless, his is the focalising consciousness of the novel. In this novel 'of forgetting', as its subtitle describes it, the figure of the old woman, whether it be Adele herself, or the retrieved memory of the soucouyant she believes she saw, is in effect without agency.

Does Gothic fiction, then, generally reiterate the prejudices of a society which finds the older woman either redundant or threatening? If we turn to comic Gothic, the answer is, no, not always. In the satiric *True Blood* television series, for example, the older woman – Sookie's paternal grandmother – is portrayed positively as energetic, kind and open-minded. She is, however, perhaps too easily assimilated into the stereotype of the loving, reliable, apple-pie baking granny (and she is also killed off in Season One [2008]). There are, however, more daring ways of portraying the older woman. For example, in her short story, 'Miss Mary Pask' (1925), Edith Wharton parodically appropriated the Gothic in order to raise questions about the older woman and sexual desire. As in du Maurier's 'Don't Look Now', the story is focused through an unreliable male – this time a well-connected young man from New York – who, travelling through Europe, decides to visit a friend's unmarried sister-in-law, Mary Pask. Knocking on the door of her cottage on the Brittany coast, he is greeted by Mary – but is suddenly struck by the thought that she had died the previous year. Looking with horror on her 'blue fingernails' and her hands like 'pale freckled toadstools' (Wharton 2001: 315) he assumes he must be seeing a ghost. Mary Pask plays up to this, intimating that she has become a vampire:

> I hate the light … And so I sleep all day … Do you know where I usually sleep? Down below there – in the garden … There's a shady corner at the bottom where the sun never bothers one. (Wharton 2001: 317)

The narrator, by now thoroughly terrified, seeks to escape, but Mary Pask flirts with him, pleading with him to stay, although her pleas reflect loneliness as much as sexual frustration. In effect, of course, Mary's status as unmarried and ageing has rendered her invisible and easily forgettable in the homosocial American scene of which the narrator is part. However, the story challenges such values. Mary, while playing 'undead', feels licensed to speak 'what the living woman had always had to keep dumb and hidden' (319); she articulates clearly both her sexual desire and her sadness at the loneliness imposed on her as an older woman. The narrator, associating Mary's behaviour with old tales of vampires, flees the cottage. We learn that subsequently he undergoes a breakdown and retreats to a sanatorium in Switzerland. While the experience has shaken his faith in the boundaries between life and death, he also talks of an awakening, describing 'the revelation of the dead Mary Pask who was so much more real to me than the living one had been' (320). The storyline is resolved neatly in a Radcliffean explanation of a cataleptic trance being mistaken for death, combined with his friend's wife's failure to give her friends and relatives news of her sister.[13] Wharton was 63 years old when she published this story – the same age as du Maurier when she finished 'Don't Look Now'. Exploiting what she called elsewhere 'the fun of the shudder', she offers a comically transgressive portrait of the older woman – as, of course, does Angela Carter in her 1991 novel *Wise Children*, in which the 75-year-old Nora and Dora Chance express their sexual desires in energetic and no uncertain terms.

Such challenges to the seemingly inevitable association of age with decline and withdrawal are repeated in many other comic Gothic texts, some of them indeed presenting the ageing process as a time of new beginnings. Stella Gibbons, in *Cold Comfort Farm*, published in 1932, for example, has Aunt Ada, the elderly Gothic matriarch who has controlled the household from her dark bedroom for many years, embark on a personal adventure when, clad in black leather and accompanied by a dashing young pilot, she takes off in an aeroplane for Paris. Similarly, Molly Keane's *Time After Time*, published in 1983, which focuses on a group of elderly siblings living in a decaying Irish mansion and stuck in their various grooves, has the arrival of a blind and devious cousin disturb their web of malicious co-dependency. Her attempt to seduce the elderly (and closeted homosexual) male of the group fails utterly and she returns to the convent where she had previously been confined by her daughter; nevertheless her visit has disrupted the siblings' lives and results in fresh beginnings, especially for one of the sisters, whose obsession with giving local talks on flower arranging is abandoned for a new and lucrative career as a restorer of antiques.

Finally, we turn our attention to an example of the reclamation of the older woman in a contemporary example of 'comic Gothic', Paul Magrs's *Never the Bride* (2006). Amid what Magrs calls 'silliness and fun', there are some serious ideas. The central figure of the novel is the 'bride' Frankenstein made for his monster (a creature that he tips overboard in pieces in the seas around Scotland, but which is a manifest entity in some of the adaptations of Mary Shelley's novel). That makes her nearly 200 years old, although, unlike an immensely old female vampire such as Carmilla, she does not possess eternal youth and beauty but looks as though she has had plenty of life experiences. In Magrs's gloriously weird world she is here in the present day, called Brenda and running an immaculate seaside bed-and-breakfast in Whitby. Covering the scars of her construction with heavy make-up and a wig and keeping a few spare parts in the attic, she manages to lead a fulfilling life catering for her guests and spending her spare time with her friend Effie. Like latter-day Miss Marples,[14] they love a mystery, and prove more than a match for the dark doings of the figures of Gothic fiction and film that leach into the pages of the novel to disturb the peace of Whitby.

Brenda is a reclaimed Gothic heroine in more senses than one. She has survived the violence of men to the body parts in her former selves that now make up her composite whole. She has no mother and her father is a dim memory. She is done with flight and handles fright with great resourcefulness and humour. Mr Alucard (whose name should be read backwards for full impact) is no match for her. Perhaps more importantly, like Mary Pask, she is the reclaimed female grotesque, the monstrous made knowable, lovable and estimable. That split within female subjectivity – dramatised so powerfully by Margaret Atwood in the characters of *The Robber Bride* – is there in the form of her scars but they hold her together in a self that has been forged over a long period. Most importantly, in this comic Gothic text, the older female self has benign agency. Known also for some powerful fiction about contemporary gay experience, Magrs has, with his 'Brenda' books, succeeded in queering/querying not only gender but also age.

In these comic Gothic texts, the formal play of surface effects works to disturb established conceptions about age and gender, offering the reader a position of detachment and scepticism towards received narratives about the older woman. Their authors self-consciously use Gothic's propensity to bare the device in order to allay the reader's learnt response of fear and anxiety when confronting the inevitable prospect of the ageing female body. Such fictions offer entertaining and potent critiques of late capitalism's construction of the older woman. We need more of them.

Notes

1. W. B. Yeats, 'Sailing to Byzantium' (1928; see Yeats 1992: 239). The opening phrase of this poem, 'That is no country for old men' was used by Cormac McCarthy for his novel *No Country for Old Men* (2005) and has inspired the title of this chapter.
2. Miriam O'Reilly, for example, successfully took the BBC to an employment tribunal in 2011 for their refusal to renew her contract for *Countryfile* when the programme was moved to a prime-time television slot in 2010, citing discrimination on grounds of age and sex. Other older women who have found themselves in similar situations include Moira Stuart, Selina Scott, Arlene Phillips, Anna Ford and Olenka Frenkiel.
3. We owe this observation to Angela Wright.
4. For a more detailed reading of this story, see Horner and Zlosnik 1998: 173–83.
5. The word 'crone' means literally a useless old ewe and derives from Middle Dutch and Middle English. It later came to mean a cantankerous or mischievous and withered old woman.
6. Cf. 'Without a mythology that includes the crone, representations of female experience are bound to remain incomplete' (Brennan 2004: 153).
7. Spivak 1985 is regarded as the seminal text in this line of criticism.
8. For a more detailed reading of this story, see Horner and Beer 2011: 162–4.
9. Interestingly, of course, there is no shortage of older women sleuths in crime fiction, a genre in which the older woman is accorded a rare respect for her intelligence and acuity. For more on this, see Brennan 2004, chapter 5: 'The Wise and Archetypal Older Woman', where she notes, nonetheless, that 'feminist theory makes relatively little of the fact that a thriving sub-genre in which the older woman is a central character constitutes a literary anomaly' (135).

Bibliography

Anatol, Giselle Liza (2004), 'A Feminist Reading of Soucouyants in Nalo Hopkinson's *Brown Girl in the Ring* and Skin Folk', *Mosaic*, 37(3): 33–50.

Anolik, Ruth Bienstock (2003), 'The Missing Mother: The Meanings of Maternal Absence in the Gothic Mode', *Modern Language Studies*, 33(1): 24–43.

Brennan, Zoe (2004), *The Older Woman in Recent Fiction*, Jefferson, NC, and London: McFarland.

Chariandy, David (2007), *Soucouyant*, Vancouver: Arsenal Pulp Press.

Davison, Carol Margaret (2009), *Gothic Literature 1764–1824*, Cardiff: University of Wales Press.

de Beauvoir, Simone [1970] (1985), *La Vieillesse*, trans. Patrick O'Brien, Harmondsworth: Penguin Books.

Drabble, Margaret [1996] (1997), *The Witch of Exmoor*, London: Penguin Books Ltd.

du Maurier, Daphne (1971), 'Don't Look Now', in *Not After Midnight: Five Long Stories*, London: Gollancz, pp. 9–58.

du Maurier, Daphne (1972), *Rule Britannia*, London: Gollancz.

Faulkner, William (1992), 'A Rose for Emily' [1930], in Chris Baldick (ed.), *The Oxford Book of Gothic Tales*, Oxford: Oxford University Press, pp. 322–30.

Gaskell, Elizabeth (2000), 'The Grey Woman' [1861], in S. Lewis (ed.), *A Dark Night's Work and Other Stories*, Oxford: Oxford University Press.

Gullette, Margaret Morganroth (2004), *Aged by Culture*, Chicago: University of Chicago Press.

Haefele-Thomas, Ardel (2012), *Queer Others in Victorian Gothic*, Cardiff: University of Wales Press.

Haggard, H. Rider [1886] (2007), *She*, Harmondsworth: Penguin Books.

Heiland, Donna (2004), *Gothic & Gender: An Introduction*, Oxford: Blackwell.

Horner, Avril and Janet Beer (2011), *Edith Wharton: Sex, Satire and the Older Woman*, Basingstoke: Palgrave.

Horner, Avril and Sue Zlosnik (1998), 'Deaths in Venice: "Don't Look Now"', in Horner and Zlosnik, *Daphne du Maurier: Writing, Identity and the Gothic Imagination*, Basingstoke: Macmillan, pp. 173–83.

Keane, Molly [1983] (1984), *Time After Time*, London: Abacus Books.

King, Jeanette (2012), *Discourses of Ageing in Film and Fiction*, Basingstoke: Palgrave Macmillan.

Magrs, Paul (2006), *Never the Bride*, London: Hodder Headline.

Malet, Oriel (1993), *Letters from Menabilly*, London: Weidenfeld and Nicolson.

Meyer, Stephenie [2006] (2007), *New Moon*, London: Atom.

Munford, Rebecca [2004] (2007), '"Wake Up and Smell the Lipgloss": Gender, Generation and the (A)politics of Girl Power', in Stacy Gillis, Gillian Howie and Rebecca Munford (eds), *Third Wave Feminism: A Critical Exploration*, Basingstoke: Palgrave Macmillan.

Negra, Diane (2008), *What a Girl Wants? Fantasising the Reclamation of Self in Post-feminism*, London and New York: Routledge.

Oyeyeme, Helen (2009), *White is for Witching*, London: Picador.

Parker, Dorothy (1973), *The Portable Dorothy Parker*, New York: Viking.

Radcliffe, Ann [1790] (1993), *A Sicilian Romance*, ed. Alison Milbank, Oxford: Oxford University Press.

Radcliffe, Ann [1797] (1991), *The Italian*, ed. Frederick Garber, Oxford: Oxford University Press.

Rhys, Jean [1966] (1968), *Wide Sargasso Sea*, Harmondsworth: Penguin Books.

Rich, Adrienne (1976), *Of Woman Born: Motherhood as Experience and Institution*, New York: Norton.

Rudd, Alison (2010), *Postcolonial Gothic Fictions from the Caribbean, Canada, Australia and New Zealand*, Cardiff: University of Wales Press.

Spivak, Gayatri Chakravorty (1985), 'Three Women's Texts and a Critique of Imperialism', *Critical Inquiry*, 12: 243–61.

Sugars, Cynthia (2014), *Canadian Gothic: Literature, History and the Spectre of Self-Invention*, Cardiff: University of Wales Press.

Warner, Sylvia Townsend [1926] (2012), *Lolly Willowes*, London: Virago.

Wharton, Edith (2001), 'Miss Mary Pask' [1925], in Maureen Howard (ed.), *Edith Wharton; Collected Stories 1891–1910, Vol. 2*, New York: The Library of America.

Whitford, Margaret (ed.) [1991] (1994), *The Irigaray Reader*, Oxford: Blackwell.

Yakir, Nedira (2012), 'W. Barns-Graham and Old Age: *Celebration at 90*', in Josephine Dolan and Estella Tincknell (eds), *Aging Femininities: Troubling Representations*, Newcastle upon Tyne: Cambridge Scholars Publishing, pp. 27–41.

Yeats, W. B. (1992), 'Sailing to Byzantium' [1928], in Daniel Albright (ed.), *The Poems*, London: Everyman.

Chapter 13

Virtual Gothic Women
Catherine Spooner

Women at the Interface

Gothic and new technologies have always been closely allied, from eighteenth-century phantasmagoria shows to the digital revolution. As Jeffrey Sconce has shown, recurring fictions of uncanny disembodiment and an 'electronic elsewhere' accompany electronic media throughout the nineteenth and twentieth centuries (Sconce 2000: 9). The emergence of telegraphy, radio, television and computers each in turn produced fantasies of spectral presence and an otherworldly space from which that presence emanates or through which it travels. Women's position within this alliance is complex: often the mediums through which technologies are Gothicised, they frequently provide a hinge between the embodied human subject and a pure realm of disembodiment. This uneasy positioning of a Gothicised female subject across the Cartesian mind/body dualism is reiterated in contemporary fictions that engage with the possibilities of digital technologies. Virtual Gothic heroines seek liberation into a realm of pure mind, but remain haunted by the needs and sensations of the body. In the texts considered in this chapter – Arthur Machen's *The Great God Pan* (1894), William Gibson's *Neuromancer* (1984), Neal Stephenson's *The Diamond Age* (1995) and Scarlett Thomas's *The End of Mr Y* (2006) – virtual Gothic women are constructed as double agents, travelling through and acting upon two parallel worlds, and providing an interface between pure cerebration and sensory embodiment.

The digital culture of the late twentieth and early twenty-first centuries projects a persistent fantasy of a virtual realm, a synthetic space in which real actors may interact with varying degrees of consequence. This space is realised in video games, in Multiple User Domain (MUD) virtual environments such as Second Life, and in the space of the World Wide Web itself, in which users are freed from their immediate physical constraints to communicate with their counterparts across the globe. While these actualised forms of virtual space may be mundane, in fiction they are frequently and explicitly Gothicised. For writers such as William Gibson, the unofficial figurehead of the cyberpunk movement, the virtual realm is represented as a labyrinthine space, replete with doubles and ghosts enabled by cloning and digitalised memory. Virtual reality becomes the latest iteration of the magic lantern show or phantasmagoria which, as David J. Jones demonstrates, was a crucial context for the development of Gothic literature in the eighteenth century (Jones 2011).

In contrast to the Gothic heroine, however, the protagonist of cyberpunk is usually male. As Brian McHale suggests, 'Cyberpunk ... returns to its romance roots through its use of wandering adventurer-heroes ... Space-traveling versions of the knight-errant or cowboy abound' (McHale 1992: 249). Noel Fielding's TV sketch character, Fantasy Man, 'a modern-day Don Quixote character trapped inside an electronic operatic world that resembles Tron', is a particularly revealing parody of this genre archetype (*Noel Fielding's Luxury Comedy*: online). Nevertheless, if the virtual world in fiction and in actuality often mirrors the material one in that it is male-dominated and patriarchal in structure, nevertheless it also offers the potential to interrogate familiar gender conventions. Within it, women re-enact Gothic narrative patterns in ways that are sometimes familiar and sometimes suggestive of new possibilities for the gendered subject.

Within feminist criticism, the gendering of virtual space has been a matter of heated debate, eliciting sometimes diametrically opposed views. For Zoe Sofia, representations of cyberspace are structured according to a masculinist mythology derived from the classical myth of the goddess Athena, born directly from her father Zeus's brain. She calls this mythology 'Jupiter space', after the mystic womb-like representation of outer space in Stanley Kubrick's *2001: A Space Odyssey* (1968):

> Jupiter space iconography reinforces parallels between the fertile spaces of the masculinist/rational brain, outer space, cyberspace, as well as electronic circuitry and urban streets. Typically, a luminous grid of lines passes into infinity, a visual pun on the concept of 'matrix' as womb and as mathematical/geometrical grid, signifying the fertility of the techno-scientific intellect and corporate production. In Jupiter Space, not only technological artefacts and information circuits, as well as fembots – electro-mechanical women – but also the Earth and even the universe itself are depicted as conceptions of a masculine, rational and (increasingly) artificial brain. (Sofia 1999: 59)

In direct contrast, Sadie Plant draws on the historical figure of Ada Lovelace, who was instrumental to the development of Charles Babbage's early computer prototype, the Analytical Engine, in the nineteenth century, to suggest that computing arose from the feminine technology of weaving (the Analytical Engine borrowed much of its technology from Jacquard's mechanical loom). For Plant, this allies women and computers and offers women a privileged position within digital culture as mediators between various binaries.

> The computer was always a simulation of weaving; threads of ones and zeros riding the carpets and simulating silk screens in the perpetual motions of cyberspace. It joins women on and as the interface between man and matter, identity and difference, one and zero, the actual and the virtual. (Plant 1995: 63)

Ultimately, for Plant, Western feminism's quest to instate women as subjects is a backward movement as cyberspace, representing an extreme logical end-point of postmodernism, is built precisely on lack of subjecthood, offering a kind of utopian zone in which differences of gender are erased: 'there is no subject position and no identity on the other side of the screens' (63).

Plant's work has been controversial, and widely discredited as computer technologies have developed and subject positions and identities have proved crucial to interactions on the World Wide Web. In the 'real' world, video gamers and web users perform gender and sexuality in a variety of ways, both radical and retrogressive, which cannot be summarised here. Nevertheless, despite what might seem, in the twenty-first century, like the naïve optimism of Plant's utopian vision of a subject-free, gender-free virtual space, it is her conception of woman/computer as interface that resonates most strongly with the tenor of contemporary Gothic fiction. Plant's model can be aligned with a much earlier archetype, one that coalesced with the imagery of emerging technologies in the nineteenth century: that of the spirit medium.

As discussed at length in Jeffrey Sconce's study, the rise of spiritualism in the mid-nineteenth century was coincident with the advent of telegraphy, and the two discourses frequently exchanged concepts and vocabulary based on the shared transmission and reception of messages through the ether. Sconce notes that 'For the Spiritualists, the bodiless communication of telegraphy heralded the existence of a land without material substance, an always unseen origin point of transmission for disembodied souls in an electromagnetic utopia' (Sconce 2000: 57). Within Spiritualism, women were privileged as mediums between the material world and the world of spirits. Judith Walkowitz recognises that 'Spiritualists deemed women particularly apt for mediumship because they were weak in the masculine attributes of will and intelligence, yet strong in the feminine attributes of passivity, chastity, and impressionability' (Walkowitz 1992: 176–7). This reification of conventional gender paradigms could, however, result in uneasy forms of empowerment for women. For Alex Owen, 'The medium's power lay in her ability to absent herself in order to become the vessel for spiritual possession, and this was a species of power which must remain, apparently by definition, contained' (Owen 1990: 11). Owen documents the numerous ways in which women, frequently from working-class backgrounds, not only were able to make a living through mediumship, but also gained influence over their immediate spiritualist circles 'and in rare cases ... gained some notoriety both amongst spiritualists and the public at large' (5).

In her construction as intermediary, the medium augured a new kind of feminine subjectivity. For Owen, this consisted of a subtle subversion of existing gender paradigms, so that 'the Victorian séance room became a battle ground across which the tensions implicit in the acquisition of gendered subjectivity and the assumption of female spiritual power were played out' (11). The medium became a hinge or portal between two different spaces, able to move within and between the two. As such she anticipated the peculiar form of consciousness associated in the late twentieth and early twenty-first centuries with accessing virtual realms. Sconce suggests that 'Long before our contemporary fascination with the beatific possibilities of cyberspace, feminine mediums led the Spiritualist movement as wholly realised cybernetic beings – electromagnetic devices bridging flesh and spirit, body and machine, material reality and electronic space' (Sconce 2000: 27).

The female subject as conduit between worlds appears in nineteenth-century Gothic fiction such as Arthur Machen's *The Great God Pan* (1894), in which a doctor, Raymond, performs an operation on the brain of a young woman named Mary in order to grant her perception of the 'real world ... beyond'. The novella offers a deeply problematic representation of the woman as medium that anticipates the tensions between body and spirit in twentieth-century narratives of the virtual realm. Raymond possesses a cavalier disregard for Mary's agency: on being warned of the risks of the experiment, he assures his friend Clarke that 'I rescued Mary from the gutter, and from almost certain starvation, when she was a child; I think her life is mine, to use as I see fit' (Machen 2005: 186). Raymond has created Mary as a subject; she is the absent vessel that Owen describes and her passivity paradoxically enables her mobility between worlds.

Machen explicitly uses telegraphy as a metaphor for this process of communication across 'the unthinkable gulf that yawns profound between two worlds, the world of matter and the world of spirit', imagining in graphic terms Sconce's 'electronic elsewhere'.

> this world of ours is pretty well girded now with the telegraph wires and cables; thought, with something less than the speed of thought, flashes from sunrise to sunset, from north to south, across the floods and the desert places. Suppose that an electrician of today were suddenly to perceive that he and his friends have merely been playing with pebbles and mistaking them for the foundations of the world; suppose that such a man saw uttermost space lie open before the current, and words of men flash forth to the sun and beyond the sun into the systems beyond, and the voice of articulate-speaking men echo in the waste void that bounds our thought. (Machen 2005: 185)

In fact, Raymond's vision, in which he sees 'mapped out in lines of light a whole world', uncannily anticipates Gibson's description of cyberspace as 'Lines of light ranged in the nonspace of the mind' (Machen 2005: 185; Gibson 1993: 67). The iconography of cyberspace has its roots in a long tradition of occult imaginings.

Raymond's attempt to span the abyss between the worlds by allowing Mary to cross the 'bridge of light' is doomed to failure, as Mary herself becomes the bridge, becoming impregnated by the god Pan and bringing his demonic child Helen into the world (Machen 2005: 185). Mary's name (and the fact that she is not, Clarke hints, a virgin) indicate that her pregnancy is to be read as a demonic inversion of the immaculate conception; while Raymond's plan is evidently intended to confirm, in Sofia's terms, 'Jupiter space' or the fertile spaces of the rational brain, its mediation through the polluted female body perverts and distorts this process, leading to a monstrous birth. Although Mary does perceive the other world, she is left a 'hopeless idiot' by the operation, doubly absented and reduced to mere flesh, anticipating the 'meat puppets' of Gibson's cyberpunk fiction, empty bodies vacated by their owners' consciousness (Machen 2005: 190). The novella thus raises crucial themes of embodiment and transcendence that are replicated in the developing discourses of digital culture in the so-called 'Information Age'.

The three novels considered in the remainder of this chapter were published at intervals of just over ten years and have been selected to represent the development of virtual Gothic femininity across three decades. The first, William Gibson's *Neuromancer*, is regarded as the foundational text of cyberpunk fiction and in its envisioning of cyberspace (a term coined by Gibson himself two years earlier) determined the way that virtual environments would subsequently be represented. Cyberpunk is notable for being a highly Gothicised form of science fiction, characterised by labyrinthine spaces (both urban and virtual), a concern with criminal and subcultural underworlds and sinister corporations, and a

Frankensteinian emphasis on the body reconstructed through science. It is the culmination of a Gothic concern with and mediation through new technologies that dates back to the phantasmagoria shows of the late eighteenth century, and takes in photography, cinema, television and digital media. In *Neuromancer*, the iconography Gibson uses in his depiction of cyberspace is decidedly Gothic: a burnt-out male computer hacker, the digital 'ghost' of his ex-partner and a technologically augmented female assassin carry out a digital heist within a simultaneously material and virtual mansion presided over by the mad, cloned daughter of a corporate dynasty.

Neal Stephenson's *The Diamond Age: Or, A Young Lady's Illustrated Primer* also has its heroine undertake a virtual quest, but despite the fact that this quest takes place in a series of fantasy castles, the novel is less overtly Gothic than *Neuromancer*, lacking its *noir* aesthetic. In fact it animates two different kinds of Gothic. In a world of advanced technology, where 'matter compilers' allow almost anything to be composed from atoms at the push of a button, the inhabitants of New Atlantis value authentic objects, which become a signifier of high status. They have returned to Victorian values as a means of preserving social order, and employ communities of craftspeople, recalling the nineteenth-century Arts and Crafts movement, to make real furniture and fabrics, and even paper, using traditional methods. They therefore are undergoing a Gothic Revival reminiscent of Pugin, Ruskin and Morris, seeking to restore an authentic relationship between humans and objects, while the world around them is a networked urban dystopia, recalling the threatening labyrinthine spaces of Gothic fiction.

Crucially, the central artefact of *The Diamond Age* is a book. As I have argued elsewhere, the flourishing of the Information Age in the late twentieth and early twenty-first centuries resulted in a repeated concern in fiction with the Gothic properties of knowledge itself and an enhanced awareness of the book itself as Gothic artefact (Spooner 2014). In *The Diamond Age*, the book is a technically redundant but fetishised retro technology, revamped into a sophisticated hand-held device that immerses the reader literally in a fictional world. As the book is programmed to respond to only a young female reader, *The Diamond Age* implicitly recalls the debates over the educational properties of young women's reading matter that dogged the Gothic novel in the eighteenth and nineteenth centuries. Moreover, it reflects this concern at the level of form as well as content, marrying the characteristic concerns of cyberpunk fiction with the nineteenth-century form of the *Bildungsroman*, or novel of education.

The Gothicisation of knowledge recurs in Scarlett Thomas's *The End of Mr Y* (2006), which retro-fits the interactive book to resemble much more closely the found manuscript of Gothic tradition. The eponymous book is an apparently cursed nineteenth-century novel containing a homeopathic formula that enables access to the 'troposphere', a virtual realm in which the participant can inhabit and travel between other minds. The device of the troposphere enables Thomas to explore the experience of fear in creative new ways, from the heroine inhabiting the body of a series of laboratory mice, to the 'train of fear', which draws on the collective unconscious to crystallise cultural anxieties into a single overwhelming journey through horror imagery. Thomas jettisons the genre trappings of science fiction for what could be called 'literary' fiction, but her presentation of a female character traversing a labyrinthine virtual world, in which the relationship between body and mind is interrogated, puts similar themes and concerns to the other two novels into play.

In all three of these novels, a Gothic sensibility is signalled through the positioning of a female character at the centre of the labyrinth. In *Neuromancer*, Molly remains embedded in the material world while her male partner Case inhabits the virtual one and, at the same time, vicariously experiences her physical sensations through the medium of 'simstim', a technology that enables the user to 'ride' another's body. Nevertheless, while in many ways this confirms a conventionally gendered dynamic, there are interesting things about the presentation of Molly, notably her artificial augmentation and her resistance to the male gaze, that complicate a comfortably gendered reading. *The Diamond Age* presents Nell as an active female subject equally at home in the physical and virtual world, but one whose agency has nevertheless been scripted by a benevolent paternalistic authority. Finally, *The End of Mr Y* sees Ariel escape the confines of her body to be liberated into pure mind – or in the Derridean world the novel constructs, pure language. In each case, the access to an 'electronic elsewhere' is predicated on the feminine subject in flight, the heroine outrunning her tormentors in a digital version of the Gothic castle. The female subject is the medium, or interface, who stands on the threshold between the virtual and the material.

'Mirror into mirror': *Neuromancer*

Neuromancer's Molly, a black-clad assassin with surgically enhanced reflexes, retractable razor-blades implanted beneath her nails and mirrorshades implanted over her eyes, offers a new kind of Gothic heroine, one who decidedly rejects victimhood. Her convoluted journey through the corridors of the Villa Straylight, the 'Gothic folly' inhabited by the cloned Tessier-Ashpool dynasty, is a freely chosen professional engagement, not a flight from terror (Gibson 1993: 206). The mirrors that conceal her eyes repel the gaze: the windows to her soul are barred, deflecting the viewer back on themselves. She sees, but is not fully seen. In Turkey, Molly has a face-off with an Armenian agent who also is wearing mirrorshades:

> He seemed to stare pointedly at Molly, but at last he removed the silver glasses. His eyes were a dark brown that matched the shade of his very short military-cut hair. He smiled. 'It is better, this way, yes? Else we make the *tunel* infinity, mirror into mirror …' (Gibson 1993: 109; ellipsis in original)

In this exchange, Molly has the upper hand, forcing the agent to choose between an infinite play of replications (in Lacanian terms, refusing the recognition of the 'I' as a unique and coherent whole) or relinquishing the power of the gaze and revealing his own eyes. The agent saves face with a series of sexist jibes that results in Molly accidentally shooting off his middle finger, a blackly comic symbolic castration. Even when Case 'rides' her body through simstim, sharing her sensory experiences, he does not have access to her thoughts, and 'found himself wondering about the mind he shared these sensations with' (72). Moreover, while Molly can communicate with Case by speaking aloud, he cannot speak directly to her. In their artificially simulated alliance, she becomes the active partner, he the passive one.

Nevertheless, Molly's subordination of her body to her will through the use of technology remains ambivalent in feminist terms. The body cannot be jettisoned so easily, Gibson demonstrates. Molly remains haunted by bodily trauma: she has financed her modifications, it transpires, by a spell as a 'meat puppet' in a brothel, in which women are implanted with a 'cut-out chip' that removes their memory and consciousness while they rent out their bodies. Her ongoing modifications make the chip lose efficacy and she regains consciousness in the midst of a violently exploitative sexual encounter, retaliates with her newly weaponised body and is forced to go on the run. The event catches up with her, however, in the form of a 'dreaming real' show put on by her nemesis, Riviera, an illusionist who creates hallucinations by manipulating the subconscious. In this show, he appears to have sex with Molly before an audience, putting her body together piece by piece, before she in turn violently takes him apart. Whereas Molly is supremely in control of her body, manipulating it to do her bidding, Riviera threatens that control, subordinating her to a kind of mental rape in which he publicly takes possession of her body, to the extent of redesigning it: 'it wasn't Molly; it was Molly as Riviera imagined her. The breasts were wrong, the nipples larger, too dark' (168). This bodily threat culminates at the climax of the novel in Riviera smashing one of Molly's mirrored lenses, a direct assault on her psychic integrity and a symbolic violation.

Commentary on the novel has frequently pointed out that Molly is flesh to Case's mind, reifying a conventionally gendered division. Sherryl Vint explains that:

> Cartesian dualism has a misogynistic heritage. The transcendence of pure mind is a position available to the male subject, while the female subject must remain immanent, absorbing all the limits of materiality that man has cast off in his construction of his own subjectivity. (Vint 2007: 104)

Molly's materiality, however, is not straightforward: her flesh is artificially augmented so that she is part machine. She anticipates the cyborg envisioned by Donna Haraway in her iconic essay, 'The Cyborg Manifesto' (1985): 'a hybrid of machine and organism' (Haraway 1991: 149). For Haraway, the cyborg is the 'illegitimate offspring of militarism and patriarchal capitalism', but is liable, like many illegitimate children, to be unfaithful to its origin (151). In its artificially constructed quality, the cyborg recalls Frankenstein's Creature, but Haraway makes clear that unlike the Creature, 'the cyborg does not expect its father to save it through a restoration of the garden; that is, through the fabrication of a heterosexual mate, through its completion in a finished whole' (151). *Frankenstein*, for Haraway, is tied to the project of liberal humanism and therefore cannot provide a model for a monstrous being that confuses boundaries 'between natural and artificial, mind and body, self-developing and externally-designed, and many other distinctions that used to apply to organisms and machines' (152). Haraway proposes her cyborg as 'a myth system waiting to become a political language', a utopian figure who offers the possibility of a 'post-gender world' (181, 150).

Gibson's Molly does not realise the full potential of Haraway's utopian being, but she does provide the '*pleasure* in the confusion of boundaries and for *responsibility* in their construction' that Haraway advocates (Haraway 1991: 150; emphasis in original). Although ultimately the plot does not allow her to be much more than a vessel or a vehicle for Case's narrative consciousness, her presence begins to deconstruct and problematise the mind/body dualism in interesting ways, setting the template for subsequent virtual Gothic women.

'Flight to the Land Beyond': *The Diamond Age*

In Neal Stephenson's *The Diamond Age: Or, A Young Lady's Illustrated Primer*, twenty-first-century society has developed into a series of enclaves or tribes, dispersed in discrete communities across the globe. The most dominant is that of the New Atlantans, who have revived Victorian manners and morals in order to preserve social order in the face of extreme technological advance. The heroine is a young girl called Nell from an ignominious background, who, through a series of plot twists, comes into possession of an interactive book, the *Young Lady's Illustrated Primer* of the title, designed to educate young women into self-reliant adulthood. *Primer* is in some ways a disingenuous title, as while it is certainly an introductory text, the education it provides is comprehensive, making other books redundant. It works by immersing the reader in an interactive world, constructed from a combination of fantasy and fairy-tale archetypes and the designated reader's own experiences, which the Primer absorbs through smart technology. In it, rather like a video game, the reader progresses by discovering information, acquiring skills and making decisions – but these skills do not remain 'virtual' but are carried into the 'real' world. The doubleness of the novel's title directly reflects the dual narrative that unfolds within it, one of which is set in 'the diamond age' of advanced nanotechnology and one of which plays out in the fantasy world depicted in the Primer.

Stephenson's world aggressively asserts the value of nurture over nature. Nell's beginnings are inauspicious: her father is a low-life executed for violent crime early on in the novel; her mother is inattentive and takes up with a series of boyfriends who are more or less abusive. In the early part of the novel, Nell is a version of the sentimental Dickensian heroine from whom she takes her name, in flight from domestic entrapment, poverty and abuse. However, unlike Dickens's Little Nell, she receives ongoing training and a kind of substitute parenting from the Primer, which inculcates resilience, social intelligence, survival skills, martial arts expertise and eventually advanced digital programming skills. These learning objectives are scripted by the benevolent paternalistic authority of John Hackworth, the programmer who designs the book. His paternal authority is supplemented by the maternal role of the woman employed to narrate it. *The Diamond Age* depicts an industry of virtual entertainment, closely recalling Gibson's simstim, populated by 'ractors' who have been implanted with neural transmitters in order to create personally tailored interactive narratives for audiences across a digital network. The ractor who animates the Primer for Nell, a young woman called Miranda, explicitly takes on a maternal role towards her, although they do not know each other's identities and do not meet until Nell is fully adult. It is this relationship, Stephenson implies, that makes Nell's use of the Primer so successful. Two other young girls who also receive copies of the Primer produce less satisfactory results, despite more privileged backgrounds, because they only receive one side of the virtual parenting relationship (Hackworth narrates his own daughter's copy) or because their relationships with their ractors are less consistent. The importance of the mother – who explicitly gives up her promising racting career in order to parent Nell – is insisted upon, but the mother is not biologically or even physically linked to the child, existing only in a virtual space.

By presenting itself metafictionally as a novel of education, *The Diamond Age* recalls debates on the educational properties (or lack of them) of the first wave of Gothic novels in the late eighteenth century. The notorious satire 'Terrorist Novel Writing' published by an anonymous critic in 1798, proposed that:

> A novel, if at all useful, ought to be a representation of human life and manners, with a view to direct the conduct in the most important duties of life, and to correct its follies. [...] Can a young lady be taught nothing more necessary in life, than to sleep in a dungeon with venomous reptiles, walk through a ward [wood] with assassins, and carry bloody daggers in their pockets, instead of pin-cushions and needle-books? (Anon. 2000: 184)

The *Young Lady's Illustrated Primer* embodies this teaching experience to an improbably literal degree – one of Princess Nell's early travelling companions during her imprisonment in various castles is a dinosaur. As an early incident in the Primer demonstrates, Gothic fiction can, recalling Austen's *Northanger Abbey* (1818), comment effectively on material abuses of women. Nell's physical and sexual abuse at the hands of her mother's boyfriend Burt is translated into her incarceration in the Dark Castle, where she is assaulted by Baron Burt. The Primer, voiced by Miranda, instructs her to run away while her companion Dinosaur attacks Burt. Nell misinterprets the information provided her and attempts to attack Burt herself with a screwdriver, with nearly catastrophic results. The Primer uses Gothic/fantasy tropes to script real-life trauma and provide strategies for surviving it, but its meaning is not always transparent and requires correct interpretation.

The Diamond Age's Gothicism becomes most apparent in the subjectivity of Nell and to a lesser extent Miranda, poised between embodiment and disembodiment. Nell and Miranda simultaneously inhabit two worlds: a technologically enhanced, material world and a magical, virtual one. However, these worlds, connected by the media net, are not comfortably distinct. Relationships forged in the virtual world are as strong or stronger than those in the material world; skills learned in the virtual world can be brought to bear on the material world; the lived experience of the virtual world comes to comprise the shared reality of the actors in it. If the Primer is scripted by Hackworth as a means of producing an ideal daughter, then the relationships forged by the women who animate and use the book, whether Nell and Miranda or the 'Mouse Army' of abandoned Chinese girl-children who have been brought up via cut-price copies of the Primer, exceed and confound the script. At the climax of the novel, Nell finds her virtual mother Miranda and saves her with a kiss, transmitting nanotechnology to her body through the exchange of fluids. Ultimately, the novel reasserts the value of the physical world, allowing the virtual and material to exist in balance through the enlightened figure of Nell.

Becoming Bibliorg: *The End of Mr Y*

Like *The Diamond Age*, Scarlett Thomas's *The End of Mr Y* is focused on a book, the mysteriously cursed novel of the title. Its heroine is Ariel Manto, named for the Sylvia Plath poem, describing a transcendent flight towards death and the simultaneous realisation and dissolution of the 'I' in the 'red/Eye, the cauldron of morning'. This 'Suicidal ... drive' towards transcendence is one that Ariel's own narrative embraces (Plath 1981: 240). A PhD student working on nineteenth-century thought experiments, she discovers a rare copy of a supposedly cursed book by obscure author Thomas Lumas in a second-hand bookshop, and through reading it is able to recreate a homeopathic potion that enables access to a world of pure thought that Lumas names the 'troposphere'. In this world, the subject inhabits the minds of others, experiencing their thoughts and sensations while retaining their own thoughts and agency. They can travel through the world by 'jumping' between minds, and by 'jumping' from one generation to another can effectively go back in time. The troposphere comprises a merger of Gibson's cyberspace and simstim: like Case, Ariel 'rides' other people's bodily sensations while simultaneously travelling through a virtual landscape that is structured like a video game. Although the troposphere allows access to almost unlimited knowledge, it is dangerous for two reasons: because there are people who seek to control that knowledge and destroy anyone who threatens their own access to it; and because, while their minds are active in the troposphere, subjects' bodies enter into a kind of coma in which they do not attend to their physical needs and therefore can die.

Like Nell, therefore, Ariel inhabits both a material world and a virtual one. Ariel's material world is one in which the body's needs are insistent and troublesome. As a PhD student, she survives on an extremely limited budget, her next meal in constant jeopardy. She spends a significant amount of time making elaborate calculations how to spin out her last remaining cash, and devising cheap meals of lentils or baked potatoes with olive oil and salt, enlivened with the odd square of chocolate. She smokes, sometimes choosing cigarettes over food, and drinks endless quantities of coffee and red wine. She has increasingly degrading sex with a married Linguistics professor, culminating in him paying her for sodomising her in a Little Chef toilet: 'And I'm thinking whatever he does next doesn't matter', she says, 'I don't mind how fucked my body gets as long as my mind's OK' (Thomas 2008: 324). In fact, she realises, she desires the pain, which supplements her personal history of self-harm. Like a religious ascetic (and the comparison is not misplaced, as Ariel increasingly turns to religious questions), Ariel seeks the mortification of the flesh as a means of achieving spiritual revelation.

When Ariel begins to fall in love with a theology lecturer called Adam, she reflects on the unreality of the romance myth, setting up a distinction between the physical deprivations of 'real life' and the disembodied world of books. She dreams of merging with books in a retro-fitted version of Haraway's cyborg:

> This isn't real life. Real life is letting men fuck you over their desks (and enjoying it, which is somehow the worst thing). Real life is regularly running out of money, and then food. Real life is having no proper heating. Real life is physical. Give me books instead: give me the invisibility of the contents of books, the thoughts, the contents, the images. Let me become part of a book; I'd give anything for that. Being cursed by *The End of Mr Y* must mean becoming part of the book; an intertextual being: a book-cyborg, or, considering books aren't cybernetic, perhaps a bibliorg. (Thomas 2008: 147)

As Ariel begins to leave 'real life' and the body that accompanies it behind for increasingly long spells in the troposphere, she undergoes the process of becoming the bibliorg she envisions. In the final revelation of the novel, her journey through the troposphere takes her, and the 'virtual' Adam (who has died in the real world), to 'the edge of consciousness' (501). Here she finds herself in a garden: 'And there's one tree, standing by the river, and we walk towards it. And then I understand' (502).

Just as it seems Ariel has finally transcended the body and achieved the heavenly realm of pure thought, or become fully bibliorg, she returns to the moment of the Fall. To preserve the knowledge she values so highly she will have to choose expulsion to the material world. Here Thomas recalls Haraway's insistence that 'The cyborg would not recognise the garden of Eden' (Haraway 1991: 151). Ariel, of course, a fully intertextual being, does recognise Eden (even if she does not name it); but in recognising it, she implicitly realises that it is only by choosing to reject it that difference comes into being and meaning is made. Despite all her attempts to abstract herself from the flesh, mind and body are proved inextricable.

Conclusion

Each of the contemporary texts considered here offers, in different ways, a feminist critique of the Cartesian mind/body dualism, and an argument for the sustained importance of an embodied femininity. As Sherryl Vint points out, despite the ascendance of digital technologies offering access to virtual worlds:

> The body remains relevant to critical work and 'real' life, both because 'real' people continue to suffer or prosper in their material bodies, and because the discourses that structure these material bodies continue to construct and constrain our possible selves. (Vint 2007: 9)

In these texts, virtual Gothic women move between embodied and disembodied selves, and their ability to travel asserts the co-dependence of virtual and material realms. For Elizabeth Grosz, the body constitutes 'a kind of hinge or threshold: it is placed between a psychic or lived interiority and a more sociopolitical exteriority that produces interiority through the inscription of the body's outer surface' (Grosz 1993: 196). She proposes the analogy of the Möbius strip, a continuous three-dimensional figure with one surface and one edge, to demonstrate the inextricability of outer and inner layers. This analogy provides an apt model for the way that virtual Gothic women act as mediums between a material world and a virtual one. Whether cyborgs or bibliorgs, they provide an interface for multiple border-crossings.

Bibliography

Anon. (2000), 'Terrorist Novel Writing' [1798], in E. J. Clery and Robert Miles (eds), *Gothic Documents: A Sourcebook 1700–1820*, Manchester: Manchester University Press.

Gibson, William [1984] (1993), *Neuromancer*, London: HarperCollins.

Grosz, Elizabeth (1993), 'Bodies and Knowledges: Feminism and the Crisis of Reason', in L. Alcoff and E. Potter (eds), *Feminist Epistemologies*, New York and London: Routledge, pp. 187–216.

Haraway, Donna (1991), *Simians, Cyborgs and Women: The Reinvention of Nature*, New York and Abingdon: Routledge.

Jones, David J. (2011), *Gothic Machine: Textualities, Pre-cinematic Media and Film in Popular Visual Culture, 1670–1910*, Cardiff: University of Wales Press.

Machen, Arthur (2005), *The Great God Pan* [1894], in Roger Luckhurst (ed.), *Late Victorian Gothic Tales*, Oxford: Oxford University Press, pp. 183–233.

McHale, Brian (1992), *Constructing Postmodernism*, London and New York: Routledge.

Noel Fielding's Luxury Comedy: Fantasy Man: http://www.channel4.com/pro grammes/noel-fieldings-luxury-comedy/profiles/all/fantasy-man (accessed 8 April 2015).

Owen, Alex (1990), *The Darkened Room: Women, Power and Spiritualism in Late Victorian England*, Philadelphia: University of Pennsylvania Press.

Plant, Sadie (1995), 'The Future Looms: Weaving Women and Cybernetics', in Mike Featherstone and Roger Burrows (eds), *Cyberspace, Cyberbodies, Cyberpunk: Cultures of Technological Embodiment*, London: Sage.

Plath, Sylvia (1981), *Collected Poems*, London: Faber and Faber.

Sconce, Jeffrey (2000), *Haunted Media: Electronic Presence from Telegraphy to Television*, Durham, NC: Duke University Press.

Sofia, Zoe [1992] (1999), 'Virtual Corporeality: A Feminist View', in Jenny Wolmark (ed.), *Cybersexualities: A Reader on Feminist Theory, Cyborgs and Cyberspace*, Edinburgh: Edinburgh University Press, pp. 55–68.

Spooner, Catherine (2014), 'Twenty-first Century Gothic', in Dale Townshend (ed.), *Terror and Wonder: The Gothic Imagination*, London: The British Library, pp. 180–205.

Stephenson, Neal [1995] (1996), *The Diamond Age: Or, A Young Lady's Illustrated Primer*, Harmondsworth: Penguin.

Thomas, Scarlett [2006] (2008), *The End of Mr Y*, Edinburgh: Canongate.

Vint, Sherryl (2007), *Bodies of Tomorrow: Technology, Subjectivity, Science Fiction*, Toronto: University of Toronto Press.

Walkowitz, Judith R. (1992), *City of Dreadful Delight: Narratives of Sexual Danger in Late-Victorian London*, London: Virago.

Chapter 14

Formations of Player Agency and Gender in Gothic Games

Tanya Krzywinska

Digital games are an established feature of contemporary popular culture. They are no longer confined to desktop computers or consoles. We find them embedded in social media, on our smartphones and tablets. While digital games were once designed for and played by those with high levels of technological and gaming literacy, they now reach into a far wider market, with elements of games employed in advertising, business, training and education, as well as consumer and communications cultures. Freed from the constraints of interfaces such as keyboards or game-pad controllers and from expensive, dedicated hardware, games have extended their invitation to a more varied range of people. In addition, it is also increasingly easier to make games, with simplified drag-and-drop interfaces provided by game engines such as Unity. As a result, games are losing their technological opacity and extend beyond the tastes and competencies of the traditionally male-dominated market (Ofcom 2014). While these developments are positive and create a broader and more gender-inclusive participation in digital game media, game development companies are nonetheless still largely populated and led by men. Resistance to equality-driven change is also in evidence, with mainstream news channels in the closing months of 2014 featuring misogynist voices claiming to represent gamers angrily expressing a minority desire to preserve games from 'feminist insurgents'. Representations of gendered embodiments, psychological profiles and role functions within games commonly make use of stereotyped and often gender-exaggerated modes to attract players. This is particularly the case in big-budget high-risk games made for the 'Triple A' market, which target male players (such as the Grand Theft Auto or Call of Duty series, for example). Less risk-averse and lower-budget games do design for other markets, however. Indeed, powerful, agentic and often complex female characters are not completely absent from the field of games.

Within this group there is a particularly high proportion that draws on the Gothic, often sold under the rubric of horror or fantasy. Game development companies often use Gothic as form of branding to attract a pre-established market; in so doing they take advantage of Gothic fiction's appeal across the gender divide to reach beyond the usual male market for games. As distinct from other games, a relatively high percentage of Gothic games are designed by women. An early example is the story-rich point-and-click game *Phantasmagoria*, released in 1995, designed by Roberta Williams, in which the female protagonist battles with a demon who has possessed her husband. Another later example is *Primal* (2003), designed by Katie Lea, in which a young woman discovers during her search for a kidnapped boyfriend that she has a range of demonic powers. Gothic games that provide powerful and complex female playable characters are not limited to female lead designers, however, as indicated by *American McGee's Alice* (2000) and *Bayonetta* (2009).

The Gothic mode provides these particular games with a basis for departure from the dominant use of either male playable characters or playable characters designed simply to function as empty vehicles for entry into a game's diegetic space. Gothic games generally call on the generative traditions and forms of previous Gothic fictions, but *Phantasmagoria*, *Primal*, *American McGee's Alice* and *Bayonetta*, in particular, draw on those narratives that are told from a woman's point of view and which, as a result, can be claimed under the cultural rubric of 'Female Gothic' (Moers 1976). Very specifically, they call on Ann Radcliffe's imprisoned and pursued heroines, the stand-and-fight heroines found in some of Angela Carter's work and perhaps more directly those featured in Joss Whedon's *Buffy the Vampire Slayer*. In all these cases, including Radcliffe, agency – enacted, imagined and constrained – is pivotal to the narrative and character arc, as well as the types of resonances that are likely to be read into and off these configurations. Not only do such characteristics explain the considerable appeal of Gothic for game developers and audiences, they also motivate the creation of representations that break with conventional alignments of function and gender that are more commonly present in games, even if such disruptions are ameliorated through some form of conditionality. While the 'subversions' of game conventions cannot be claimed as 'Feminist Gothic', they nonetheless express issues and tensions around gender and agency current in contemporary culture through the medium of participatory media, and they are games that actively invite the interest of women and girls. Given that games have very often been designed by men to appeal to the pleasures and competencies of men and boys, it is noteworthy that aspects of Gothic have been used to seek to engage what the industry called a few years ago a 'new' market, that of women and girls. Within this context, the deployment of Gothic formations can therefore enact a form of agency for female players that provides, in this relativist sense, an extra power to fracture conventional gender alignments that have consolidated within the risk-averse context of digital games. The core argument of this chapter is that certain iterations of Gothic *can* be used very effectively in games to disquieten and demythologise the thoughtless formations of agency and gender that are perpetuated by many games.

It might prove helpful to readers unfamiliar with digital games to sketch out the diverse use of the scope of the Gothic in games. Gothic formations can be found across game genres such as Role-playing, First- and Third-Person Shooters, Survival Horror, Casual, Action-Adventure, Stealth and Strategy, as well as various platforms: mobile, console, PC, or in games made by any size of development studio. It is, therefore, clear that Gothic offers useful cultural capital for game developers and designers, acting often as form of branding. To make some sense of this field, I'll begin by dividing Gothic-inspired games into five distinctive groups which span game genre divides.

The first includes those games that are designed to appeal to the traditional shoot-'em-up and beat-'em-up market, such as *Outlast* (2014), *Painkiller* (2004), *Quake 4* (2005) and the dandyesque 'Devil May Cry' franchise.[15] These games offer fast-paced action, affording a strong but easily acquired sense of conquest for the player. Characters are often quickly sketched and the storyline is linear and minimal, usually a zombie apocalypse or similar. These games tend to privilege action and have mainly male playable characters who are in pursuit, rather than pursued. As such, in a game context as well as in a performative sense, such games can be claimed aesthetically as male, but their muscular and triumphant nature splits them off from Robert Miles's definition of 'Male Gothic' as scopophilic (Miles 2009: 55), typified by Lewis's *The Monk* (1796), and locates them more appropriately within 'hero'-based fictional formations, which have great purchase in contemporary culture through Hollywood's action movies.

The second group are those games that combine an action-adventure format with Gothic storylines and iconography, such as *American McGee's Alice* and *Primal*, although *Bayonetta* draws on elements of both groups. In this group there is a good proportion of games with female protagonists, and all adopt a female point of view; as such I claim them as 'Female Gothic' in the context of games and it is from this group that most of the games discussed in this chapter are taken. Games within these two groups are often made by established studios and require considerable investment.

The third group includes those games that employ Gothic iconography and which are designed for the casual game market. Examples include the 'Plants versus Zombies' series and 'Zombies, Run!', a suite of gamified, motivational running apps. 'Casual games' is a generic term used within games journalism and by publishers to describe games that are easy to pick up and play, games that do not have complex interfaces and which do not demand much time commitment from their players. They are defined in opposition to 'hardcore' games. There is an implicit, rhetorical gendered distinction here that should be noted, whereby casual games are feminised as a means of trivialisation (Kubik 2012). Often casual games are small-scale productions that require less investment, expertise and labour to make, yet are designed to appeal across a wide market. As might be expected because of their casual nature, few such games take the Gothic route in more than a superficial sense.

The fourth group comprises 'indie' style games that seek experimentally to explore and reinvent both Gothic and game-structures, such as *Among the Sleep* (2014), in which the player takes on the guise of a toddler; *Dear Esther* (2012), a game expressly made to approach horror games from an atmospheric rather than action perspective; *Limbo* (2010) which calls on the aesthetic visual style of Lotte Reiniger's silhouette fairy-tale films and where the central character, coded as male, is pursued, Radcliffe-style, and frequently dies; and *The Path* (2009), a multi-outcome, minimal-action game version of Little Red Riding Hood. Most 'Indie' games are made by small teams of game designers for a niche market and often trade on their non-standard art work or game mechanics; this means that they can take more risks and are likely to be more experimental in terms of their deployment of Gothic formations.

The last, and fifth, group is made up of games that seek to undermine the agency of the player, and provide, therefore, a counter-weight to the more conventional approach of the first group. This 'Weird' group draws on the discomfiting aesthetic of H. P. Lovecraft and equates to the 'horror' which is typified by Lewis's *The Monk* aesthetic that Radcliffe suggests is different from her own brand of Gothic, and which Robert Miles, using the words of Coleridge, describes as 'physicality observed with "libidinous minuteness"' (Miles 2000: 41). There is no muscular, noisy and spectacular action or triumph in this group as there is in the first group, and it therefore cannot be claimed as a 'Male Gothic' aesthetic in the context of games. Examples include: *I Have No Mouth and I Must Scream* (1995); *Deadly Premonition* (2010), a homage to David Lynch's *Twin Peaks*; and the multi-player online game *The Secret*

World (2012); to which we might add the various game adaptations of Lovecraft's stories, such as *Call of Cthulhu: Dark Corners of the Earth* (2005).

While games draw on traditions of the Gothic found in other media, there are certain features of game media that shape the way that Gothic elements might be articulated. Unlike other media, games require physical participation as well as certain literacies that are unique to digital games. In a game, a player's actions and choices are contingent upon the design of a game's core mechanics. This instrumental feature means that the type of experience that games are able to offer players is well-disposed to themes that revolve around agency and mastery. Every game is comprised of an array of different systems that define, address and manage a player's actions. The implications of the ways that a game controls and manipulates a player's behaviour will, however, signify in diverse ways for different players, with gender differences likely to play a part in the way that control is understood and interpreted. Most digital games possess an interface and are composed of rules, progress arcs and winning conditions. These elements are tailored according to each game's own design logic, which, in turn, governs the disposition of a game's spatiality and perspective. Therefore, to progress within a game, a player must engage actively with the particular demands set by the design of a game's mechanics and semiotic cues. Such mechanics range from the simple to the complex, encompassing what a player has to do in a game as well as the various elements of computing behind delivering the game to screen in concert with the effects of using the interface controls. These mechanics dictate the specific horizon of interactivity, the particular scope of managerial feedback mechanisms delivered by the game and the precise arrangement of the interface. These aspects are all configured around an individual overarching game concept. Negotiation of the meanings of these structures for both player and developer tie, whether unconsciously or not, into often implicitly gendered definitions of action, ineptitude, mastery and failure, the meanings of which are situational.

As is evident in Gothic fiction throughout its history, agency and its lack are among the principal verbs (and 'anti-verbs') on which a vocabulary of gender and sexual difference is produced, reproduced and acquires currency. What types of agency, how they signify and in what sphere they acquire currency may, however, change. This lacing together of formations of agency and gender has sources in foundational texts such as the Bible and the Koran and is operative rhetorically and socially. While not immanent but constructed through social, cultural and economic paradigms, such alignment is still nonetheless evident across many of the world's cultures. It might therefore be thought of as a grand narrative on which Gothic rests. Materialist, feminist, structuralist and psychoanalytic critics approach agency and gender from different perspectives, yet they share the premise that gender difference (much like other modes of difference such as class and race) is organised around an economics of agency. Hélène Cixous makes the agenda plain:

> Organisation by hierarchy makes all conceptual organisation subject to man. Male privilege, showing in the opposition between activity and passivity, which he uses to sustain himself. Traditionally, the questions of sexual difference is treated by coupling it with the opposition activity/passivity. (Cixous 1989: 102)

She is careful to historicise oppositional troping of gender according to passivity and activity, yet such convergences persist in mimetic fashion, thereby allowing fiction to find dramatic effect in playing with such roles and in exploring divergence between gender expectations and experience. As Eve Kosofsky Sedgwick (1980) argues, a central plank of Gothic is its thematic and iconographic focus on inaction and lack of agency, emblemised by claustrophobia and burial alive. Given that games promise players action and agency, this discrepancy seems somewhat unpromising. Yet often it is by working with this discrepancy that game designers can begin to challenge what might be thought of as a central pleasure of gaming, a sense of agency as mastery. Agency can, however, be cast in diverse ways – contingent or individualist, for example – and can be operative across different spheres: in terms of character and/or story, or in terms of ludic mechanics and/or player agency. Moral choices, for example, might be centralised to the ludic design of a game, rather than simply sidelined as they often are in the fast-paced zombie-style shooters. Gender contextualises the articulation of agency in games, feeding back into the design logic of a game, and playing a role in the way that player choice is managed. Gothic can influence the ways in which this might occur.

Radcliffe's foundational model of the pursued and terrified heroine is acted out in a range of different Gothic games, in the interactive context of *Phantasmagoria* (1995), for example. This point-and-click game worked with limited computing resources and its innovation was to overlay filmed footage of the player's character, Adrienne Delaney, being played by Victoria Morsell, onto computer-generated images. The use of real footage made more convincing Adrienne's frightened reactions to events than was possible with computer animation at that time. In accord with the Radcliffean model, Adrienne is pursued by her demonically possessed husband until she is killed by him or dispatches the demon through right actions enabling her to leave the house. The player is aware that the game provides a way to do this and has to work through the clues on a trial-and-error basis. Adrienne is thus likely to 'die' at the hands of her husband-demon many times, a repetition that diminishes both death and dramatic tension, and which, importantly, places agency with players who can also, if they wish, sadistically side not with Adrienne but with the demonic; players can of course have it both ways – killing her and saving her at the same time. In a Carter-esque twist on Radcliffe's model, Adrienne finally lures the demon into a subterranean bloody chamber where, in concert with a player, she is able to dispatch it and finally leave the confines of the house. In this sense Adrienne has agency on the external world and events in narrative terms, through her active, investigative approach, which is practically focused towards coping, prevailing and expressing herself. Here there is a clear departure from Radcliffe's model, where agency for the heroine lies mainly within the sphere of the imagination. This departure is partly related to the nature of game media, whereby players act through the mediation of characters. In addition, it is also fuelled by Angela Carter's reconception of the Gothic 'heroine', made in the mode of Sade's active Juliette rather than the passive, suffering Justine, anticipating Whedon's contemporary expression of the Female Gothic in *Buffy the Vampire Slayer* (1997–2003).

Making use of Manuel Aguirre's analysis of Shelley's *Frankenstein* (Aguirre 2013), I have argued elsewhere (Krzywinska 2015) that the notion of the false hero, as a figuration of tragedy and entropy, is impor-tant to understanding the way that a Gothic game can work against the convention of unqualified mastery as a dominant mode of figuring agency in play in many video games. For Aguirre, 'a key to Gothic ... resides in its centering the flawed character as protagonist ... [while] the standard hero of traditional tales is often demoted to a helpless or passive stance' (Aguirre 2013: 11). Through the use of such weirdling figurations, games can move from the conventional alignment of agency and action with representations and embodiments coded as masculine through to enabling all players the ability to act decisively and master-fully on and in situations. In *American McGee's Alice*, for example, the active, rational position is represented not by a scientist or muscled hero, nor by a caring Dad coping with the Apocalypse as in *The Last of Us* (2013), nor even by a protective maternal female of the type discussed by Yvonne Tasker (1993). This game's Alice is not going about rescuing anyone at all, as Tasker argues is the condition for the action heroine in Hollywood, and there are no explicit surrogate children. Alice encoun-ters situations and characters that cannot be made sense of, yet she retains a clear-sighted yet contrarian grumpiness which establishes her individuality for the player. While Alice is dependent upon the player for her agency to play out, the players are also dependent upon her for their agency in the game. The designers did, however, miss a trick here. If this contingency had been noted *diegetically*, then the game could have moved widdershins in relation to the usual hero-style game conception of agency as individualist action. Alice has a helper, the Cheshire cat, who comments on progress and gives hints; yet just as Alice is a false hero, so her helper is a false helper: he's unpredictable and sarcastic, and with his silky tones and demonic features, is closer to the Radcliffean villain than a positive character.

Contingency-based agency that counters the hero model goes a little further in *Primal*, as Jen works more fully in partnership with her gargoyle companion to solve puzzles in order to act on the world and to help save her boyfriend. While actions used in playing as Alice bear comparison to that used to play Lara Croft in the 'Tomb Raider' games, the meaning of those actions are recast through the Gothic milieu of *American McGee's Alice* and acquire a strange, quietly desperate and deeply unheroic cast. And, while Lara Croft is merely a one-dimensional hero-machine with few signs of possessing subjectivity, Alice is most clearly possessed of a wilful subjectivity, in part by virtue of her textual relationship to Lewis Carroll's *Alice in Wonderland*. Her subjectivity and will are strongly signified verbally and in terms of the way she is animated, revealing her reactions to the topsy-turvy world that she seemingly unwillingly inhabits. In addition, it is hinted at that this world is of her own imaginative making. And, unlike Lara, Alice talks throughout game play. Alice, Bayonetta and Jen share their thoughts and feelings with their companion helpers, in all cases assuring the player that they are meant to be regarded as separate, living, breathing and thinking others. These characters express how gender and agency are often figured in contemporary culture; not through civic or political action, but instead filtered through the lens of Gothic culture, through the display and performance of quirky, conventionally unconventional individualism.

Alice, Bayonetta and Jen are not therefore just false heroes because they differ from the mass-produced, masculinised hero-cyborgs found in many games. Through deployment of Gothic grammar, each has something demonic or witchy about them that shapes the articulation of their agency. Physically small and slender, Jen of *Primal* discovers that she can transform into different, clawed and muscular demonic forms that allow her to fight physically. Alice uses her toys to destroy without remorse and inhabits a world that is not formed around a simple good-versus-evil binary. Bayonetta is a laconic witch working on the side of darkness who, in graceful balletic moves, kills untold numbers of aggressive angelic beings before breakfast. These formations are figured around worlds and scenarios that permit the transformation of the false hero into empathetic women and girls, rather than narrative cyphers. They provide examples of how, when placed within weirdifying quotation marks, a more diverse figuration of character agency can be drawn. While the condition for agency here seems to be some kind of madness, recalling the debate between Clément and Cixous (1986) on whether hysteria can be regarded as a feminist strategy, what *is* clear is that the Gothic role of false hero provides an alternative model to hero-based games for the building of a wider, more diverse vocabulary of character agency than that typified within shooter and adventure game format.

However, for all these characters agency comes at the cost of some aspect of their humanity as each acquires something monstrous. Agency, as in Angela Carter's animalistic versions of fairy stories ('The Tiger's Bride', for example), may certainly be liberating and libidinal, but there is a palpable, Frankenstein-styled, cost. That cost is sanity and family in the case of Alice and the female protagonist of *Phantasmagoria*, both of whom are simply trying to survive a nightmare. In contrast, Jen comes off the best of the bunch. She is able to transform *at will* and her powers are deployed in the pursuit of saving her beleaguered boyfriend. This is not successful, however, preserving her status as false hero. This ending is interesting, certainly Gothic in tone, and must be understood in a medial context, within which most games allow players to triumph over adversity and therefore master potential threats to their ego. Apart from the more Radcliffean ending of *Phantasmagoria*, in which Adrienne bests the demon male presence and steps out of the bloody chamber house into sunlight, these other 'Female Gothic' games offer no resolution, coupling or triumphant pay off. Alice might even be her own enemy, cast as Other through the image of the Red Queen, and the game *Bayonetta* is a quirky oddity, perhaps by virtue of its Japanese authorship, whereby the traditional western iconography of angels versus demons is reversed. However, it is only in this game that the denouement involves Bayonetta killing her father and being spared death, saved by a queen who punches the Creator into the sun in an echo of the rescue of the girl in Angela Carter's version of the tale of Bluebeard, 'The Bloody Chamber' (1979).

The notion of a 'Female Gothic' in the context of games is not meant to suggest that gender or sex is immanent. Instead it is used to show how gender is constructed and performed through the texts that comprise culture. It also provides a means of bringing gender back to the (game) design board in a theoretical milieu, where some critics, in a premature application of Donna Haraway's speculative post-human model, emphasise and celebrate digital game players as post-human (Keogh 2014). While such a position is tantalising, and even hinted at when playing online in the skin of an avatar of no-gender or differently gendered, it nonetheless elides the pervasively embodied and experiential nature of gameplay itself (Kirkpatrick 2011; Carr 2007; 2013), as well as the rhetoric in which that embodiment is conventionalised and understood socially and culturally. When playing a game we might not be represented in the game space as 'woman' or even as human at all, but our lived, socialised experience interweaves with the pervasive constructions that name and claim us and how we use our bodies as women or men, even if we resist or contradict such constructions. If games often articulate agency in terms of heroism and individualism, there are, however, other economies of agency that are at work on games generally and which acquire something further through a Gothic frame.

Left 4 Dead 2 (2009) is a Zombie Apocalypse game that by virtue of its cooperative nature seems to represent a challenge to the usual conception of agency as individualist, found in many shooter-style games. Working in teams of four, players are represented in the game by an unlikely alliance between a redneck teenaged boy, a twenty-something African-American woman, a large, middle-aged African-American man, and a wide-boy white man. Together they must survive various scenarios of a Zombie Apocalypse. Ostensibly they work together and in concert with their players to clean up the mess, listening out for different types of special monsters that threaten in different ways to wipe out the team. While cooperation is certainly required, effect agency is often contingent upon concerted action and there is no distinction between the differently embodied characters in terms of their capacity to act effectively. The game nonetheless deploys attributes found in more conventional shooter games that encourage competition between players in terms of kill rate. Should one player-character die, then there is no game mechanism to ensure that the other players will go back to retrieve them, weakening the game's claim to agency through contingency. In the end it's still about individual survival, even if the characters exhibit some attributes of the false hero (a feature that calls on Romero's anti-heroic *Night of the Living Dead* [1968]). Here we see the pull of the gamic convention to figure agency in a way that emphasises competition and individualism.

By contrast, in *Buffy the Vampire Slayer: Chaos Bleeds* (2003), a solo player game, 'the big bad' can only defeated with the help of *all* the Buffy gang, whom the player plays one at a time. Contingency is perhaps most apparent in multi-player games with large worlds, where it is difficult for every player inhabitant to be figured as hero/saviour, and it takes on a Gothic form in the multi-player online game *The Secret World* (2012). In this game players have to work together supporting each other with their different skills in order to escape from dungeons. This ensemble-playing is derived from classic table-top Role-Playing Games rather than specifically from Gothic literature, although Joss Whedon's *Buffy* series is informed by the practice and directly referenced. *The Secret World* does, however, give the player a strong sense of weird isolation and humility and, even though players are chosen by a faction to fight, their efforts are contingent on that faction's resources and support. A player is also just one among many and while small victories might be won, there is a strong pessimistic sense that no amount of fighting will prevent the demise of the human world, so limiting any sense of personal agency. It is also extremely difficult to ascertain the moral alignment of factions or groups for whom the player works; this makes choices seem random and therefore alters the 'heroic' condition of agency more usually found in games. This is an excellent example of how a game makes use of contingency and moral ambiguity to drain meaning from any winning condition and its concomitant sense of unbounded agency and mastery. Power is localised and contingent for humans, and put into perspective in relation to the Big Other that stalks the defiles of the game. In this context conventional alignments of masculinity and power suffer most, and it is perhaps no coincidence that it is long-term resident Norma Creed who holds out longest, when all the 'menfolk' of Solomon Island have died or turned inhuman. In this game and in the other games discussed above that emphasise a contingent model of agency, an untroubled, unilateral approach to power becomes untenable and, by virtue of the Gothic frame, is both bounded and comes at a cost, felt palpably within the agency offered to a player.

I want now to turn to the value of games in which player agency is eroded and undermined in terms of a 'Male Gothic'. In a media context which sells itself on giving players agency in a game, Gothic can be deployed in such a way as to undermine the standard pretence of unconditional agency for a player. In these games the player is often embodied in the game not as a woman but instead as a man and it seems logical to assume that this is because women are less potent signifiers of effective agency than men. Game media has some unique, characteristic seductions, the principal one of which is that it offers (at least) the illusion of agency and action to a player, of whom more appropriately controlled physical action is demanded than that of the reader or spectator. Agency and action are the core affordances of games, while in thematic terms a lack of either is integral to the Gothic, at least for many female characters. While this might appear to be a severely contradictory, dissonant show-stopper, an apposite combination can produce a visceral and engaging experience. Giving players the capacity to act, to become an agent, indeed promising them that pleasure, provides the context within which any abrupt curtailment of that agency can have potentially a powerful, visceral emotional and psychological impact. For example, in *Call of Cthulhu: Dark Corners of the Earth*, fear is used as a mechanism to prevent a player from taking action, placing that player very palpably in the shoes of a Radcliffean heroine who can only imagine resistance and in a game convention sense gendering the player as female/feminine. Such a possibility arises because games are far more than simply representational artefacts: a player's performance and physicality are deeply implicated in the equation.

Games are commonly defined by the presence of a winning condition. Winning conditions afford players an unconditional sense of progress and achievement. They might be temporary or terminal affairs. Games generally work, in an operant conditioning sense, on the basis of giving a player positive feedback that leads to the achievement of a set goal. Players win in *A Vampyre Story* by working through the puzzles one by one, to release Mona from the island-castle where she has been imprisoned by the Dracula figure, so that she can pursue her aspiration to become an opera singer; the narrative alongside the feedback mechanics work to make players feel good to have done so. The systems and structures of games such as these are also designed to create an appetite to continue playing by giving bursts of pleasure as challenges are overcome, thereby shoring up a player's sense of agency. As such, games can be regarded as highly loaded performance-management devices, wherein certain behaviours are enforced and reified. But it is possible in games to play *on and with* such devices. The manipulative nature of games and the illusion of player agency within the diegesis is revealed and wryly deployed in the Deco-Gothic-styled, dystopian, first-person game *Bioshock* (2007), a game that I claim here for 'Male Gothic'. Player-characters are told half way through the game, to great dramatic effect, that they've been mind-controlled throughout: what of agency now? Rather than accruing a bolstered sense of agency for the player, as is commonly pursued by games, it is clear that the player has instead been played. This manoeuvre certainly pulls the rug out from under any allegiance between the pleasurable experience of mastery and control and conventional definitions of masculinity. The game's various endings are far from triumphant and two of the three endings culminate in condemnation of the actions of the player-character – who will have just followed the expected path used within most games – by killing the threatening and demonic-looking Little Sisters that populate the game. This play on conventional gamic agency reveals it as contingent, fragile and illusory.

Call of Cthulhu: Dark Corners of the Earth also operates with a different, decidedly weird, model of agency for its players. Players are highly vulnerable throughout and for a large part of the game they can only run from dangerous situations and try to avoid being paralysed by fear in the face of the monstrous Other. Winning is simply surviving rather than triumphantly overcoming. Breaking the definition of agency as player mastery is also themed in *Eternal Darkness* (2002) which tries to convince players – not just the characters they play – that they are going mad and are haunted: the player is addressed *as* a player during the game when it appears that the game console has been switched off and agency over the game's controller has been removed. More recently, horror games for the Oculus Rift, a virtual-reality head-mounted display, such as *Alone in the Rift* (2014) and *Dreadhalls* (2014), have exploited the physical and perceptual effects of a 360-degree immersive virtual space to play with and on player agency. In so doing, such horror games call on the aesthetics of 'Male Gothic' by placing emphasis on scopophilia – the rift is strapped around the eyes and thereby re-embodies players in their own skins, creating an experience that finds its thrill in putting players beyond their own physical and perceptual agency. At a time when agency is so contested and contingent in our real lives, it is perhaps no small wonder that the virtual offerings of mastery within games has proved so seductive; yet games and, in particular, Gothic games that actively engage with entropy – the arch-enemy of agency and progression – are capable of figuring agency and mastery against dominant game conventions. Such games can provide the affective and embodied experience that lead us to ask if we have any personal or social agency or whether meaning and identity have just simply been co-opted in order to boost the overweening consumerist ego.

Note

1. I use italics for individual titles and single quotation marks for franchises.

Bibliography

Aguirre, M. (2013), 'Gothic Fiction and Folk-Narrative Structure: The Case of Mary Shelley's *Frankenstein*', *Gothic Studies*, 15(2) (November): 1–18.

Carr, D. (2007), *Un-Situated Play? Textual Analysis and Digital Games*, Digital Games Research Association: http://www.digra.org/hardcore-18-un-situated-play-textual-analysis-and-digital-games-diane-carr (accessed 20 August 2015).

Carr, D. (2013), *Digital Games: Representations of Ability and Disability Project Update atGames*, London: Institute of Education.

Cixous, Hélène [1989] (1997), 'Sorties: Out and Out: Attacks/Ways Out/Forays', in C. Belsey and J. Moore (eds), *The Feminist Reader: Essays in Gender and the Politics of Literary Criticism*, Basingstoke: Macmillan, pp. 91–103.

Clément, Catherine and Hélène Cixous (1986), *The Newly Born Woman*, Minneapolis: University of Minnesota Press.

Keogh, B. (2014), 'Cybernetic Memory and the Construction of the Posthuman Self in Videogame Play', in D. M. Weiss, A. D. Propen and C. Emmerson Reid (eds), *Design, Mediation and the Posthuman*, New York: Lexington Books, pp. 233–46.

Kirkpatrick, G. (2011), *Aesthetic Theory and The Video Game*, Manchester: Manchester University Press.

Krzywinska, T. (2015), 'The Gamification of Gothic Coordinates', *Revenant: Critical and Creative Studies of the Supernatural*, 1(1), online journal: http://www.revenantjournal.com.

Kubik, E. (2012), 'Masters of Technology: Defining and Theorising the Hardcore/Casual Dichotomy in Video Game Culture', in R. Gajjala and Y. J. Oh (eds), *Cyberfeminism 2.0*, NewYork: Peter Lang Publishing, pp. 135–52.

Miles, Robert (2000), 'Ann Radcliffe and Matthew Lewis', in David Punter (ed.), *A Companion to the Gothic*, Oxford: Blackwell, pp. 41–57.

Miles, Robert (2009), '"Mother Radcliff": Ann Radcliffe and the Female Gothic', in Diana Wallace and Andrew Smith (eds), *The Female Gothic: New Directions*, Basingstoke: Palgrave Macmillan, pp. 42–59.

Moers, E. (1976), *Literary Women*, London: The Women's Press.

Ofcom (2014), *The Communications Market Report* (7 August 2014): http://stakeholders.ofcom.org.uk/binaries/research/cmr/cmr14/2014_UK_CMR.pdf (accessed 24 October 2014).

Sedgwick, E. K. (1980), *The Coherence of Gothic Conventions*, London and New York: Methuen.

Tasker, Y. (1993), *Spectacular Bodies: Gender, Genre, and the Action Cinema*, London and New York: Routledge.

Notes on Contributors

Lucie Armitt is Professor of Contemporary English Literature at the University of Lincoln. Her principal publications include: *Twentieth-Century Gothic* (2011); *Fantasy Fiction* (2005); *Contemporary Women's Fiction and the Fantastic* (2000); (ed.) *George Eliot: A Reader's Guide to Essential Criticism: Adam Bede, The Mill on the Floss, Middlemarch* (2000); *Theorising the Fantastic* (1996); (ed.) *Where No Man Has Gone Before: Women and Science Fiction* (1991). She is currently working on a co-edited book (with Scott Brewster) on Gothic literary tourism.

Ginette Carpenter is Senior Lecturer in the Department of English at Manchester Metropolitan University. Her doctorate assessed the shifting relationships between reading and romance in contemporary women's writing and she has published on textual seductions in the work of Jeanette Winterson and Elizabeth Jane Howard. She is currently researching the figure of the mother in the work of Hilary Mantel, in addition to working on a longer-term project that addresses cultural representations of the childfree.

Sue Chaplin is Senior Lecturer in Romanticism and Gothic Studies at Leeds Beckett University. She is the author of several books in her field, including *The Gothic and the Rule of Law* (2007), *Gothic Literature: Texts, Concepts, Contexts* (2011) and *The Romanticism Handbook*, co-edited with Joel Faflak (2011).

Ardel Haefele-Thomas is currently the Chair of Lesbian, Gay, Bisexual, Transgender and Queer Studies at City College of San Francisco. She has published numerous articles on Queer Gothic and the monograph *Queer Others in Victorian Gothic: Transgressing Monstrosity* (2012). She is currently working with Columbia University Press on an introduction to Transgender Studies textbook, forthcoming in 2017.

Avril Horner is an Emeritus Professor of English at Kingston University, London. Her research interests include women's writing and Gothic fiction. With Sue Zlosnik she has co-authored many articles and several books, including *Daphne du Maurier: Writing, Identity and the Gothic Imagination* (1998) and *Gothic and the Comic Turn* (2005). Her edited books include *European Gothic: A Spirited Exchange, 1760–1960* (2002) and (with Anne Rowe) *Iris Murdoch and Morality* (2010), *Iris Murdoch: Texts and Contexts* (2012) and *Living on Paper: Letters from Iris Murdoch, 1934–1995* (2015). She has also written several articles with Janet Beer, with whom she co-authored *Edith Wharton: Sex, Satire and the Older Woman* (2011).

Tanya Krzywinska is a Professor in Digital Games at Falmouth University and an artist. She is the author of several books and many articles on different aspects of digital games, including, most recently, exploring the affect of remediations of Gothic by game media. She is currently working on a monograph, *Gothic Games*, and on an interactive Gothic fiction, 'The Witch's Room'; she is also researching the Gothic possibilities offered by augmented reality.

Marie Mulvey-Roberts is an Associate Professor in English literature at the University of the West of England, Bristol. She is the editor of the journal *Women's Writing* on women writers up to the long nineteenth century and has edited many books, including *The Handbook to the Gothic* (2nd edition, 2009). She is the author of several monographs, the most recent being *Dangerous Bodies: Historicising the Gothic Body* (2015), along with numerous chapters and articles in the field of Gothic, gender and the body.

Rebecca Munford is a Senior Lecturer in English Literature at Cardiff University. Her research focuses on modernist and contemporary experimental women's writing, the Gothic in its European and erotic modes, and the relationship between gender, fashion and dress. She is the author of *Decadent Daughters and Monstrous Mothers: Angela Carter and European Gothic* (2013) and co-author, with Melanie Waters, of *Feminism and Popular Culture: Investigating the Postfeminist Mystique* (2013). She is currently writing a literary and cultural history of women in trousers.

Catherine Spooner is Reader in Literature and Culture at Lancaster University and co-President of the International Gothic Association. She has published widely on Gothic literature, film and popular culture, including the books *Fashioning Gothic Bodies*, *Contemporary Gothic*, *The Routledge Companion to Gothic* (with Emma McEvoy), *Monstrous Media/Spectral Subjects: Imaging Gothic from the Nineteenth Century to the Present* (with Fred Botting) and *Return to Twin Peaks: New Approaches to Materiality, Theory and Genre* (with Jeffrey Weinstock). Her next book will be *Post-Millennial Gothic: Comedy, Romance and the Rise of Happy Gothic* (2017).

Laurence Talairach-Vielmas is Professor of English at the University of Toulouse Jean Jaurès, and associate researcher at Alexandre Koyré Centre for the History of Science and Technology. Her research specialises in the interrelations between Victorian literature, medicine and science. She is the author of *Fairy Tales, Natural History and Victorian Culture* (2014), *Wilkie Collins, Medicine and the Gothic* (2009) and *Moulding the Female Body in Victorian Fairy Tales and Sensation Novels* (2007). She has also edited several collections of articles on the popularisation of science, as well as two novels by Mary Elizabeth Braddon: *Thou Art the Man* [1894] (2008) and *Dead Love Has Chains* [1907] (2014), both published by Valancourt Books.

Diana Wallace is Professor of English Literature at the University of South Wales. She is the author of *Female Gothic Histories: Gender, History and the Gothic* (2013), *The Woman's Historical Novel: British Women Writers, 1900–2000* (2005), *Sisters and Rivals in British Women's Fiction, 1914–39* (2000) and co-editor (with Andrew Smith) of *The Female Gothic: New Directions* (2009). She has also produced an edition of Hilda Vaughan's *Here Are Lovers* [1926] for the Welsh Women's Classics series, published by Honno in 2012.

Anne Williams is Professor of English Emeritus at the University of Georgia. She is author of *Prophetic Strain: The Greater Lyric in the Eighteenth Century* (1984) and *Art of Darkness: A Poetics of Gothic* (1995). She has edited *Three Vampire Tales* (2002) and, with Christy Desmet, *Shakespearean Gothic* (2009). She has written numerous essays on Gothic and Romantic topics and is completing a psychobiography of Horace Walpole, 'Monstrous Pleasures: Horace Walpole's Gothic Operas'.

Gina Wisker is Professor of Higher Education and Contemporary Literature at the University of Brighton. Her principal research interests are contemporary women's Gothic and postcolonial writing. She has published *Postcolonial and African American Women's Writing* (2000);

Key Concepts in Postcolonial Writing (2007); *Horror* (2005); *Margaret Atwood, an Introduction to Critical Views of Her Fiction* (2012); and has just completed *Contemporary Women's Gothic Fiction*. Other interests are postgraduate study and supervision: *The Postgraduate Research Handbook* (2001, 2008); *The Good Supervisor* (2005, 2012); *Getting Published* (2015). She edits *Innovations in Education and Teaching International* and online literary journals *Dissections* and *Spokes*. She is currently chair of the Contemporary Women's Writing Association, a Higher Education Academy Principal Fellow and a National Teaching Fellow.

Angela Wright is Professor of Romantic Literature at the University of Sheffield and currently co-President of the International Gothic Association. She is the author of *Gothic Fiction* (2007), *Britain, France and the Gothic: The Import of Terror* (2013) and co-editor (with Dale Townshend) of *Ann Radcliffe, Romanticism and the Gothic* (2014) and *The Edinburgh Companion to Romantic Gothic*. Current projects include a study of Mary Shelley for the University of Wales Press series *Gothic Literary Authors* and preliminary research for her next project, which carries the provisional title 'Fostering Romanticism'.

Sue Zlosnik is Emeritus Professor of Gothic Literature at Manchester Metropolitan University, UK and former co-President of the International Gothic Association. With Avril Horner, she has published five books, including *Daphne du Maurier: Writing, Identity and the Gothic Imagination* (1998) and *Gothic and the Comic Turn* (2005), as well as numerous essays and articles. Alone, she has published essays on writers as diverse as J. R. R. Tolkien and Chuck Palahniuk and a monograph, *Patrick McGrath* (2011). She is co-editor (with Agnes Andeweg) of *Gothic Kinship* (2013).

Index

abjection, 4, 6, 7, 46–52, 55–8, 68–9, 140–1, 150–1, 153–4, 157, 163, 187

ageing, 9, 25, 94, 102, 110, 131, 154–5, 159–60, 163, 184–97

agency, 1, 7, 10, 96, 101, 133, 139–40, 147, 157, 159, 161–3, 193, 195, 202, 205, 210, 214–27

Aguirre, Manuel, 220

Alcock, Mary, 'A Receipt for Writing a Novel', 15–16, 17, 22

Amirpour, Ana Lily, *A Girl Walks Home Alone at Night*, 8, 159, 161, 162

Anatol, Giselle, 192

apocalypse, 79, 216, 220, 223

Appignanesi, Lisa et al., *Fifty Shades of Feminism*, 2

asylum, 3, 6, 35, 110

Atwood, Margaret
  Lady Oracle, 101–2
  The Blind Assassin, 102–3
  The Journals of Susanna Moodie, 187
  The Robber Bride, 195

Auerbach, Nina
  Our Vampires Ourselves, 150
  Woman and the Demon, 42

Austen, Jane, 16
  Northanger Abbey, 3, 16–18, 27, 109–10, 141, 209

Badmington, Neil, 122

Bakhtin, Mikhail, 107

Ball, Alan, *True Blood* (television series), 193

Bathory, Elizabeth, 151–2, 154

Baudelaire, Charles, 6, 120

Baum, L. Frank, *The Wonderful Wizard of Oz*, 91

Beauvoir, Simone de, 184, 185

Bentham, Jeremy, *A Fragment on Government*, 137–8

Blackstone, William, *Commentaries on the Laws of England*, 136–7, 139

Blake, William, 163

Bluebeard, 6, 77, 84, 109–10, 191, 222

Botting, Fred, 46, 138, 153

Bowen, Elizabeth, 'The Cat Jumps', 110

Braddon, Mary Elizabeth, 6, 36, 38, 42–3
  Dead Love Has Chains, 42, 43
  Eleanor's Victory, 42
  Lady Audley's Secret, 3, 34–5, 110, 155, 156
  The Golden Calf, 42
  'The Good Lady Ducayne', 7, 113, 152, 154–5, 186
  Thou Art the Man, 42

Brite, Poppy Z., 150, 165
  Lost Souls, 158
  Love in Vein, 151

Brontë, Charlotte
  Jane Eyre, 3, 34–5, 38, 98, 110, 143, 191
  Villette, 9, 38–9, 186

Brontë, Emily, *Wuthering Heights*, 62–3, 110–11

brothers, 4, 7, 43n, 51, 64–5, 83, 84, 91, 100, 144, 146–7, 170, 176, 190

Brownworth, Victoria, *Nite Bites*, 157, 158, 159, 162

Bruhm, Steven, 51

Buffini, Moira, *A Vampire Story*, 8, 159, 161, 162

Bulwer Lytton, Edward, 6, 110
Bulwer Lytton, Rosina, 6, 110
Burney, Frances ('Fanny')
   Cecilia, 19
   Evelina, 19
   The Wanderer, 19
Burton, Robert, *The Anatomy of
   Melancholy*, 96
Buse, Peter, 124
Butler, Judith, 116,127, 187
Byron, Lord, *The Giaour*, 95–6

Califia, Pat, 'The Vampire', 158
Carr, Helen, 67
Carroll, Lewis, *Alice in Wonderland*,
   221
Carter, Angela, 6, 71, 76, 84, 85, 86,
   115, 150, 157, 158, 163, 215,
   220
   The Bloody Chamber, 70
   'The Bloody Chamber', 191, 222
   'The Lady of the House of Love', 8,
      115, 157
   'The Loves of Lady Purple', 8, 157
   The Magic Toyshop, 66–8
   The Passion of New Eve, 115–16
   'The Tiger's Bride', 222
   Wise Children, 194
   'Wolf-Alice', 70
Case, Sue Ellen, 158
Castle, Terry, 6–7, 120, 121, 128
castration, 6, 48, 91, 92, 94, 97, 107,
   113–16, 206
Catholicism, 93, 94, 98, 140
Chambers, Jane, *Burning*, 171–2, 177
Charcot, Jean-Martin, 40, 41, 111
Chariandy, David, 9, 192–3
child, Gothic, 4–5, 49, 51, 53–8, 59–73,
   100–1, 112, 175, 189, 203
Cixous, Hélène, 154, 219, 222
class, 8, 19, 56, 66, 71, 75, 79, 98, 133,
   155, 161, 170–1, 176–7, 179, 180,
   182n, 202, 219
Clément, Catherine, 222
Clery, E. J., 18
Coleridge, Samuel Taylor, 217
   'Christabel', 96
Collins, Wilkie, 6
   Heart and Science, 39–40
   Jezebel's Daughter, 40
   The Woman in White, 9, 35, 36, 186
Comyns, Barbara, 5
   The Skin Chairs, 76
   The Vet's Daughter, 76, 85–6

Condé, Maryse, 171, 174
   I, Tituba, Black Witch of Salem, 171,
      172–3
Conolly, John, 35
corpses, 3, 22, 32, 37, 40, 56, 109, 125,
   131–2, 187
Craciun, Adriana, 95, 108, 109
Creed, Barbara, 47, 55, 57, 65, 107,
   154
Culpepper, Cate, *A Question of Ghosts*,
   177, 178
cyberpunk, 200, 203–4
cyberspace *see* virtual
cyborg, 207, 211–12, 221

Dacre, Charlotte, 92, 109
   Zofloya, or The Moor, 2, 27–8, 95,
      108–9, 117
Daly, Mary, 91, 103
daughters, 6, 21, 23, 25, 26, 28, 40,
   51, 56, 64, 69, 71, 75, 76, 77, 80,
   82, 82, 85–6, 91, 94, 97, 102, 112,
   126, 140–1, 145, 161–2, 174, 176,
   178, 180, 189, 191, 194, 204, 209,
   210
Davison, Carol Margaret, 186
death, 19–20, 22, 25, 37, 40, 44n, 49,
   56–7, 60, 63, 65, 66, 71, 76, 78,
   79, 83–5, 95–7, 100, 102–3, 108,
   114–15, 117, 118n, 121, 126,
   128–9, 130, 132, 136, 139, 142–3,
   151, 155, 158, 159, 162, 173, 175,
   186, 189, 191, 194, 210, 220,
   220
Delamotte, Eugenia, 31, 32, 125
demonisation, 2, 11, 106, 163
Derrida, Jacques, 6–7, 120–1, 125,
   126–7, 130, 131
desire, 4, 5, 7, 52, 55, 68, 84, 93, 109,
   114, 117, 128–9, 132–3, 151–4,
   156–8, 162–3, 179, 188, 193–4,
   211, 214, 224
Dickens, Charles
   Great Expectations, 35, 37–8, 186
   The Old Curiosity Shop, 208
Dijkstra, Bram, 97, 107, 153
domestic, the, 5, 6, 21, 47, 52, 53,
   54, 56–7, 74–88, 107, 108, 117,
   125–6, 129, 132, 143, 208
Donoghue, Emma, 5
   Room, 86–7
double, 4, 5, 33, 34, 35, 75, 82, 85, 86,
   93, 122, 200
   doppelgänger, 4, 117

Drabble, Margaret, *The Witch of Exmoor*, 190
Drake, Nathan, 17
dungeons, 26, 41, 86, 116, 209, 224

Ellis, Havelock, 97
Ellman, Mary, 186
Eve, 5, 106, 109
Everyday Sexism Project, 2
evil, 5–6, 22, 32, 57, 94, 96, 101, 106–7, 108, 114, 186, 191, 192, 222

family, 2, 5, 8, 13, 19, 25, 33, 50, 51, 54, 63, 64, 71, 76, 77, 79–85, 93, 96, 100, 110, 116, 126, 139, 145–6, 150, 151, 169, 177, 190, 222
  Family Reform Law, 61
  Family Romance, 85
fantasy, 82, 92, 96–7, 102, 145, 199, 204, 208, 209, 215
Fanu, Le Sheridan
  'Carmilla', 150, 152, 153–4
  Uncle Silas, 186
fathers, 32, 49, 51, 52, 53, 56, 65, 66, 76–80, 83, 84–6, 92–4, 96, 101, 102, 103, 112, 115, 116, 140–1, 144–6, 153, 156, 195, 200, 207, 208, 222
Faulkner, William, 'A Rose for Emily', 187
Faye, Deirdre Le, 16–17
'Female', the, 5, 51, 94
female body, 6, 9, 49, 50, 51, 78, 81, 82, 95, 98, 106–17, 147, 154, 189, 195, 203
Female Gothic, 1, 6, 7, 8, 10, 33, 43n, 51, 62, 76, 77, 80, 87, 101, 102, 109, 135–48, 154, 169, 177, 182, 186, 215, 216, 220, 222
female subjectivity, 6, 7, 9, 91, 112, 121, 126, 129, 130, 135–6, 139, 142, 144–5, 147, 195, 199, 202, 205, 207
Femicidal plots, 147
femininity, 6–7, 10, 16, 34, 36, 39, 46–7, 49–51, 57–8, 75–6, 79, 80–1, 83, 98, 101, 106–8, 110, 115, 117, 120–34, 135, 137–8, 140–1, 153–4, 201, 202–3, 212, 225
feminism, 1–2, 46, 68, 69, 173, 179, 182, 187, 201
  Fourth-Wave Feminism, 2

Lesbian Feminism, 69, 177
Post-Feminism, 1, 2, 9, 187, 188
Second-Wave Feminism, 1, 83, 86, 125, 170–1, 179, 182, 187, 188, 191
Third-Wave Feminism, 187
Trans*Feminism, 179
femme fatale, 97, 103, 106, 108, 113, 114, 153, 157
Fielding, Noel, 200
fin-de-siècle, 42, 64, 97, 107, 112, 153, 179, 180
Firestone, Shulamith, 2
Fleenor, Judith, 33
Forrest, Katherine, 'O Captain, My Captain', 158
freakishness, 181, 189
Freeman, Mary E. Wilkins, 'Luella Miller', 152, 156
Freud, Sigmund, 78, 82, 92, 96, 107, 111, 113, 144, 156, 158–9
  'Medusa's Head', 114–15
  Studies in Hysteria, 99–100
  'The Uncanny', 5, 6, 61, 67, 75, 94
Friedan, Betty, 75, 80–1, 83, 125

Galt, John, 'The Buried Alive', 39
games, 69, 71, 180
  digital, 1, 10, 199, 201, 208, 210, 214–27
Gaskell, Elizabeth, 6
  'The Grey Lady', 110, 190–1
  'The Old Nurse's Story', 4, 62–3, 64
Gavron, Hannah, *The Captive Wife*, 75
Gelder, Ken, 158–9
gender, 1, 2, 8–9, 10, 21, 34, 36, 40, 43, 47, 77, 78, 81, 91, 113, 116–17, 121, 137, 138, 144, 147, 150, 153, 155, 158–9, 161, 169–70, 173, 179, 181, 182n, 184–5, 187–8, 190, 195, 200–2, 205, 207, 214–27
genderqueer, 8, 190
Georgieva, Margarita, *The Gothic Child*, 61, 64
Germanà, Monica, 130
ghosts *see* spectrality
Gibbons, Stella, 9
  Cold Comfort Farm, 194
Gibson, William, 199, 200
  Neuromancer, 203–4, 205–7, 208, 210
Gilbert, Sandra and Susan Gubar, 31, 34, 42, 156

Gilman, Charlotte Perkins, *The Yellow Wallpaper*, 143
Gomez, Jewelle, 150
  The Gilda Stories, 158, 171, 175
Gottlieb, Sherry, 8, 158, 162
  Love Bite, 159
Grosz, Elizabeth, 212
grotesque, 50, 65, 68, 82, 85, 107, 181, 188, 189, 195
Gullette, Margaret Morganroth, 184

Haefele-Thomas, Ardel, 190
Haggard, Rider, 43
  She, 9, 189–90
Halberstam, Judith, 48, 50
Hand, Elizabeth, 6
  The Bride of Frankenstein: Pandora's Bride, 112
Haraway, Donna, 207, 211, 212, 223
Harris, Charlaine, 7, 146–7, 150
  The Southern Vampire Mysteries, 147
haunting *see* spectrality
Hawthorne, Nathaniel, *The Scarlet Letter*, 172–3
Heggarty, George E., 56
Heidt, Yvonne
heimlich, homely, 5, 75, 67, 87
  Sometime Yesterday, 177–8
hero, Gothic, 22, 24, 38, 42, 43, 141, 188, 220, 222, 224
heroine, Gothic, 3, 6, 9, 10, 15–28, 31, 33–4, 37, 38–9, 49, 62, 72, 76, 80, 87, 102, 103, 108–10, 114, 115, 116, 120, 140, 142, 147, 154, 162, 172, 178, 185, 186, 188, 190, 195, 199, 200, 204, 205, 208, 210, 215, 219–20, 225
Hill, Susan, *The Woman in Black*, 114
Hoeveler, Diane, 94, 142
Hoffmann, E. T. A., 94
Hogle, Jerrold. E., 20
Holland, Norman and Leona Sherman, 77, 78, 86
home, the, 3, 5, 54, 57, 74, 75–6, 78, 80–1, 84, 85, 94, 110, 125–7, 133, 143, 151, 160, 176
homosexuality, 97, 151
  'apparitional lesbian', 119, 128, 132
  lesbianism, 8, 71, 120, 128, 132, 133n, 152–3, 157–9, 163, 169, 170–2, 176–9, 182n

Hopkinson, Nalo, 'Greedy Choke Puppy', 8, 150, 155, 159–60, 162
Horner, Avril and Sue Zlosnik, 9, 85, 122–3
Horney, Karen, 164
horror, 3, 4, 15, 21, 32, 46, 47, 48, 50–1, 53–8, 62, 67–70, 77, 78, 81–2, 84, 95, 107, 109, 114, 116, 117, 153, 154, 158, 171, 172, 184, 189, 193, 205, 215–17, 226
hysteria, 36–40, 42, 92, 99–100, 110, 155–6, 222

illegitimacy, 18, 94, 112, 140–1, 207
incarceration/imprisonment 3, 6, 15, 21, 25, 26, 33, 34, 54, 103, 108, 133n, 141, 142–3, 186, 191, 209
incest, 21, 76, 84–5, 95–6, 174, 176
inheritance, 6, 11, 79, 99, 108, 112, 120, 130, 136, 139–40
Irigaray, Luce, 4, 47–8, 52, 53, 97, 106, 154, 186

Jackson, Shelley, *Patchwork Girl*, 111–12
Jackson, Shirley, 6, 78–9
  The Haunting of Hill House, 7, 80, 121, 125–9, 132
  The Sundial, 76, 79, 84
  We have Always Lived in the Castle, 76, 79–80, 83, 84, 100
James, Henry, 6
  The Turn of the Screw, 4, 64–5, 68, 100
James, William, 100–1
Johnson, Samuel, 28
Jones, David J., 200
Jordan, Neil, 8
  Byzantium, 161–2

Keane, Molly, *Time After Time*, 194
Keesey, Pam, 157, 158
Kincaid, James R., 61
King, Stephen, 6
  Carrie, 68–70
Kipling, Rudyard, 'The Female of the Species', 111
Kirkpatrick, Nancy, 8
  Sunglasses After Dark, 159
Kristeva, Julia, 4, 47–8, 50, 55, 68, 151, 154, 157
Kubrick, Stanley, *2001: A Space Odyssey*, 200

Lang, Fritz
  Metropolis, 112
  Secret Beyond the Door, 110
law, 7, 26, 27, 47, 48, 61, 93, 135–49,
    172, 173, 177, 185, 186
'Law of the Father', 26–8, 33, 47, 51,
    55, 58, 92–5, 97, 144, 197
Lea, Katie, *Primal*, 213
Lee, Dennis, Civil Elegies', 187
Lee, Sophia, 136, 139, 143
  The Recess, 140
Lee, Tanith, 'The Gorgon', 114
Lee, Vernon, 179
  'A Wicked Voice', 179–80
  'Prince Alberic and the Snake Lady',
    180
Lewis, Matthew 'Monk', 92, 185
  The Monk, 5, 19–21, 26, 28, 93, 95,
    98, 108–9, 117, 185, 186, 216,
    217
Lidoff, Joan, 75–6, 77, 80, 81
Lochhead, Liz, *Dracula*, 113
Locke, John, 138
Lofts, Norah, 76, 77
  'A Curious Experience', 74–5
  'A Visit to Claudia', 78
  Is Anybody There?, 77
  'Mr Edward', 78
  'Pesticide', 84
  'The Watchers', 78
Lovecraft, H. P., 217, 218
Lovelace, Ada, 200–1
Lynch, David, 217

MacCannell, Juliet, 7, 144, 147
McCullers, Carson, 179
  The Ballad of the Sad Café, 181
Macfie, Sian, 153
McHale, Brian, 200
Machen, Arthur, *The Great God Pan*,
    199, 202–3
MacKenzie, Henry, 17, 27
  Julia de Roubigné, 24, 25
madness, 3, 31–44, 56, 92–9, 101, 103,
    110, 112, 130, 156, 204, 222, 226
Magrs, Paul, 9
  Never the Bride, 195
Maguire, Gregory, *Wicked*, 101
Marbod of Rennes, Bishop, 106–7
Marryat, Florence, 179
  The Blood of the Vampire, 112–13,
    152, 155–6, 162, 180–1
masculinity, 6, 9, 10, 16, 27, 28, 43, 51,
    92–4, 98, 99, 108, 136, 138, 146,
    153, 176, 179, 180, 184, 189, 200,
    201, 220, 221, 224, 225
Matthias, Thomas, 138
Maudsley, Henry, 36, 40
Maurier, Daphne du, 184, 188, 190
  'Don't Look Now', 9, 188–9, 190,
    193, 194
  Rebecca, 99, 121, 122–5, 128, 131,
    132–3
  Rule Britannia, 188
  'The Pool', 65–6
medicine, 3, 4, 8, 34–9, 41–2, 69–70,
    99, 100, 111, 126, 128, 156, 169,
    180, 184–5, 193
Melzer, Patricia, 49–50
menstruation, 4, 65, 66, 69, 70, 113,
    115
metamorphosis, 107, 151, 189,
    192
Meyer, Stephenie, 9, 163
  Twilight tetralogy, 9, 114–16,
    116–17, 144–6, 148, 150, 161,
    188
Meyers, Helene, 147–8
Miles, Robert, 108, 216, 217
misogyny, 2, 106, 107, 117, 171, 185,
    190
Mitchell, Juliet, 92
Mitchell, Weir, 156
Moers, Ellen, 33, 46, 52, 62, 72, 154,
    215
monks, 93, 109, 117
monstrosity, 4, 6, 46, 47, 49, 50–8, 76,
    82, 106–8, 110, 115, 117, 154,
    158, 191, 192, 195, 203, 207, 222,
    226
Moore, C. L., 'Shambleau', 6, 114
Mootoo, Shani, *Cereus Blooms at
    Night*, 160
Morpurgo, Michael, 63
Morrison, Toni, 86
  Beloved, 171, 173–5
Mortimer, Penelope
  The Pumpkin Eater, 76, 82–3
  'The Skylight', 80
mothers, 3–6, 23–8, 41, 46–58, 64–7,
    71, 75–6, 79–81, 84–7, 91, 93,
    95–6, 100, 102–3, 111–12, 114,
    120, 126, 128, 141, 145, 154, 156,
    158–9, 161–3, 174, 176–8, 180,
    186, 189, 191–2, 195, 208–10
Mulvey-Roberts, Marie, 156
Munford, Rebecca, 187
Murphy, Bernice, 79

myth, 4, 6, 11, 33, 42, 87, 102, 106, 114–16, 118n, 136, 140, 151, 156–7, 160–3, 200, 207, 211

necrophilia, 187
Negra, Diane, 188
Nestle, Joan, 169
Norton, Lady Caroline, *English Laws for Women in the Nineteenth Century*, 143
Novak, Kim, 188
nuns, 5, 19–21, 23, 28, 41, 91, 93, 95, 98, 107–8, 186
nymphomania, 109

Oliphant, Margaret, 'The Library Window', 64
'Other', the, 4, 11, 46, 47–51, 55–8, 92, 94, 117, 120–4, 127, 144, 151, 154–7, 158, 161, 163, 184–5, 192, 222, 224, 226
Owen, Alex, 37, 63, 202
Oyeyeme, Helen, 9
White is for Witching, 192

Palmer, Paulina, 67–8, 158
Parker, Dorothy, 184
parody, 3, 15, 16, 18, 21, 24–8, 35, 50, 54, 85, 116, 157, 193, 200
Parsons, Eliza, 7, 16, 135, 136, 139, 143, 144
The Castle of Wolfenbach, 26, 141–2
Patmore, Coventry, *The Angel in the House*, 107
patriarchy, 3, 5, 6, 8, 11, 18, 32–3, 46, 47, 48, 50, 51, 52, 58, 61, 75–7, 79–80, 83–6, 91–5, 97–8, 100–3, 106–9, 115, 128–9, 132, 135, 139–42, 144–6, 152, 154, 162–3, 169, 172–5, 177, 182, 185–6, 189–92, 200, 207
Perrault, Charles, 6
phallic/phallus, 10, 82, 107, 113–14
Phillips, Adam, 100
Plant, Sadie, 200–1
Plath, Sylvia, 76, 77, 81
'Ariel', 210
'Daddy', 77, 86
'Lady Lazarus', 87
Poe, Edgar Allan, 6, 39, 120
'Berenice', 115
'The Oval Portrait', 61–2
Polanski, Roman, 116
Polidori, John, *The Vampyr*, 96

Polwhele, Richard, *The Unsex'd Females*, 111
Pope, Alexander
'Eloise to Abelard', 5, 91–3, 97, 99
The Rape of the Lock, 92
possession, 5, 55, 63, 74–5, 78, 122, 125, 126, 133, 202, 215, 219
pregnancy, 46, 47, 50, 55, 82, 93, 107, 116, 145, 173, 203
psychoanalysis, 5, 39, 47–8, 82, 92, 93, 97, 151, 219
Punter, David, 69

Queer Gothic, 8, 60, 721, 158, 170–3, 175–82, 190, 195

race, 8, 111, 112, 155, 156, 158–9, 170, 179, 219
Radcliffe, Anne, 3, 6, 16, 17, 19, 21, 26, 34, 35, 39, 43, 98, 109, 120, 139, 141–2, 215, 217, 219, 220, 221, 222, 225
A Sicilian Romance, 21, 84, 141, 186, 191
The Castles of Athlin and Dunbayne, 21, 141
The Italian, 17, 21–3, 24, 26–7, 28, 98, 142–3, 185–6
The Mysteries of Udolpho, 17, 18, 25, 30, 32–4, 35, 37, 38, 98, 99, 109, 114, 121, 186
Ramsay, Lynne, *We Need to Talk about Kevin*, 46–7, 48, 52–8
rape, 21, 23, 95, 96, 117, 172, 206
Reade, Charles, *Hard Cash*, 35
Reiniger, Lotte, 217
repetition, Gothic, 121, 122, 124, 132, 220
Rhys, Jean, 9
Wide Sargasso Sea, 101, 156, 191
Rice, Anne, 150
Interview with the Vampire, 158, 162
Queen of the Damned, 157
Rich, Adrienne, 186
Richardson, Samuel, 17
Pamela, 18
Rigby, Elizabeth, 98
Roche, Maria Regina, 16
Clermont, 26
romance, Gothic, 31, 34, 39, 136–8, 141–2, 172, 177
Romanticism, 3, 21, 27, 28, 185
Romero, George A., *Night of the Living Dead*, 223

Rousseau, Jean-Jacques, 17, 27
  Julie, ou la Nouvelle Héloïse, 24
Royle, Nicholas, *The Uncanny*, 94–5
Russo, Mary, *The Female Grotesque*,
  65, 68

Sade, Marquis de, 84
  Juliette, 108, 220
Sconce, Jeffrey, 199, 201, 202, 203
Scott, Ridley, *Prometheus*, 4, 46–7,
  48–52, 54, 55, 57–8
Scott, Sir Walter, 17
  Marmion, 41
Sedgwick, Eve Kosofsky, 39, 219
Sexton, Anne, 'Housewife', 75, 76, 77
sexuality, 5, 8, 20, 94, 95, 98, 107–8,
  109, 121, 128, 151–4, 156, 158,
  159, 161, 163, 170, 179, 181,
  201
Shapira, Yael, 98
Shelley, Mary, 46, 185
  *Frankenstein or the Modern
    Prometheus*, 6, 28, 52, 111–12,
    195, 220
Shelley, Percy Bysshe, 95, 96
  St. Irvyne: or The Rosicrucian, 92
  The Cenci, 85
  Zastrozzi: A Romance, 92
Showalter, Elaine, 156
Silver, Anne, 144, 148
simpkins, reese, 179, 182
sisters, 4, 53, 61, 63, 68, 79, 83, 95,
  102–3, 106, 109, 114, 124, 126,
  128, 130, 140, 158, 159, 161, 163,
  174, 189–90, 194, 226
slavery, 112, 117, 155, 158, 171, 173–5
Sleath, Eleanor, 16
  The Orphan of the Rhine, 17–18,
    23–7, 28
Small, Helen, 35, 36
Smith, Ali, 6
  Hotel World, 121, 129–33
Smith, Allan Lloyd, 122
Sofia, Zoe, 200, 203
sons, 4, 25, 26, 48, 52–7, 79, 80, 86, 94,
  97, 114, 141, 147, 186, 193
soucouyant, 9, 155, 159–60, 162,
  191–3
Spark, Muriel, 132
spectrality, 4, 6–7, 19, 31–2, 34, 52, 53,
  62–5, 70–1, 75–8, 80, 83, 86, 93,
  95, 96, 100, 108, 109, 110, 114,
  120–33, 140, 142, 171–4, 177–8,
  180, 190, 193, 199, 200, 204

spiritualism, 9, 63, 75, 96, 101, 131,
  151, 172, 176, 192, 201–3, 211
Stead, Christina, 76, 77, 80, 84
  The Man Who Loved Children, 75–7,
    78, 81–2, 83, 84–5, 86
Stein, Karen F., 154
Stephenson, Neal, 10
  The Diamond Age, 199, 204, 208–10
Stoker, Bram, 153
  Dracula, 7–8, 40–2, 97, 111, 112–14,
    150
Sugars, Cynthia, 187
suicide, 101–2, 156, 173, 176, 181, 210
supernatural, 9, 21, 33, 85, 91, 97, 106,
  113, 116, 122–3, 125–6, 128, 141,
  146–7, 154, 178

Tasker, Yvonne, 220
Thomas, Scarlett, *The End of Mr Y*,
  199, 204–5, 210–12
Tourette, Gilles de la, 40
Tracy, Ann B., 93
transformation, 7, 9, 62, 70, 83, 99,
  116, 145, 146, 122
transgression, 5, 20, 49, 66, 93, 114,
  140
trauma, 5, 7, 52, 53, 69, 70, 72, 92,
  109, 142, 174, 193, 206, 209
tropes, Gothic, 3, 4, 5, 10, 26, 32, 34,
  36, 37, 38, 39, 40, 42, 47, 54, 75,
  76, 118n, 133, 133n, 143, 171,
  176–8, 209
  blood, 41–4, 54, 64, 67, 69–70, 72,
    86, 95, 96, 97, 112–13, 115, 142,
    145, 146, 151–3, 155–6, 159, 160,
    174–5, 178, 209, 220, 222
  castles, 15, 20, 25, 31, 32, 54, 70, 75,
    77, 78, 83, 94, 96, 109, 113, 115,
    136, 137, 139–42, 204–5, 209, 225
  houses, 37, 39, 41, 48, 53, 64, 67,
    75–80, 83–5, 92, 94, 97, 100, 107,
    110, 116, 122, 124, 125–9, 133,
    171, 177, 187, 190, 192, 220
  labyrinths, 10, 137, 139, 189, 200,
    203, 205
  mirrors, 4, 65–6, 70, 116, 117, 205–7
  portraits, 37, 61, 85, 99, 124, 144,
    185
  tombs, 83, 95, 140, 221

U.K. Feminista, 2
uncanny, 4, 5, 6, 9, 10, 26, 32, 38, 47,
  48, 50, 52, 54, 55, 57, 61, 64, 65,
  67, 68, 71, 75, 77, 79, 83, 85,

94–5, 98–100, 107, 121, 122, 123, 125, 158, 174, 192, 199, 203
unheimlich/unhomely, 5, 75, 77–8, 84–6, 94, 107

vagina dentate, 6, 115
vampire, 6, 7, 41, 42, 52, 77, 86, 95–7, 116, 136, 146, 147, 188, 190, 194, 215, 220, 222
  vampire facelift, 117
  vampire, female, 8, 76, 96, 97, 106, 108, 112–15, 117, 122, 146, 150–64, 173, 175, 180–1, 192, 195
  vampire romance, 136, 144–5, 148, 150, 163
villain, Gothic, 15, 17, 18, 33, 87, 221
villainess, Gothic, 5, 34, 35–8, 93, 95, 100, 110
Vint, Sherryl, 207, 212
virtual, the, 1, 9, 10, 199–213, 214–27

Wallace, Diana, 5, 136, 139
Walpole, Horace, *The Castle of Otranto*, 5, 26, 92, 94–5, 97, 185
Warner, Sylvia Townsend, *Lolly Willowes*, 190
Waters, Sarah, 71
  Affinity, 176–7
  The Little Stranger, 4, 71
Weldon, Fay, 86
  The Life and Loves of a She Devil, 117
  Rhode Island Blues, 190

Wells, H. G., *The Island of Doctor Moreau*, 112
West, Vita Sackville, *All Passion Spent*, 190
Wharton, Edith, 9
  'Miss Mary Pask', 193–4
Whedon, Joss, *Buffy the Vampire Slayer*, 215, 220, 224
White, Allon, 69
Williams, Anne, 5–6
  Art of Darkness, 26, 27, 33, 49, 51, 87
Williams, Roberta, *Phantasmagoria*, 215
Wilson, Elizabeth, 123
Wisker, Gina, 2, 7–8, 76, 81, 86, 157
witchcraft, 5, 57, 76, 81, 83, 91–2, 94, 96, 103, 106, 109, 111, 153–5, 171–3, 177–8, 186–7, 190–2, 221–2
Wolf, Naomi, 55, 155
Wolfreys, Julian, 126
Wollstonecraft, Mary, *A Vindication of the Rights of Women*, 18, 111
Woodward, Kathleen, 184
Woolf, Virginia, *A Room of One's Own*, 108

Yeats, W. B., 184

zombie, 72, 216, 217, 219, 223